Library Learning Information

Idea Store® Bow
1 Gladstone Place
Roman Road
London E3 5ES

020 7364 4332
www.ideastore.co.uk

Created and managed by
Tower Hamlets Council

FOOTBALLING FIFTIES

When the Beautiful Game was in black and white

NORMAN GILLER

Statistical sections compiled by Michael Giller

Introduced by **JIMMY GREAVES**

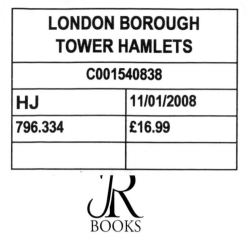

A JR Books publication

© NormanMichaelGiller Enterprises 2007

First published in 2007 by JR Books
10 Greenland Street
London NW1 0ND

A CIP catalogue for this title is available from the British Library
ISBN 978-1-906217-25-9

Typeset and designed by NMG Enterprises, Dorset, UK
Printed by MKT Print, Slovenia

Contents

Kick-off by **JIMMY GREAVES** — 5

A Decade of two Halves by **NORMAN GILLER** — 7

The Cast: 100 players waiting in the wings — 9

1949-50: Horizontal in Horizonte — 21

1950-51: From Amateurs to Shamateurs — 37

1951-52: Nat Lofthouse, the Lion of Vienna — 47

1952-53: Matthews, the Wizard of Dribble — 58

1953-54: Major Puskas and the Magical Magyars — 70

1954-55: When Ted Drake had the last laugh — 94

1955-56: Birth of the Busby Babes — 107

1956-57: Mac the Knife on a collision course — 121

6 February 1958: Death of the Busby Babes — 131

1957-58: Pele and the ball-juggling boys from Brazil — 141

1958-59: The Cloughie and Greavsie goal show — 154

1959-60 Alfredo the Great and the Real Deal — 177

The Final Bow: What the cast did next — 193

The Great Footballing Fifties Poll — 213

It's Saturday, 24 August 1957 and seventeen-year-old Jimmy Greaves makes his debut for Chelsea against Tottenham at White Hart Lane. Here he is on his way to the first of a record 357 First Division goals. It earned Chelsea a point. Four years later, on the same ground but wearing a Tottenham shirt, he scored a hat-trick against Blackpool in his first game for Spurs after his £99,999 transfer from AC Milan.

IT was the summer of 1955 when I joined Chelsea as a wide-eyed, innocent fifteen-year-old apprentice at the start of a football career that was to bring me quite a bit of fame but hardly a fortune.

Chelsea had just won the old First Division championship, and my starting wage was a princely four pounds a week. The heroes who had brought the title to the Bridge – Roy Bentley and Co – were each paid exactly seventeen pounds a week. That was the maximum allowed in an era when clubs treated players like pawns.

It was a world unrecogniseable from today's Stamford Bridge of Abramovich and Mourinho and the £100,000-a-week wages. Frank Lampard pays out more to the bloke who cleans his Bentley than I got in my weekly wage packet, even when I was banging in 30-plus goals a season for Chelsea.

But I'm not moaning. I *know* that back in those 1950s I got more fun and satisfaction from my football than any of today's so-called superstars. It was a proper man's game then, featuring loads of exciting physical contact without the referee running around waving cards like a demented Paul Daniels.

Defenders were allowed to tackle from behind (I have the scars to prove it), and the stars of the day – my heroes like Len Shackleton, Raich Carter, Wilf Mannion and, of course Matthews and Finney – had to develop nifty footwork to avoid being crippled. I am convinced we had better ball control than today's top players, mainly because we had to be quick and smart to outthink the men literally trying to mark us.

My pal of many years, Norman Giller, has done the game a service by writing this book that gives the footballing fifties the spotlight they deserve. You are in safe and caring hands with him. He has been around the game as long as me, and is nostalgic for the good old bad old days when football was literally played for kicks.

The younger generation will not believe just how much football has changed from the days when we regularly played in front of 50,000-plus crowds and scored goals by the bucket-load before the coaches got their choking stranglehold on individualists.

Enjoy the journey back into a decade when the Beautiful Game really was in black and white. Fasten your safety belts. It could be a bumpy ride.

Jim Greaves

AUTHOR'S ACKNOWLEDGEMENTS

Norman Giller wishes to thank the venerable Jeremy Robson and his friendly team at JR Books – in particular senior editor Lesley Wilson, Anna Keirnan and production manager Peter Colley – for their expert help in getting this book into the net (or, as they would have said in the footballing 'fifties, into the onion bag). I am indebted to the 'fifties genius Jimmy Greaves for his fee-free introduction, and to my son and partner Michael Giller for his safety-net checking work and his supply of statistics that help to make this one of the most exhaustive examinations of football in the 'fifties. I have dipped copiously into the many facts and figures published by my old press-box colleague Albert Sewell, of BBCtv and *News of the World Football Annual* fame, the data-crammed works of Barry J. Hugman and his team, and also several books by the doyens of football writers Brian Glanville and David Miller, both of whom would be far better equipped than me to write this book. Websites that proved particularly helpful were www.englandfootballonline.com, www.soccerbase.com and the all-embracing website set up by Leeds-based Bob Dunning (www.bobdunning.net). Thanks also to Ian Blackwell, of the premier photo agency Popperfoto, for his diligent research work, Glen Saville for well-designed advice, and to Jackie Jones for being there. Finally, the biggest thank you of all goes to all the old pros who gave me so much pleasure as a young man watching football in the 'fifties. It was a different game then, and much more thrilling and satisfying than today's soulless, sanitised football.

To the memory of the Busby Babes,
who briefly but brilliantly brought style
and a smile to the 1950s football stage,
and remembering my old mate Alan
Ball who sadly passed on (he would
approve of that phrase) before we could
properly argue the merits of the 'fifties
v. the 'sixties, the decade in which he
was a little giant. He is now reunited
with our captain Bobby Moore.

Front jacket pictures, left to right: Stanley Matthews, Tom Finney, Pele, Duncan Edwards (wearing his England schoolboy international cap), Nat Lofthouse and Billy Wright.

All photographs are published by kind permission of popperfoto.com

FOOTBALLING FIFTIES
A Decade of Two Halves by Norman Giller

FOOTBALL in the 1950s provided the best of times and the worst of times. This is the two-faced story of one of the most dramatic decades in the history of the game, when professional footballers were on appalling wages and contracts that shackled them to clubs like slaves. Yet it was also when the game was at its most exciting and adventurous, with goals galore and when wingers thrilled packed houses with their dazzling touchline runs. It truly was a decade of two halves, and I feel privileged to have been there to witness football at its most mesmerising and memorable.

A Premiership footballer from the New Millennium suddenly dropped into the 1950s would feel as if he had landed on another planet, a poverty-stricken place where the most a player could earn – even if you were Stanley Matthews or Tom Finney – was seventeen pounds a week. There was hardly a black or foreign footballer to be seen, and like everybody else in the early 1950s players needed a rationbook to get their weekly meat, milk and petrol. Only one or two players at a club owned a motorcar. Most of the rest went to the ground by public transport, rubbing shoulders and exchanging banter with rattle-waving, scarf-twirling fans, and not a hooligan in sight.

They even spoke a different language in the football world of the fifties. There were wing-halves, inside-forwards and wingers, two points for a win, and shoulder charges were allowed against goalkeepers in the days when football was a game of physical contact. Red and yellow cards were something associated with magicians, and authoritarian referees took names only for tackles that caused grievous bodily harm.

The laced ball was leather-panelled, and it was like heading a heavy pudding when matches were staged on pitches that were invariably muddy. It weighed the same as today's 'beach' balls at kick-off but was not water resistant. Dubbined football boots reached high above the ankle, and protective shinpads were, out of necessity, as thick as a rolled-up newspaper. It was a pure and simple eleven-against-eleven game, with no substitutes and everybody understood the no-nonense off-side law.

Spectators definitely got better value for their two bob (10p) entrance fee to grounds that were, generally, eighty per cent terracing. It would cost an Oxford scholar (a dollar ... five shillings ... 25p) to get your bum on a seat to watch football that was full-blooded and rich with individual skills. In today's transfer market the likes of super-gifted players such as Matthews, Finney, Lawton, Mannion, Shackleton, Lofthouse and Carter would be valued in the zillions.

Television coverage was in its infancy on nine-inch black and white screens, and we used to rely on the wireless – and the voice of football, Raymond Glendenning – for our commentaries. A goal scored on a Saturday would warm spectators and give them bragging rights over the next seven days. There were no action replays to prove that the goal was perhaps not quite as spectacular as described on the factory floor, all back in the days when parents almost literally smoked themselves to death to get their sons cigarette cards featuring the favourite footballers of the era.

As well as the roar of the crowd at grounds there was the clackety-clack of typewriters in the Press Boxes. The media masters in those days of mass circulation newspapers (led by the fourpenny *Daily Mirror* and *Daily Express* selling in excess of four million copies a day) were not sharp-suited TV know-alls but gifted columnists who could write with poisoned pens in the hot-metal days of Fleet Street. Henry Rose, Peter Wilson, Geoffrey Green, Desmond Hackett, Ivan Sharpe, Frank Butler, J.L. Manning, Sam Leitch and a young Ian Wooldridge were among the household names who had readers hanging on every word. An affable Irishman called Eamonn Andrews was the resident anchorman of a new BBC Light programme Saturday show called *Sports Report.*

The most common playing formation was 2-3-5 – two full-backs flanking a 'stopper' centre-half, two wing-halves and five forwards including specialist wingers. There was still an emphasis on the 1930s WM system introduced by manager Herbert Chapman when Arsenal ruled the old First Division. The more progressive sides boldly experimented with the 4-2-4 line-up that served Brazil so well when, Pele-propelled, they won the World Cup for the first time in Sweden in 1958. The Hungarians, the Swiss and the Austrians were playing a new style of football in which centre-forwards patrolled in midfield. It was to prove all very confusing and, ultimately, demoralising for English opposition. Puskas and Co came at us like aliens from outer-space, and eventually revolutionised the way we thought about and played the game.

In an era when amateur football was healthy and flourishing, it was claimed the game was going off its head when in 1950 Sunderland paid a British record £30,000 for Aston Villa's Welsh international centre-forward Trevor Ford. A reader's letter in *The Times* thundered: "This is an obscene amount of money to pay for somebody adept only at kicking a lump of leather around a grassy field. What on earth is the world coming to?"

To make this a complete history of the 1950s, I have (thanks to my sports statistician son, Michael) included a who-won-what breakdown for each season and have spotlighted the major players and the teams. And so that this is a shared journey, we set up a website (www.footballingfifties.co.uk) where surfers have been voting for their favourite players from the 1950s. We publish the result of the poll as a climax to a book that I hope brings back memories for those who were there and convinces the younger generations that they missed out on something very special ... the *footballing fifties.*

COME back with me to New Year's eve, 31 December 1949, to meet one hundred of the main characters in the cast of thousands who were to make the 'fifties such a memorable and at times momentous footballing decade. Just to give you a taste of the times, these were among the main talking points coming out of the dark, desolate Age of Austerity of the 1940s ...

Britain had an 'old' Labour government under the leadership of Prime Minister Clement Attlee, the railways and the coal mines were nationalised and just a year earlier Aneurin Bevan had introduced the National Health Service ... Harry S. Truman was still in the White House four years after ordering the dropping of the Atom Bombs on Japan, and was soon, in harness with the United Nations, to declare war on North Korea ... there were still bombed sites to remind Londoners of the Blitz ... the average price for a semi-detached, three-bedroomed house in the South-East had dropped to £1,250 following the 1949 devaluation of the pound ... a gallon of rationed petrol cost four shillings in old money (20p in the decimal currency that was still twenty-one years away) ... the average wage on the factory floor was £8 a week ... you could buy an Austin 40 for £450 and the sleek Jaguar XK 120 was about to hit the road at just over £1,000 ... George Orwell's novel *1984* was the talk of the literary world ... *The Third Man* starring Orson Welles was the top box office film ... *South Pacific* was the big musical on Broadway ... Ezzard Charles followed Joe Louis as world heavyweight champion ... and *Rudolph the Rednosed Reindeer* was the best-selling record.

This is what one hundred of the main Football League characters were doing at the dawn of the decade ...

JIMMY ADAMSON was completing his National Service in the Royal Air Force before resuming a career with Burnley that had started in 1947 following two years working down the coal mines in his native North-East. He would eventually be remembered as the man who turned down the England manager's job before Alf Ramsey went on to World Cup glory.

IVOR ALLCHURCH and his brother Len were starting out on their football adventure with Swansea along with the Jones boys, Cliff and Bryn. Ivor was about to be called up for the first of his 68 Welsh caps.

RONNIE ALLEN had been demobbed from the RAF and was playing on the right wing for Port Vale before his switch in March 1950 to West Bromwich Albion, where he would become one of the British pioneers of withdrawn centre-forward play.

MALCOLM ALLISON was preparing to move from Charlton reserves to West Ham, where he was to become one of the game's most radical thinkers. He had been inspired by watching Moscow Dynamo train while serving with the Army in Austria.

JIMMY ARMFIELD was playing rugby for Lancashire boys and soccer on the right wing for a local junior club. Blackpool spotted him and persuaded him after his National Service with the King's Own Regiment to switch full-time to soccer, and he developed into one of the world's classiest full-backs.

JOHN ATYEO had just left university with a degree in mathematics and was a surveyor and then a school teacher throughout his 15 years at Bristol City, during which he set all-time club appearance and goal-scoring records.

EDDIE BAILY, football's Cheeky Chappie, was steering push-and-run Spurs to the Second Division championship, and his spot-on passing would be a key factor in their League championship triumph a year later.

GORDON BANKS was about to leave school in Sheffield to work as a coal bagger before starting an apprenticeship as a bricklayer. A scout saw him playing in goal for a local side called Millspaugh and he was persuaded to sign for Chesterfield.

BILLY BINGHAM was playing for Glentoran in Northern Ireland and had drawn the attention of Sunderland, who in November 1950 paid £8,000 to take him to Roker Park as a wing partner for the Wearside wizard Len Shackleton.

DANNY BLANCHFLOWER, an RAF navigator during the war, had joined Barnsley from Glentoran, and now Aston Villa were beckoning. He and his Manchester United-based brother Jackie were to become mainstays of the Northern Ireland team.

JOHN BOND was an amateur with Colchester Casuals when West Ham signed him in March 1950. He became a fixture at right-back, earning the nickname Muffin because he hit a ball like a mule. John was a member of the famous West Ham 'think tank.'

RON BURGESS was the driving captain of push-and-run Spurs who were on their way to the First Division and the League championship. A former pit boy in South Wales, he had lost his best years to the war but was still a powerhouse of a player.

MATT BUSBY had pieced together the first of his three great teams, and was now building his own legend at Old Trafford after ground sharing at Maine Road because of bomb damage at the United HQ. The Busby Babes were just a twinkle in his eye.

ROGER BYRNE was trying to convince Matt Busby that he was more at home at left back than on the wing. He was eventually to establish himself as an exceptional England No 3, and was to become the inspiring captain of the Busby Babes.

NOEL CANTWELL had just been spotted by West Ham as a Cork Athletic left-back with great potential. He would guide West Ham to the First Division as skipper before joining Man United and captaining their 1963 FA Cup winning team.

RAICH CARTER was player-manager with Hull City after establishing himself as one of England's all-time great inside-forwards in a career that straddled the War. He was a star of the 'thirties and 'forties and still had an influence on the 'fifties.

JOHN CHARLES was about to have his football duties with Leeds interrupted by National Service, after which he developed into arguably the greatest all-round footballer ever produced in Britain. His golden years were to come with Juventus between two periods with Leeds.

BOBBY CHARLTON was a thirteen-year-old grammar school boy who was already causing excitement among North-East scouts. His older brother Jack had started working down the mines and then applied to join the police before being signed by Leeds.

RONNIE CLAYTON was discovered playing for Preston schoolboys and was about to make his League debut for Blackburn Rovers at the age of sixteeen. During his distinguished career he would become captain for his club and country.

BRIAN CLOUGH was playing with local club Great Broughton Juniors before joining Middlesbrough where he would become one of football's most prolific goal scorers. He then kept finding the target with Sunderland before becoming a legendary manager.

EDDIE COLMAN had been spotted by Manchester United playing for Salford Boys while at Ordsall school. He would be invited to join the Old Trafford groundstaff as a member of one of the most talented group of football youngsters ever assembled.

STAN CULLIS at thirty-three had, in May 1949, become the youngest manager of an FA Cup winning side, and was now poised to turn his Wolves team into giants of the 1950s. It signposted a decade of head-to-head rivalry with Manchester United.

TED DRAKE had hung up his boots after his swashbuckling playing career and was now managing at Reading. His greatest days as a manager would come at Chelsea with a League title and the introduction of Drake's Ducklings.

JOHN DICK was doing his National Service in Colchester when spotted playing for his Army team by a West Ham scout. He would eventually sign for the Hammers and become the first West Ham player to win a Scottish international cap.

JIMMY DICKINSON, Pompey's first gentleman of football, was helping Portsmouth retain the League championship and was a season away from the first of his forty-eight England caps.

TOMMY DOCHERTY had joined Preston from Celtic in November 1949, and was starting to establish himself in the club and country shirts previously worn by Bill Shankly. 'The Doc' was already outspoken and controversial with his opinions!

BRYAN DOUGLAS was recommended to Blackburn by his mother, and proved her judgment perfect by becoming the nearest thing to a 'new' Stanley Matthews. He joined the Ewood Park groundstaff and settled into the first-team after National Service.

GEORGE EASTHAM was about to leave school and follow his father to Northern Ireland where George Eastham Snr was manager-elect of Ards. After joining Newcastle in 1956 Eastham Jnr would start a one-man war against the transfer sysytem.

DUNCAN EDWARDS was fourteen at the dawn of the decade and destined to become the most famous of the Busby Babes. Manchester United were already on his trail at Dudley where he was about to win an England schoolboy international cap.

GEORGE FARM was plucked from the obscurity of Hibernian reserves in Edinburgh to become the 500-match last line of defence for Blackpool throughout the 1950s. Keeping seemed to be in his blood. On his retirement he became a lighthouse keeper.

MALCOLM FINLAYSON was into his third season at Millwall after being signed from Renfrew. His greatest challenge would be taking over in goal from the legendary Bert 'the Cat' Williams at Wolves. He was the best goalkeeper Scotland never capped.

TOM FINNEY, the Pride of Preston, was juggling two jobs, as he did throughout his distinguished career. When he wasn't running defences into dizzy disarray, he was building up his lucrative business as a plumber and electrician.

EDDIE FIRMANI had decided to try his luck in England as one of the few foreign footballers, signing for Charlton from South African club Clyde in February 1950. It was the first of three periods at The Valley in between successful sojourns in Italy.

CHARLIE FLEMING had scored 169 goals for East Fife before bringing his shooting boots to Sunderland. He was nicknamed Cannonball because of the ferocity of his shots. He topped 50 goals for three successive seasons when winding down with Bath.

RON FLOWERS was released by his local club Doncaster Rovers but quickly snapped up by Wolves, who blooded him in their Wath Wanderers nursery club. He eventually captained his club and country in a long and distinguished career at Molineux.

TREVOR FORD was about to move from Aston Villa to Sunderland for what was then a record £30,000. He and Len Shackleton formed an unpredictable (and often unhappy) partnership that baffled and bemused defences.

BILL FOULKES was working down the mines when signed by Manchester United as an amateur in 1950. It was not until he had been called up by England that he decided to become a full-time professional footballer as one of the Busby Babes. He took over as captain after surviving the Munich air disaster.

NEIL FRANKLIN, arguably the greatest ever England centre-half, was secretly negotiating to join the outlawed Colombian league as the fifties dawned. His defection left a hole in the England defence that took ages to fill.

RON GREENWOOD was settled in the middle of the Brentford defence after playing for Bradford Park Avenue in the immediate post-war years. He was already showing an interest in coaching and was a disciple of England manager Walter Winterbottom.

Preston Plumber Tom Finney shields the ball against Chile in what was an historic match for England ... their first in a World Cup finals tournament. England got their World Cup campaign off to a winning 2-0 start in this game at the Maracana Stadium in Rio de Janeiro on Sunday 25 June 1950. But humiliation was waiting around the corner for them in the shape of the unrated United States team.

HARRY GREGG was playing in goal for Coleraine before starting a career in the League with Doncaster Rovers and then Manchester United. He would survive the Munich air disaster, earning hero status for pulling team-mates from the wreckage.

JIMMY GREAVES was a ten-year-old schoolboy and top scorer for South Wood Lane under-10s team on its way to the Dagenham Schools title. Five years later Chelsea persuaded him to sign for them under the noses of Spurs and West Ham.

JOHNNY HANCOCKS was into his fourth season with Wolves after joining them from Walsall following wartime service. The 'Mighty Atom' stood just 5ft 4in in his football boots, but could destroy defences with his swift running and rocket shots.

JOE HARVEY was right-half and captain of a Newcastle team that was about to turn the 'fifties into a festival of FA Cup triumphs. He skippered them in successive victories at Wembley, and later became their long-serving manager.

JOHNNY HAYNES, the Pass Master, had just led England schoolboys to an 8-2 victory over Scotland (including Dave Mackay) at Wembley, and when all the major clubs came with their calling cards he chose Fulham simply because his best pal Tosh Chamberlain had signed for them a year earlier. It was the start of an 18-year association.

JIMMY HILL was playing for Brentford before moving to Fulham where he led the PFA wages fight. He once scored five goals at Doncaster when marked by Charlie Williams, one of the few black players in the League and a comedian in the making.

CLIFF HOLTON, a Rock Hudson lookalike but all man, had just been converted from a reserve full-back at Arsenal to a first-team centre-forward, and scored dozens of goals that were to make him a hero at Higbury and later Watford and Northampton.

DON HOWE was establishing himself as a thinking right-back in the West Bromwich Albion defence, and showing the sort of tactical intelligence that would eventually make him one of the game's outstanding coaches.

HARRY JOHNSTON came into the 'fifties as captain of the Matthews/Mortensen-motivated Blackpool team that were proving themselves FA Cup specialists. He was a composed centre-half, unlucky to get caught in the Hungarian hurricane of 1953.

JACK KELSEY had been signed by Arsenal from Welsh club Winch Wen as understudy to George Swindin, and from 1952 was to make the Gunners' goalkeeping jersey his own. Many considered him the greatest of all British goalkeepers.

DEREK KEVAN started the new decade playing for Ripon YMCA before signing for Bradford Park Avenue, His most prolific goal-scoring days were to be with West Bromwich Albion, and he took his bulldozing style into two World Cup campaigns.

DENIS LAW was a puny, squint-eyed schoolboy footballer in his hometown of Aberdeen, and hardly looking like somebody who would during the 'fifties develop into one of the most exciting goal scorers in the world.

TOMMY LAWTON was in the middle of the season in which he memorably shot Notts County back to the Second Division. His peak decades were the 'thirties and 'forties, but he still had enough ammunition left to make an impact on the 'fifties.

BILLY LIDDELL was such a formidable force at Anfield that Liverpool were known as Liddellpool when he was banging in goals from all positions. As the 'fifties arrived this super-charged Scot was about to help shoot Liverpool to the FA Cup final.

NAT LOFTHOUSE was knocking on the door of the England team as he came into the 'fifties full of running and showing the mixture of skill and physical power that was to make him a living legend at Bolton and beyond.

JIMMY LOGIE was about to enter a year in which his precise passing helped Arsenal triumph in a 1950 FA Cup final in which Reg Lewis scored two goals. His wonderful skills were rewarded with only one Scottish cap.

DAVE MACKAY started the New Year signing schoolboy forms with Hearts, and he was farmed out to Newtongrange Star to lay the foundation to a glittering career. It was fitting that he played for Hearts because he was all heart, and his shuddering tackling and skilled passing were to be vital future weapons for Tottenham and Derby County.

JIMMY McILROY was playing for Glentoran when spotted by Burnley, who signed him in the autumn of 1950. He became a Turf Moor legend, and he and Danny Blanchflower playing together in midfield for Northern Ireland was poetry in motion.

ALF McMICHAEL was into his first season at Newcastle after being signed from Linfield. He was a key member of the outstanding Northern Ireland team of the 'fifties and many considered him the finest left back in the Football League.

PETER McPARLAND had established himself in the Dundalk side as a free-scoring outside-left when Aston Villa picked him up for a bargain £3,880. He would enter into FA Cup folklore during the 'fifties.

WILF MANNION, the Golden Boy, was nearing the end of his exceptional career. Like so many of his contemporaries, he was robbed of his peak years by the War but he remained a Middlesbrough idol long after the 'fifties had faded.

STANLEY MATTHEWS came into the 'fifties with people wondering when he would retire. But the Wizard of Dribble was still casting his spell fifteen years later! Wembley was beckoning as Stanley shuffled in from the wing into a new decade.

JOE MERCER was about to kick off the year in which he would collect the FA Cup as Arsenal captain. He continued to play for the Gunners until a broken leg forced his retirement in 1953-54. 'Uncle Joe' then started a new life as a manager.

GIL MERRICK chose a career in football ahead of school teaching and followed Harry Hibbs as Birmingham City goalkeeper without being overshadowed by his famous predecessor. He was unfortunate to be on the end of 13 goals from Hungary.

JACKIE MILBURN was coming into a decade in which he established himself as a football god on Tyneside. Three FA Cup finals in five years was just part of the fairytale as he lived up to his initials JET. 'Wor Jackie' was the king of Newcastle.

BOBBY MITCHELL was in his first season at Newcastle after signing from Third Lanark. He was a darting left winger who earned the nickname Dazzler, and like Jackie Milburn and Bobby Cowell collected three FA Cup winners' medals in five years.

STAN MORTENSEN was feeding off the passes of 'the other Stanley' (Matthews) for Blackpool and England, and was three seasons away from the game that would make him a legend as the only player to score a hat-trick in a Wembley FA Cup final.

JACKIE MUDIE was three months off launching his first-team career with Blackpool to complete the M-squad, with Matthews and Mortensen. A goal-plundering Scottish inside-forward, he switched to centre-forward when Morty moved to Hull.

JIMMY MULLEN was on his way to 486 League appearances for Wolves as a left winger who was a perfect balance to the tiny, rocket-shooting Johnny Hancocks out on the right. Despite the presence of Matthews and Finney he would win 12 caps.

BILL NICHOLSON was a key man in midfield for the push-and-run Spurs, and already looking forward to a new career by taking a coaching course. His one and only cap was to follow in 1951 when he scored with his first touch of the ball against Portugal.

SYD OWEN, whose start in the game was delayed by the War until he was twenty-three, was establishing himself in the centre of the Luton Town defence after joining them from his hometown club Birmingham City. His greatest season was still ten years away when he would pick up the Footballer of the Year award at the age of thirty-six.

BOB PAISLEY was studying physiotherapy in preparation for his retirement from playing, and his dream was to get a place in the Liverpool backroom team. He was a stalwart player at Anfield but his best years lay ahead of him as a king of managers.

BILL PERRY had just joined Blackpool from Johannesburg Rangers despite a last-minute bid by Charlton to take him to The Valley. He patrolled Blackpool's left wing with pace and power while Stanley Matthews was performing his magic on the right.

ALBERT QUIXALL was about to become a professional with Sheffield Wednesday after two years as a Hillsborough amateur. He was valued at his weight in gold when sold to Manchester United for a record £45,000 in the wake of the Munich air disaster.

ALF RAMSEY was 'The General' of the push-and-run Spurs after joining them from Southampton in 1949. He was the thinking man's right-back and had already gathered a reputation as a tactical genius.

DON REVIE was operating as an orthodox inside-forward with Hull City before joining Manchester City, where his deep-lying centre-forward role would become known as 'the Revie Plan.' He had already made up his mind on a future in club management.

What the well-dressed footballer was wearing in the mid-fifties. Don Revie (left), Billy Wright (centre) and Stanley Matthews were in Paris for an international against France in May 1955. Style icons? Eat your heart out, Becks.

GEORGE ROBLEDO and his brother Ted had just joined Newcastle from Barnsley, where they had grown up after moving from Chile to Yorkshire with their Chilean father and English mother. George was to form a great partnership with Jackie Milburn.

BOBBY ROBSON had qualified as an electrician and was then rescued from a life down the mines when Fulham signed him early in 1950. He was to have two spells at Craven Cottage, but his peak playing years were with West Bromwich Albion.

ARTHUR ROWE had returned to Tottenham where he had been a pre-war player, and introduced the push-and-run tactics that were to bring Spurs back-to-back Second and First Division titles.

ARTHUR ROWLEY was building his goals mountain at Fulham before moving on to Leicester in 1950. He would eventually take his total to an all-time record 434 League goals. His older brother Jack was a scoring machine with Manchester United.

JIMMY SCOULAR was playing a tough-tackling role in bringing Portsmouth two successive League titles before moving on to Newcastle, where he found more success in the FA Cup. Scotland's selectors rewarded him with a meagre nine caps.

MAURICE SETTERS had just won England schoolboy international honours and was about to be signed by his nearest League club Exeter City. He would become one of the country's outstanding wing-halves with West Brom and then Manchester United.

JACKIE SEWELL was discovered playing for his local club Whitehaven at the age of fifteen by Notts County, and as the 'fifties dawned he was on the brink of becoming the game's most expensive player. Sheffield Wednesday paid a record £34,000 for him in 1951, and he was poised for the first of six England caps.

LEN SHACKLETON was at Sunderland, adding to his reputation as one of the game's great entertainers. The Clown Prince of Soccer had the skill to dismantle any defence. It is outrageous that he won only five England caps.

BILL SHANKLY was in the middle of his first season as a manager with Carlisle United after an energetic playing career with Preston and Scotland. A much bigger stage lay in waiting at Anfield.

ALF SHERWOOD was winning fame at Cardiff as 'the king of the sliding tackle.' Stanley Matthews paid him the compliment of calling him the best full back he had ever faced. The ex-miner won 41 Welsh caps.

RONNIE SIMPSON was about to turn pro with Third Lanark after playing for Great Britain in the 1948 Olympics. His astonishing goalkeeping career would take in FA Cup winning finals with Newcastle and the European Cup final with Celtic in 1967.

BILL SLATER was at university studying for his teacher's degree while playing as an amateur for Blackpool. Even after joining Wolves for his peak years he was never more than a semi-professional, with equal interest in teaching as in playing.

BOBBY SMITH was spotted by Chelsea scouts while playing for Redcar Boys' Club and started his professional career at Chelsea in 1950. It was only after his move to Tottenham in 1955 that he became recognised as a world-class centre-forward.

BOB STOKOE was to make his Newcastle debut on Christmas Day 1950 as centre-forward, but later established himself as a driving half-back. He would later become a legend in the North East for his managerial exploits with Sunderland.

ERNIE TAYLOR was creating chances for Newcastle and with such style and panache that Stanley Matthews advised Blackpool to sign him as his partner. He collected FA Cup winners' medals with Newcastle and Blackpool, and was a finalist with Man United.

TOMMY TAYLOR had started his career with Barnsley after being discovered playing with a local colliery side. Manchester United would come calling in 1953 and at Old Trafford he would develop into one of the great centre-forwards.

BERT TRAUTMANN, the former German prisoner of war, was one of the few foreign players in the Football League in the 'fifties. There was huge controversy when he signed for Man City from St Helen's in 1949, but he won over the fans and proved himself more than worthy to take over from the great Frank Swift.

DENNIS VIOLLET was an England schoolboy international about to come through the Manchester United junior squad to establish himself as a potent first-team striker.

CHARLIE WAYMAN, small but lethal, was poised for a move from Southampton to Preston after banging in goals galore for the Saints and his local club Newcastle.

LEN WHITE was making such an impact at Rotherham that Newcastle came calling, and he played in four forward positions while scoring 153 goals for the Magpies.

RAY WILSON was discovered by Huddersfield while working as an apprentice railwayman. Bill Shankly was a huge influence in making him a world-class left-back.

BERT WILLIAMS was just establishing himself as England's goalkeeper in succession to the great Frank Swift. A series of stunning goalkeeping performances for Wolves earned him the fitting nickname 'the Cat.'

WALTER WINTERBOTTOM was the England team manager preparing for the 1950 World Cup challenge, and what would become a huge embarrassment.

RAY WOOD had been playing for Darlington for just three months when Manchester United took him to Old Trafford where he developed into an exceptional goalkeeper.

BILLY WRIGHT was on the brink of a decade when he became a legend of the game as captain for his club and country. He would lead England 90 times on his way to becoming the first footballer to win 100 international caps.

They are the main players in the cast of thousands ... and now it is curtain up on the footballing 'fifties.

Billy Wright proudly leads out his team-mates from the bowels of the gigantic Maracana Stadium in Rio for England's first ever World Cup finals match against Chile on 25 June 1950. His Wolves clubmate Bert 'the Cat' Williams is directly behind him. A 2-0 victory was a little over 90 minutes away. It was the calm before the storm.

OUR first dip back into the footballing 'fifties collides with one of the darkest days in the history of English football: the humiliating 1-0 World Cup defeat in Belo Horizonte by a United States team that we in our arrogance thought did not belong on the same planet, let alone the same pitch as the game's proud Old Masters. It was a result that could be measured on the Richter scale.

All these years on it is pointless seeking excuses, but hindsight is a wonderful gift and it is possible to trace the seeds of the debacle to a controversial event two months before the finals in Brazil. Centre-half Neil Franklin, arguably the finest player ever to wear the No 5 England shirt, literally walked out on his country, and left a hole in the middle of the defence that took years to fill.

Franklin was the best known and most talented of a cluster of League footballers who joined the outlawed Colombian league in Bogota. Sick to death of his slave-labour wages in Britain, Franklin went to seek his fortune on foreign fields only to find frustration. The disillusioned Stoke City captain soon returned home with empty pockets and to a ban from international football. It was four years before England found an adequate replacement for the cultured Franklin, in the shape of skipper Billy Wright. He had been playing his heart out at right-half while the selectors tried no fewer than eleven players in their fruitless search for the man who could command the centre of the defence.

Franklin's last match for England was against Scotland in the 1950 Home Championship that had been nominated as a World Cup qualifying group. The top two teams were guaranteed a place in the finals.

The Scottish FA decided that they would only send a team if they won the domestic title, putting enormous pressure on their players before the final deciding match against England. With Franklin masterful in defence, England beat them 1-0 thanks to a second-half Roy Bentley goal that suddenly silenced a crowd of 133,250 Hampden Park spectators trying to roar Scotland to Rio.

England went to Brazil, and the Scots stayed behind even though a final place had been booked for them. It is hard to fathom who was the more stupidly stubborn in those days, the Scottish or English rulers. It was the blind leading the bland.

There is no question that the England team captained by Billy Wright had the players with the ability to win the World Cup when they first entered that 1950 tournament but the Football Association made a complete hash of it. Let me lay out the evidence, and see what you think.

The FA saw fit to organise a goodwill tour of Canada at the same time as the World Cup finals in Brazil, and then ummed and ahhed when Manchester United requested that none of their players should be considered because they had arranged a trip to the United States.

Team manager Walter Winterbottom, battling against this blinkered club-before-country attitude, almost had to get on his knees to have first choice for the World Cup. As it was, he had to go to Brazil without England's most famous player, Stanley Matthews, who was sent on the totally meaningless Canadian trip as a footballing ambassador. Special arrangements had to be made to fly him down to Rio for the World Cup, and he arrived after England had won their opening match 2-0 against Chile.

Winterbottom wanted to play Matthews in the second game against the United States, and the then FA secretary Sir Stanley Rous argued the case for him with the chairman of the selectors, a Grimsby fish merchant called Arthur Drewry, who had been appointed the lone selector for the World Cup. 'My policy is that I never change a winning team,' the dogmatic Drewry said dismissively. Winterbottom could advise but not pick the team!

It is etched into the record books that England were beaten 1-0 by the United States with Stanley Matthews among the spectators. It was like leaving Wellington on the bench at Waterloo.

Billy Wright, a great personal friend of mine, once told me a story from that 1950 World Cup tournament which captures the amateurish way in which we approached international football. Nobody had bothered to check what food the hotel would serve in Brazil, and the players complained that they could not eat it because it was too spicy. Winterbottom decided the only way round the problem was to go into the hotel kitchen and do the cooking himself. Talk about head cook and bottle washer!

England had made a far from impressive start to their World Cup campaign against Chile but got away with a victory. The vast Maracana Stadium, with workmen still putting the finishing touches, held 200,000 spectators and it looked and sounded deserted with fewer than 30,000 watching the game. Playing against England was Newcastle United forward George Robledo, who could hardly speak a word of Spanish but had been called in to help the country of his birth. He rattled the England crossbar with a 30-yard free-kick before goals from Jimmy Mullen and Stan Mortensen lifted England to a 2-0 victory that neutral observers considered flattering.

Then came England's humiliation by the United States in Belo Horizonte which was not, as reported at the time, against a team imported from overseas by the Americans. The football writers failed to do their homework, and wrote inaccurate stories that England had been beaten by a side that had come from Ellis Island, with only a couple of true Americans among them. But research has since proved this to be false information. All but three of the team were born in the United States. They were boosted by immigrants

England goalkeeper Bert Williams looks back in anger as he is beaten by the deflected Joe Gaetjens header that sent shock waves through the World Cup. It gave English football a new low point by which to measure disaster.

Joe Maca from Belgium, Ed McIllveney from Scotland, and the goal scorer, Joe Gaetjens from Haiti who had a Belgian father.

It was a deflected header from Gaetjens eight minutes before half-time that gave the United States a victory that sent shock waves through the World Cup. England hit the woodwork three times, and what seemed a certain face-saving goal from a Ramsey free-kick in the closing minutes was miraculously saved by the diving goalkeeper Borghi, a professional baseball catcher. Another Ramsey free-kick had earlier found the back of the net, but the referee whistled for an infringement. England spent eighty-five per cent of the game in the American half but finished up the losers. Nobody could have felt more frustrated than Stanley Matthews, who sat watching impassively from the sidelines. It was if the Indians had upped and massacred John Wayne and his men.

The goal-scoring hero Gaetjens was later reported to have died in jail in Haiti after helping to organise a guerrilla movement against the island's dictator, 'Papa' Doc

Duvalier. His name is certain to live on in football history.

A victory against Spain in the next match could still have sent England through but they surrendered dismally, even with Matthews and Finney operating on the wing.

While England took the long haul home, Uruguay went on to win the World Cup. They beat hosts Brazil in front of a world record crowd of 199,854 in a frantic match refereed by England's George Reader, a 53-year-old schoolteacher who later became chairman of Southampton. His linesmen were Scot George Mitchell and Yorkshireman Arthur 'It's A Knockout' Ellis.

Strictly speaking this was not a Final but a deciding match of a league-style pool involving Uruguay, Brazil, Sweden and Spain. Brazil, urged on by their fanatical fans, needed only a draw to take the trophy. They seemed certain to be crowned champions when right winger Friaca shot them into the lead two minutes after half-time. But Uruguay, superbly marshalled by skipper Obdulio Varela, stayed calm and composed. They equalised eighteen minutes later with a neatly taken goal by Juan Schiaffino, who would later play for AC Milan and Italy before returning to Uruguay as national manager.

With just eleven minutes to go hurtling winger Alcide Ghiggia exchanged passes with hs partner Julio Perez before crashing a winning shot nto the net to send a Brazilian nation into mourning. Ghiggia was an unlikely looking hero. He was the 'Matchstick Man,' of Uruguayan football, with spindly legs and a narrow, hunched frame. But his ball control and speed on the right wing demoralised many a full-back and his rocketing right-foot shooting was Uruguay's most devastating weapon in the 1950 finals. Eight years after his triumph in Rio Ghiggia played in the World Cup qualifying rounds for Italy and got himself ordered off against Northern Ireland.

The Brazilians were so devastated by their defeat by Uruguay that they looked around for reasons for their failure to win the World Cup for the first time. They decided their blue and white shirts were to blame, and switched for future games to yellow and green, the colours in which they were set to dominate world football. Perhaps England should have thought of switching to red shirts?

Many years later I asked the man who had been at the heart of the game what the atmosphere was like. This is what referee George Reader, by then chairman of Southampton, told me:

'At the final whistle it was suddenly like being at a mass funeral. I have never in my life seen so many grown men crying and sobbing. The Brazilian fans and their players were absolutely heart broken. They had been convinced they were going to win, but I think the tension of the occasion got to them. Neutral spectators would admit that the Urguayans deserved their victory with football that was simple, economical and ideally suited to the conditions. I felt very privileged to be part of it, particularly as the game was watched by a world record crowd.'

THE LEAGUE CHAMPIONSHIP 1949-50
Portsmouth still rule the waves

RARELY has there been a closer finish to a League championship race than the 1949-50 title battle. Any one of three teams could have won it coming into the final straight, with defending champions Portsmouth, Wolves and Sunderland all within shooting distance of the championship trophy.

The young Wolves team – the Cullis cubs – had set the early pace, going thirteen matches before their first defeat. They were then overhauled by Billy Liddell-inspired Liverpool, who went nineteeen matches unbeaten.

Manchester United, back home at Old Trafford after ground-sharing with Manchester City because of bomb damage to their ground, were always in the hunt, with Portsmouth, Blackpool and Sunderland on their heels.

Matt Busby's United caught up with Liverpool in the spring, but over the crucial Easter programme it was Sunderland who came through to lead the exciting, unpredictable title race.

Just one point seperated the three top clubs on the final day of the season, 6 May 1950, with Portsmouth and Wolves level on points and Sunderland one point behind. Pompey, at home to Aston Villa, knew that a win would clinch the championship. Fratton Park resounded to the sounds of Pompey chimes as a hat-trick from rugged Scot Doug Reid inspired a 5-1 victory.

Wolves hammered bottom club Birmingham City 6-1 to become only the second side to miss the title on goal average. Sunderland crushed Chelsea 4-1 but had to settle for third place one point behind. Only six points separated the first nine clubs, and Portsmouth edged out Wolves by 0.393 of a goal.

Portsmouth were the first club to retain the title since the Arsenal hat-trick of the mid-1930s, but the good times would soon be over for Pompey. So many servicemen had been based in the chief naval port during the war that they could recruit the cream of the players, but as Britain's war machine was dismantled so Portsmouth suddenly found their pool of potential players shrinking.

But for two years they ruled the football waves with football that was fast and direct. under the no-nonsense management of Bob Jackson. They had a VIP President in Field Marshal Montgomery, who collected the trophy at Fratton Park when they won it for the first time in their golden jubilee year of 1948-49.

The remarkable thing about their first championship success is that they achieved it without a single international player in their squad, but the following year caps came tumbling in for the likes of Jimmy Dickinson, Jimmy Scoular, Jack Froggatt, Peter Harris and Len Phillips. They were happy days at Pompey.

Arsenal skipper Joe Mercer (above) receives the FA Cup from King George VI, with FA secretary Sir Stanley Rous looking on. Denis Compton (right) played the penultimate football match of his career in the 1950 final against Liverpool at Wembley. He made his last appearance against League champions Portsmouth at Highbury a week later when Arsenal paraded the FA Cup.

THE 1950 FA CUP FINAL
A Compton double-act rescues Arsenal

A RSENAL's veteran stars dragged a mighty performance out of their tiring legs to beat Liverpool 2-0 in a superbly contested 1950 FA Cup final on a skidding-wet Wembley surface. The match provided a fitting finale for England's favourite cricketing footballer Denis Compton.

It was thanks to left winger Denis and his giant centre-half bother Leslie that Arsenal made it to the final. They were trailing 2-1 to Chelsea in the semi-final at White Hart Lane when Denis took a last-minute corner. Leslie Compton ignored skipper Joe Mercer's orders to stay back in defence and ran upfield to get his head to his brother's expertly flighted corner-kick and guide it into the Chelsea net.

It earned Arsenal a replay and eventual victory, bringing Denis Compton to the Wembley stage for what he knew would be his last major match. He was thirty-two, his knee was giving him long-lasting problems and he was overweight. Some years later, when Denis and I were colleagues with *Express* newspapers, he told me:

'I decided that the final would be the last football game of my career. My knee would no longer stand the strain of playing a season of football on top of the Test and County cricket. I badly wanted to go out a winner, but the way I played in the first-half I think I would have been pulled off if substitutes had been allowed. I was a stone or so overweight for football at around thirteen and a half stone, and I was quickly out of puff. Manager Tom Whittaker knew that I was struggling, and gave me a good pep-talk at half-time. "This is the last forty-five minutes of your career," he said. "Go out there and make every one of them count. Go out a winner." My old idol, Alex James, who was helping out in the dressing-room, called me into the bath area. "Get this down you," he whispered, handing me a small glass of liquid. I looked at it, smelt it and pulled a face. It was neat brandy. I decided that Alex had been around in the game long enough to know what he was doing, and so I drank the brandy in one go. Whether it was psychological or what I don't know, but it certainly put the snap back in my game in the second-half and I felt quite pleased with my contribution to our 2-0 victory.'

Arsenal always had a slight edge against Liverpool, who had reached Wembley at the expense in the semi-finals of their deadly rivals Everton. It was the half-back line of the fiery Alex Forbes, the rock-like Leslie Compton and the inspirational Joe Mercer that strangled Liverpool's victory hopes. Little Jimmy Logie was the man of the match with his probing passes, one of which made the first of two match-winning goals for Reg Lewis. The Gunners had won the Cup without once leaving London!

ENGLAND FOOTBALL DIARY
Summary of their 1949-50 matches

Republic of Ireland, Goodison Park, 21.9.49. England lost 2-0

England were beaten on English soil by a non-British team for the first time in their history. Nine of the Irish players were with Football League clubs and two from Shamrock Rovers but all of them were born in Ireland. Johnny Carey was a magnificent captain, and Con Martin (penalty) and Peter Farrell scored in each half to produce a stunning result. Derby dfender Bert Mozley made his England debut at right-back on his 26th birthday. It was an unhappy dcbut, too, for Wolves centre-forward Jesse Pye and Pompey's Peter Harris, who struck a shot against the bar with the score at 1-0. It sounded as if the majority of the 52,000 fans packed into Goodison were supporting the Irish as they battled their way to an amazing victory. Even big-hearted Billy Wright could not turn back the green tide that swept across the Goodison pitch. It was one of those days when nothing would go right for England. They had a strong wind at their backs in the second half, but still could not break down the Irish defence in which captain Johnny Carey was a colossus. England might have had three or four goals, but the ball just would not go into the net. *Team: Williams Mozley Aston Wright* Franklin Dickinson Harris Morris Pye Mannion Finney.*

Wales, Ninian Park, 15.10.49. England won 4-1

The four home countries had agreed to take part in the World Cup for the first time, and FIFA dictated that the Home Championship should be the qualifying stage for the finals in Brazil in the summer of 1950. The first two teams were to qualify, but Scotland announced that they would only go if they won the Home Championship. This was the first ever World Cup qualifying match in which England or Wales had taken part. Jackie Milburn scored a spectacular hat-trick, and England won comfortably despite having Billy Wright struggling on the wing for most of the second-half with a torn thigh muscle. The game was virtually settled during an England blitz midway through the first-half when they scored three goals in twelve minutes. Milburn made it 4-0 when he completed his hat-trick to puncture an attempted revival by Wales, who had to be content with a late goal by Mal Griffiths after goalkeeper Bert Williams had saved brilliantly from Trevor Ford. The injury to Wright completely upset the balance of the Englan team, and a talking point was whether substitutes should be allowed. *Team: Williams Mozley Aston Wright* Franklin Dickinson Finney Mortensen (1) Milburn (3) Shackleton Hancocks*

Northern Ireland, Maine Road, 16.11.49. England won 9-2

Jack Rowley, deputising for injured Jackie Milburn, hammered four goals against an Irish team that had gone down 8-2 against Scotland in their previous match. Pompey's Jack Froggatt scored on his debut. England Test cricketer Willie Watson won the first of four caps at right-half, and former amateur international Bernard Streten got his only full England call while playing in the Second Division with Luton. Fulham's Irish goalkeeper Hugh Kelly had to pick the ball out of his net 28 times in five successive international matches. *Team: Streten Mozley Aston Watson Franklin Wright* Finney Mortensen (2) Rowley (4) Pearson (2) Froggatt J (1).*

Italy, White Hart Lane, 30.11.49. England won 2-0

England were outplayed for long periods by an over-elaborate Italian team, and only a series of fine saves by Bert Williams kept them in the game in a goalless first half. England snatched an undeserved lead fourteen minutes from the end when Jack Rowley scored with one of his typical thunderbolt left foot shots that the Italian goalkeeper could only wave to on its way into the net. The match was settled by a goal in a million from Billy Wright. His second goal for England was a complete freak. He lobbed the ball forward from a position just over the halfway line. It was intended for the far post. The Italian goalie, unchallenged, came out to collect it just as a gust of wind made the ball change direction. He grasped at thin air as it curled over his head and into the net. *Team: Williams Ramsey Aston Watson Franklin Wright* (1) Finney Mortensen Rowley (1) Pearson Froggatt J.*

Scotland, Hampden Park, 15.4.50. England won 1-0

Chelsea centre-forward Roy Bentley, playing a twin spearhead role with Stan Mortensen, scored the winning goal midway through the second half of his international debut. The goal confirmed England's entry into the World Cup finals. The 133,250 Hampden Park spectators were left screaming their frustration because the Scottish Football Association had surrendered their chances of a World Cup finals place by electing to go only if they won the Home Championship. Soon afterwards came the bombshell news that master centre-half Neil Franklin did not want to be considered for the World Cup because he was joining an outlawed club in Bogota in a bid to earn decent wages. Like his partner Billy Wright, he had played in all twenty-seven England matches since the war and they had a terrific understanding on the pitch. Now England had lost their lynchpin with the World Cup finals just weeks away. It put England's amateur selectors in a complete dither. *Team:Williams Ramsey Aston Wright* Franklin Dickinson Finney Mannion Mortensen Bentley (1) Langton.*

Wilf Mannion, Will o' the Wisp of Middlesbrough and England.

Portugal, Lisbon, 14.5.50. England won 5-3

Four goals from Tom Finney, including two from the penalty spot, and a spectacular effort from Stan Mortensen lifted England to victory. But there were worrying signs that the defence was creaking without the steadying influence of Neil Franklin. Laurie Hughes was the original choice to fill the centre-half vacancy, but he pulled out at the last minute because of injury and the job went to his Liverpool team-mate Bill Jones. Portugal, after trailing 3-0 at half-time, had battled back and England were struggling to hold on at 4-3 when Finney settled it with his second penalty. There was disturbing evidence that Billy Wright was missing that all-important understanding that he had with Neil Franklin. The Portuguese had been promised a trip to the World Cup finals if they beat England, and they played their hearts out. Their African-born centre-forward Ben David scored two of their goals, and as well as Bill Jones played it was obvious that England had lost a lot of stability in the middle of their defence. England had major problems, and the World Cup finals were just a few weeks away. *Team: Williams Ramsey Aston Wright* Jones Dickinson Milburn Mortensen (1) Bentley Mannion Finney (4).*

Belgium, Brussels, 18.5.50. England won 4-1

Wolves winger Jimmy Mullen became England's first ever substitute when he replaced injured Jackie Milburn, and he scored one of the goals as England staged a second-half recovery after trailing 1-0 at half-time. Roy Bentley had a foot in three of the goals and scored the last one himself in this final warm-up before the World Cup. The Belgians, trained by ex-Blackburn and Northampton goalkeeper Bill Gormlie, scored their goal through centre-forward Joe Mermans. It exposed the fact that England were still struggling at the heart of their defence. The match was virtually won for England by a half-time tactical talk from Walter Winterbottom. He was often accused of being too long winded and technical with his instructions, but he got straight to the point and made it clear how England should tighten at the back and push forward in midfield. England followed his orders and comfortably outplayed the Belgians in the second half. Poor Bill Jones. pitched into the international arena because of injuries, failed to impress the selectors, and was not even in the squad named the following week for the trip to Brazil. *Team: Williams Ramsey Aston Wright* Jones Dickinson Milburn (Mullen, 1) Mortensen (1) Bentley (1) Mannion (1) Finney.*

For the record, the squad selected for the World Cup: Williams (Wolves), Ditchburn (Spurs), Ramsey (Spurs), Scott (Arsenal), Aston (Man United), Eckersley (Blackburn), Wright (Wolves, capt.), Hughes (Liverpool), Dickinson (Portsmouth), Watson (Sunderland), Nicholson (Spurs), Taylor (Fulham), Cockburn (Man United), Milburn (Newcastle), Mortensen (Blackpool), Bentley (Chelsea), Mannion (Middlesbrough), Finney (Preston), Mullen (Wolves), Baily (Spurs), Matthews (Blackpool).

Chile, World Cup, Rio de Janeiro, 25.6.50. England won 2-0

Laurie Hughes replaced his Liverpool clubmate Bill Jones at centre-half for this opening match of England's World Cup campaign. He won three England caps, all in this World Cup tournament. Stan Mortensen gave England a thirty-eighth minute lead against the run of play when he headed in a Jimmy Mullen cross. Mullen turned goal scorer just after the hour when he drove the ball into the net following neat approach work by Mortensen and Tom Finney. It was barely a satisfactory start to England's World Cup challenge, but a dream performance compared with the nightmare that was to follow. *Team: Williams Ramsey Aston Wright* Hughes Dickinson Finney Mannion Bentley Mortensen (1) Mullen (1).*

USA, World Cup, Belo Horizonte, 29.6.50. England lost 1-0

The most humiliating defeat since England started playing international football back in 1872. Joe Gaetjens settled the match with his thirty-seventh minute deflected header that is reported on page twenty-three. Skipper Billy Wright said: 'It was a completely freak result. We might easily have had five or six goals if the ball had run for us. We camped in their half for most of the game, but the ball just wouldn't go into the net.' *Team: Williams Ramsey Aston Wright* Hughes Dickinson Finney Mannion Bentley Mortensen Mullen.*

Spain, World Cup, Rio de Janeiro, 2.7.50. England lost 1-0

England needed to win this match to stay in the World Cup following their embarrassing defeat by the USA. Spain took the lead through centre-forward Zarra in the forty-seventh minute and then dropped back into deep defence. Even with Matthews and Finney operating, England could not make the breakthrough and their World Cup challenge was over. Jackie Milburn had a legitimate-looking equaliser ruled off-side. Alf Ramsey and Bill Eckersley started a fifteen-match full-back partnership, and Tottenham pass master Eddie Baily got a long overdue cap. Tom Finney was tripped twice in the penalty area, but each time the referee waved play on. It was one of those games, one of those tournaments. England played their best football of the finals against Spain, but their finishing left a lot to be desired. Eddie Baily had a cracking debut, and his passing cut huge holes in the Spanish defence. Stan Mortensen and Jackie Milburn might have had a couple of goals each but for some brilliant saves by Barcelona goalkeeper Ramallets. There were calls for the head of team manager Walter Winterbottom, but he got a vote of confidence from the FA. *Team: Williams Ramsey Eckersley Wright* Hughes Dickinson Matthews Mortensen Milburn Baily Finney.*

WHEN Arsenal skipper Joe Mercer tossed up before the FA Cup final against Liverpool the coin landed on the soaking-wet surface and sat upright. Joc said later: 'I joked to Liverpool captain Phil Taylor that I had been practising that trick for years and just wanted to put him in a spin. It was the only time I ever saw that happen throughout my career. I had to toss again.'

Arsenal were the first club to reach an FA Cup final at Wembley without playing outside their own city, and they were the first to allow their players to spend the night before the Final at home in their own beds.

Liverpool received more than 100,000 applications for their allocation of 8,000 tickets for the FA Cup final against Arsenal. They held a ballot, open only to supporters living within a twenty-five mile radius of the city.

Tottenham led the Second Division promotion race from start to finish, included a run of twenty-three matches without defeat and won the championship by nine points. Sheffield Wednesday (1.395) just edged out neighbours Sheffield United (1.387) and Southampton 1.333) on goal average for the runners-up promotion spot.

At eighteen years 71 days, Leeds prospect John Charles became the youngest Welsh international in the goalless draw with Northern Ireland at Wrexham's Racecourse Ground on 8 March 1950.

In the Scottish League, Rangers completed their second hat-trick of Cup wins and won the championship, but a surprise defeat by East Fife in the League Cup semi-final cost them their hopes of a treble.

The Professional Footballers' Association announced a closed shop as they stepped up the pressure on the Football League and FA over the players' restrictive contracts and the 'soccer slave' wages. At the dawn of the 'fifties the maximum wage was £12 a week in the season and £10 a week in the summer. This was gradually pushed up to £17 a week and then, under threat of mutiny, the Football League bosses increased it to £20 a week in 1958-59. It would be another two years before the maximum wage was booted out and Fulham captain Johnny Haynes became the first £100-a-week footballer.

1949-50 WHO WON WHAT
All the champions and runners-up

First Division: Portsmouth, 53pts. **Runners-up:** Wolves, 53 pts.
Portsmouth record: P42 W22 D9 L11 F74 A38 Pts53
Representative team: Butler; Hindmarsh, Ferrier; (from) Spence, Scoular, Flewin (capt.), Dickinson; Pickett, Harris, Reid, Clarke, Phillips, Froggatt.
Top scorer: Clarke (17).
Manager: Bob Jackson.

Second Division: Tottenham, 61pts. **Runners-up:** Sheffield Wednesday, 52pts.
Third Division (South): Notts County, 58pts. **Runners-up:** Northampton, 51pts.
Third Division (North): Doncaster Rovers, 55pts. **Runners-up:** Gateshead, 53pts

FA Cup final: Arsenal 2, Liverpool 0
Arsenal: Swindin; Scott, Barnes; Forbes, Compton L, Mercer (capt.); Cox, Logie, Goring, Lewis, Compton D. **Scorer:** Lewis (2)
Liverpool: Sidlow; Lambert, Spicer; Taylor (capt.), Jones, Hughes; Payne, Baron, Stubbins, Fagan, Liddell

Top First Division marksman: Dickie Davis (Sunderland), 25 goals
Footballer of the Year: Joe Mercer (Arsenal)

Scottish First Division: Rangers 50pts. **Runners-up:** Hibernian, 49pts.
Scottish Cup final: Rangers 3, East Fife 0
Scottish League Cup final: East Fife 3, Dunfermline 0

FA Amateur Cup final: Willington 4, Bishop Auckland 0

World Cup deciding match: Uruguay 2, Brazil 1 (Rio, attendance: 199,854)
Uruguay: Maspoli, Gonzales, Tejera, Gambetta, Varela (capt.), Andrade, Ghiggia, Perez, Miguez, Schiaffino, Moran. **Scorers:** Schiaffino, Ghiggia
Brazil: Barbose, Augusto (capt.), Juvenal, Bauer, Danilo, Bigode, Friaca, Zizinho, Ademir, Jair, Chico. **Scorer:** Friaca
Referee: George Reader (England)
Third place: Sweden 3, Spain 1 (final pool match)
Leading scorer: Ademir (Brazil) 9 goals in 6 games

THE LEAGUE TABLES
Where they finished in 1949-50

FIRST DIVISION

		P	W	D	L	F	A	Pts
1	Portsmouth	42	22	9	11	74	38	53
2	Wolverhampton W.	42	20	13	9	76	49	53
3	Sunderland	42	21	10	11	83	62	52
4	Manchester United	42	18	14	10	69	44	50
5	Newcastle United	42	19	12	11	77	55	50
6	Arsenal	42	19	11	12	79	55	49
7	Blackpool	42	17	15	10	46	35	49
8	Liverpool	42	17	14	11	64	54	48
9	Middlesbrough	42	20	7	15	59	48	47
10	Burnley	42	16	13	13	40	40	45
11	Derby County	42	17	10	15	69	61	44
12	Aston Villa	42	15	12	15	61	61	42
13	Chelsea	42	12	16	14	58	65	40
14	West Bromwich A.	42	14	12	16	47	53	40
15	Huddersfield Town	42	14	9	19	52	73	37
16	Bolton Wanderers	42	10	14	18	45	59	34
17	Fulham	42	10	14	18	41	54	34
18	Everton	42	10	14	18	42	66	34
19	Stoke City	42	11	12	19	45	75	34
20	Charlton Athletic	42	13	6	23	53	65	32
21	Manchester City	42	8	13	21	36	68	29
22	Birmingham City	42	7	14	21	31	67	28

SECOND DIVISION

		P	W	D	L	F	A	Pts
1	Tottenham Hotspur	42	27	7	8	81	35	61
2	Sheffield Weds.	42	18	16	8	67	48	52
3	Sheffield United	42	19	14	9	68	49	52
4	Southampton	42	19	14	9	64	48	52
5	Leeds United	42	17	13	12	54	45	47
6	Preston North End	42	18	9	15	60	49	45
7	Hull City	42	17	11	14	64	72	45
8	Swansea Town	42	17	9	16	53	49	43
9	Brentford	42	15	13	14	44	49	43
10	Cardiff City	42	16	10	16	41	44	42
11	Grimsby Town	42	16	8	18	74	73	40
12	Coventry City	42	13	13	16	55	55	39
13	Barnsley	42	13	13	16	64	67	39
14	Chesterfield	42	15	9	18	43	47	39
15	Leicester City	42	12	15	15	55	65	39
16	Blackburn Rovers	42	14	10	18	55	60	38
17	Luton Town	42	10	18	14	41	51	38
18	Bury	42	14	9	19	60	65	37
19	West Ham United	42	12	12	18	53	61	36
20	Queens Park R.	42	11	12	19	40	57	34
21	Plymouth Argyle	42	8	16	18	44	65	32
22	Bradford Park A.	42	10	11	21	51	77	31

THIRD DIVISION (NORTH)

		P	W	D	L	F	A	Pts
1	Doncaster Rovers	42	19	17	6	66	38	55
2	Gateshead	42	23	7	12	87	54	53
3	Rochdale	42	21	9	12	68	41	51
4	Lincoln City	42	21	9	12	60	39	51
5	Tranmere Rovers	42	19	11	12	51	48	49
6	Rotherham United	42	19	10	13	80	59	48
7	Crewe Alexandra	42	17	14	11	68	55	48
8	Mansfield Town	42	18	12	12	66	54	48
9	Carlisle United	42	16	15	11	68	51	47
10	Stockport County	42	19	7	16	55	52	45
11	Oldham Athletic	42	16	11	15	58	63	43
12	Chester	42	17	6	19	70	79	40
13	Accrington Stanley	42	16	7	19	57	62	39
14	New Brighton	42	14	10	18	45	63	38
15	Barrow	42	14	9	19	47	53	37
16	Southport	42	12	13	17	51	71	37
17	Darlington	42	11	13	18	56	69	35
18	Hartlepools United	42	14	5	23	52	79	33
19	Bradford City	42	12	8	22	61	76	32
20	Wrexham	42	10	12	20	39	54	32
21	Halifax Town	42	12	8	22	58	85	32
22	York City	42	9	13	20	52	70	31

THIRD DIVISION (SOUTH)

		P	W	D	L	F	A	Pts
1	Notts County	42	25	8	9	95	50	51
2	Northampton Town	42	20	11	11	72	50	51
3	Southend United	42	19	13	10	66	48	51
4	Nottingham Forest	42	20	9	13	67	39	49
5	Torquay United	42	19	10	13	66	63	48
6	Watford	42	16	13	13	45	35	45
7	Crystal Palace	42	15	14	13	55	54	44
8	Brighton & Hove A.	42	16	12	14	57	69	44
9	Bristol Rovers	42	19	5	18	51	51	43
10	Reading	42	17	8	17	70	64	42
11	Norwich City	42	16	10	16	65	63	42
12	Bournemouth	42	16	10	16	57	56	42
13	Port Vale	42	15	11	16	47	42	41
14	Swindon Town	42	15	11	16	59	62	41
15	Bristol City	42	15	10	17	60	61	40
16	Exeter City	42	14	11	17	63	75	39
17	Ipswich Town	42	12	11	19	57	86	35
18	Leyton Orient	42	12	11	19	53	85	35
19	Walsall	42	9	16	17	61	62	34
20	Aldershot	42	13	8	21	48	60	34
21	Newport County	42	13	8	21	67	98	34
22	Millwall	42	14	4	24	55	63	32

Devoted followers of football in the fifties will instantly recognise the distinctive player on the right exchanging pennants before the start of an England-West Germany amateur international at White Hart Lane in 1955. He is England and Bishop Auckland captain Bob Hardisty, considered by many the finest amateur footballer of his generation.

FOOTBALLING FIFTIES
1950-51: From Amateurs to Shamateurs

YOUNGER readers will find it difficult to believe that amateur football teams often drew bigger attendances than the professionals in the 'fifties. A combined side of Oxford and Cambridge University players formed a club in 1948-49 called Pegasus. They caught the public imagination to such an extent that they twice pulled full 100,000 houses to Wembley when winning the FA Amateur Cup in 1951 and 1953.

Pegasus had barely a dozen years at their peak before disbanding, but in their short life span revived the days of the Corinthians with a game based on skill and, above all, good sportsmanship. They had two professional coaches giving them advice for free in Arthur Rowe and Vic Buckingham, two of the architects of push-and-run football, and it was the pleasing-on-the-eye style that they adopted.

Tony Pawson, an elegant and multi-skilled forward, was their outstanding player and many years later after becoming a distinguished football writer with the *Observer* said: 'It was all the idea of Professor Harold Thompson, a Fellow of the Royal Society, who was obsessed with the Corinthian ideal that a code of appropriate behaviour on the pitch was every bit as important as the playing tactics. We smiled our way through our games, win lose or draw, and the team spirit that we engendered spread to the terraces. There was almost a glow over us in our peak years, and it was an absolute pleasure and a privilege to be part of it all.'

Bishop Auckland were a club as well known as Pegasus, but from a far different background. The North East side created an incredible record in the FA Amateur Cup, appearing in eighteen finals and winning ten of them, including a memorable three years in a row in 1955, 1956 and 1957. Players such as Bob Hardisty, Harry Sharrat, Lol Bradley, Seamus O'Connell and Jimmy Nimmins were as good as any professionals with their technique and artistry. Their national status was so high that after the Munich air disaster, three of the players were asked to join Manchester United to help them through the team rebuilding process. The showdown between Pegasus and Bishop Auckland in the 1951 Amateur Cup Final was considered on a par with the professional final. Pegasus won 2-1, but football was the real winner.

But the Pegasus true blue amateur spirit hid the fact that something was rotten beneath the surface in amateur football. It was well-known that players were accepting illegal payments – often cash left in their boots – and the word 'shamateur' became commonplace to describe amateurs who played for money.

The days of the 'amateur' footballers were numbered, but throughout the 'fifties the play-for-nothing game flourished alongside the professional leagues.

THE art of push and run football was born against the walls of North London. It's main architect Arthur Rowe remembered playing with a tennis ball against the walls as a schoolboy and suddenly thought to himself : 'That's how easy and simple the game should be!'

It was some years after Arthur had entered the land of football legend by steering Spurs to back-to-back Second and First Division titles that he told me:

'My philosophy was that the easier you made the game the easier it was to play it. So I used to tell the players to push the ball to a team-mate and then run into space to take the instant return pass. It was making the most of the 'wall pass' or the 'one-two.' Make it simple, make it quick. It was easier said than done, of course, but I got together a squad of players with the football intelligence to make it work. We used to operate in triangles, with Eddie Baily, Ronnie Burgess and Les Medley particularly brilliant at the concept out on the left. It was amazing to watch as they took defenders out of the game with simple, straightforward passes and then getting into position to receive the return. Over on the right Alf Ramsey, Billy Nicholson and Sonny Walters were equally adept at keeping possession while making progress with simple passes.'

Arthur, as modest and likeable a man as you could wish to meet, used to often reminisce when in charge of the short-lived London Football Hall of Fame after ill health had forced him out of management. Never one to want to take credit for his own genius, he would always stress that the real father of push-and-run was his old Tottenham manager Peter McWilliam, who had been a noted tactician in two spells in charge at White Hart Lane.

It was McWilliam who had launched Arthur's playing career with the Spurs nursery team Gravesend and Northfleet. He developed into a thinking man's centre-half for Tottenham throughout the 'thirties until a knee injury forced his retirement, after an international career confined to one England cap. He travelled through Europe as a full-time coach and was on the verge of accepting the Hungarian team manager's job when war was declared.

On his return to England he became an army physical training instructor and then manager of non-League Chelmsford, making him ideally placed to take over at White Hart Lane as successor to Joe Hulme in 1949. His first major signing was Southampton right-back Alf Ramsey, a player he knew shared his keep-it-simple principles.

Spurs waltzed away with the Second Division title in Rowe's first full season in

Arthur Rowe (extreme left, back row) proudly poses with his push-and-run Spurs after they had captured the League championship in 1951. Alf Ramsey and Bill Nicholson, who would go on to become master managers, sit alongside each other on the left of the second row.

charge, but sceptics said their playground push-and-run tactics would be exposed in the First Division. Wrong!

They powered to the top of the table, eventually taking the League champoinship with 60 points, four ahead of Manchester United and the highest total since Arsenal's record 66 twenty years earlier. It was their attack, led aggressively by Channel Islander Len Duquemin, that took the eye, but the defence was a vital part of the jigsaw. It featured the safe hands and acrobatics of goalkeeper Ted Ditchburn, the towering presence of centre-half Harry Clarke, the perfect balance of full-back partners Alf Ramsey and Arthur Willis, and two of the finest half-backs in the League in Bill Nicholson and skipper Ronnie Burgess. There are many of a certain age who will argue that Welsh international Burgess was the most productive player ever to pull on a Tottenham shirt. Even the great White Hart Lane guru Bill Nicholson used to offer this opinion.

Eddie Baily's inch-perfect passing from midfield was a key factor as Spurs took apart the best defences in the land, scoring seven goals against Newcastle, six against Stoke, five against West Brom and champions Portsmouth and four in three of the first four matches of the season.

Push and run became more like push and punish. It was wonderful to watch, provided you were not the team on the receiving end.

THE 1951 FA CUP FINAL
'Wor Jackie' wows Wembley

NEWCASTLE arrived at Wembley for the 1951 FA Cup final against Stanley Matthews-motivated Blackpool wondering which of their teams would turn up. They had been a Jekyll and Hyde side, winning only one of their last eleven League matches and stuttering on the way to the Twin Towers.

They scraped through 3-2 against Bolton in the fourth round, survived a Stoke rally with a 4-2 victory in the fifth round, and were then taken to a replay before overcoming Third Division Bristol Rovers. They also needed a replay against Wolves in the semi-final. Most worrying for the Magpies is that their star centre-forward Jackie Milburn had suffered such a loss of form and confidence that acting manager Stan Seymour did the unthinkable and dropped him.

Milburn was recalled in time to lead the attack against Blackpool for a battle royal with England defender Harry Johnston, who had just been elected Footballer of the Year.

It was the footballer for all seasons, thirty-six-year-old Stanley Matthews, who claimed the stage early on with a series of dazzling runs as he tried to collect his first FA Cup winners' medal in what most people thought would be his last club appearance at Wembley. But the Newcastle defence, with Joe Harvey a colossus at centre-half, managed to stop Stan Mortensen from feeding off the maestro's work and it was the Geordies who took the lead five minutes into the second-half.

Blackpool surprisingly played the off-side game, a dangerous policy against a player with Milburn's pace. He gave them a couple of scares in the first-half, and then raced on to a superbly timed pass from Chilean George Robledo in the fiftieth minute. Blackpool's defenders hesitated, waiting for an offside-flag that never came as 'Wor Jackie' ran from the halfway line and beat advancing goalkeeper George Farm with a low right foot shot that found the net like a perfect putt to the hole. Milburn had kept up his record of scoring in every round.

Four minutes later Milburn scored a second killer goal. Tommy Walker found pint-size schemer Ernie Taylor with a through ball, and he cleverly back-heeled it into the path of Milburn who netted from twenty five yards, this time with his left foot.

'We had to wait seven weeks from the semi-final,' man of the match Milburn said after the game. 'I think we lost our nerve a bit during the build-up, and our League form went to pot. But we always knew that Wembley would bring the best out of us. Our plan was to keep Stan Mortensen tightly marked and make Stanley Matthews come inside. It worked a treat. But I hope Stanley gets his winners' medal one day.'

Skipper Joe Harvey holds the Cup, and Ernie Taylor leans across and congratulates two-goal hero Jackie Milburn. That's Tommy Walker looking in over his captain's shoulder. They would be back at Wembley to do it all again twelve months later.

ENGLAND FOOTBALL DIARY
Summary of their 1950-51 matches

Northern Ireland, Windsor Park, 7.10.50. England won 4-1

Eddie Baily scored two goals and big Jackie Lee, a Leicestershire cricketer, marked his only international with a goal as England tried to shake off the misery of their World Cup failure. Northern Ireland were chasing an equaliser with the score at 2-1 when England scored twice in the last five minutes. Billy Wright netted his third and final goal for England with a shot that went into the net through a forest of legs, and Baily finished the Irish off with a clever hook shot. Man United centre-half Allenby Chilton had to wait until he was thirty-two for this first cap as the selectors continued to hunt for a successor to Neil Franklin. *Team: Williams Ramsey Aston Wright (1) Chilton Dickinson Matthews Mannion Lee (1) Baily (2) Langton.*

Wales, Roker Park, 15.11.50. England won 4-2

Injured Billy Wright missed his first international after 33 successive matches. Alf Ramsey took over as skipper. Eddie Baily repeated his two-goal act. Arsenal centre-half Leslie Compton made his England debut at the age of thirty-eight alongside County cricketing colleague Willie Watson. Leslie remains the oldest player ever to have made an England debut. Les Medley partnered his Tottenham team-mate Baily on the left wing. Lionel Smith, converted from centre-half by Arsenal, came in at left-back. Goalkeeper Bert Williams kept his place in goal to maintain the Wolves record of having at least one player in the England team in every international match since the war. Trevor Ford, playing for Wales in front of his Sunderland fans, scored twice in the second half and it was not until Jackie Milburn netted a fourth goal in the final seconds that England felt they had the game won. *Team: Williams Ramsey* Smith L Watson Compton Dickinson Finney Mannion (1) Milburn (1) Baily (2) Medley.*

Yugoslavia, Highbury, 22.11.50. Drew 2-2

Bolton centre-forward Nat Lofthouse announced his arrival on the international stage with two goals. It was the first time in post-war football that England had gone into action without either Matthews or Finney. Leslie Compton deflected the ball into his own net, and Yugoslavia forced a late equaliser to become the first Continental side to avoid defeat in England in a full international. Lofty scored his two goals in a decisive five minute spell midway through the first-half. *Team: Williams Ramsey* Eckersley Watson Compton Dickinson Hancocks Mannion Lofthouse (2) Baily Medley.*

Scotland, Wembley, 14.4.51. England lost 3-2

Wilf Mannion was carried off with a fractured cheekbone in the eleventh minute after a collision with Billy Liddell. Manager Walter Winterbottom elected to accompany Mannion to hospital, and it was skipper Billy Wright who took the decision to switch Finney to the right to partner Matthews and the two wing wizards often made the Scottish defenders think they were seeing double. The ten men of England made the Scots battle all the way after debutant Harold Hassall had given them a twenty-fifth minute lead. Hibs partners Bobby Johnstone and Lawrie Reilly netted for Scotland and then the barnstorming Liddell, the idol of Liverpool, made it 3-1. England, briefly reduced to nine men after Stan Mortensen had been knocked out, refused to give in and Tom Finney conjured a goal in the eightieth minute. But the Scots held on for a deserved victory. *Team: Williams Ramsey Eckersley Johnston Froggatt J Wright* Matthews Mannion Mortensen Hassall (1) Finney (1).*

Argentina, Wembley, 9.5.51. England won 2-1

Goals in the last ten minutes from Stan Mortensen and Jackie Milburn (following the two he had scored for Newcastle on the same pitch in the FA Cup final four days earlier) gave England a scrambled victory. Eccentric Argentinean goalkeeper Rugilo, nicknamed 'Tarzan', had the crowd roaring with laughter as he swung on the crossbar and clowned his way through the match, which was staged as part of the Festival of Britain celebrations. Fulham centre-half Jim Taylor won the first of two caps at the age of thirty-three. Argentina were only the second country other than Scotland to play England at Wembley. *Team: Williams Ramsey Eckersley Wright* Taylor Cckburn Finney Mortensen (1) Milburn (1) Hassall Metcalfe.*

Portugal, Goodison Park, 19.5.51. England won 5-2

For the only time in his career, Billy Wright was dropped because of loss of form. Tottenham right-half Bill Nicholson took over in the No 4 shirt, and had the distinction of scoring with his first kick in international football in what was to prove his only match for England. Portugal were a goal down in twenty seconds and level a minute later in a blistering start to the match. Jackie Milburn restored England's lead in the eleventh minute. Alf Ramsey, skippering the side for a third time, mishit a back pass that let Portugal in for a second equaliser soon after half-time. Tom Finney then took over and ran the Portuguese into such dizzy array that at the after-match banquet their entire team stood and toasted 'Mr. Finney, the Master.' He scored a magnificent solo goal, and then laid on goals for Milburn and Harold Hassall. *Team: Williams Ramsey* Eckersley Nicholson (1) Taylor Cockburn Finney (1) Pearson Milburn (2) Hassall (1) Metcalfe.*

THE triumphant players of Newcastle were hoping for a hush-hush bonus from the club as reward for their FA Cup victory, and at the after-match banquet the whisper went around that each player was going to be presented with a bag stuffed with white fivers. The players were called up one by one to receive their gifts, and for ten minutes there was nothing but the sound of parcels being ripped open and the 'white fivers' being fished out. It turned out that it was tissue paper inside the parcel protecting a handbag for the wives and girlfriends of each of the players. It was Jackie Milburn who told the story, and he added: 'To really rub things in we later found out that the handbags had been bought on the cheap as a job lot.'

The Two Third Divisions – North and South – were each extended to 24 clubs, with Colchester and Gillingham and Scunthorpe and Shrewsbury winning Football League status.

Trials of a new type of football were dismissed as a failure when two balls went flat in a try-out at Southampton. But the Football Association did agree to the introduction of a white ball for matches played in poor visibility.

Alec Herd, thirty-seven-year-old Scottish international, and his seventeen-year-old son David played alongside each other for Stockport County in their final game of the season. David would later become a star striker with Arsenal and then Manchester United.

Scotland lost at home for the first time to overseas opposition when Austria won 1-0 on a frost-bitten Hampden pitch on 13 December 1950. Five months later the Scots were beaten 4-0 by Austria in Vienna, a game in which Billy Steel became the first Scottish player sent off in an international match.

The first day of the new Football League season attracted a record aggregate attendance of 1,189,401 spectators, yet at the end of the season the overall total was down by more than a million.

Nottingham Forest scored 110 goals on their way to the Third Division South title, and Preston equalled the League record of fourteen successive Second Division victories.

First Division: Tottenham, 60pts. **Runners-up:** Manchester United, 56 pts.

Tottenham record: P42 W25 D10 L7 F82 A44 Pts60

Representative team: Ditchburn; Ramsey, Willis; Nicholson, Clarke, Burgess (capt.); (from) Walters, Murphy, Bennett, Duquemin, Baily, Medley.

Top scorers: Duquemin (15), Walters (15).

Manager: Arthur Rowe.

Second Division: Preston, 57pts. **Runners-up:** Manchester City, 52pts.

Third Division (South): Nottingham Forest, 70pts. **Runners-up:** Norwich, 64pts.

Third Division (North): Rotherham 71pts. **Runners-up:** Mansfield Town, 64pts.

FA Cup final: Newcastle United 2, Blackpool 0

Newcastle: Fairbrother; Cowell, Corbett; Harvey (capt.), Brennan, Crowe; Walker, Taylor, Milburn, Robledo, Mitchell. **Scorer:** Milburn (2)

Blackpool: Farm; Shimwell, Garrett; Johnston (capt.), Hayward, Kelly; Matthews, Mudie, Mortensen, Slater, Perry

---

Top First Division marksman: Stan Mortensen (Blackpool), 30 goals

Top Second Division marksman: Cecil McCormack (Barnsley), 33 goals

Top Third Division North marksman: Jack Shaw (Rotherham), 37 goals

Top Third Division South marksman: Wally Ardron (Nottm Forest), 36 goals

Footballer of the Year: Harry Johnston (Blackpool)

Scottish First Division: Hibernian, 48pts. **Runners-up:** Rangers, 38pts.

Top Scottish First Division marksman: Lawrie Reilly (Hibernian), 22 goals

Scottish Cup final: Celtic 1, Motherwell 0

Scottish League Cup final: Motherwell 3, Hibernian 0

FA Amateur Cup final: Pegasus 2, Bishop Auckland 1

THE LEAGUE TABLES
Where they finished in 1950-51

FIRST DIVISION

		P	W	D	L	F	A	Pts
1	Tottenham Hotspur	42	25	10	7	82	44	60
2	Manchester United	42	24	8	10	74	40	56
3	Blackpool	42	20	10	12	79	53	50
4	Newcastle United	42	18	13	11	62	53	49
5	Arsenal	42	19	9	14	73	56	47
6	Middlesbrough	42	18	11	13	76	65	47
7	Portsmouth	42	16	15	11	71	68	47
8	Bolton Wanderers	42	19	7	16	64	61	45
9	Liverpool	42	16	11	15	53	59	43
10	Burnley	42	14	14	14	48	43	42
11	Derby County	42	16	8	18	81	75	40
12	Sunderland	42	12	16	14	63	73	40
13	Stoke City	42	13	14	15	50	59	40
14	Wolverhampton W.	42	15	8	19	74	61	38
15	Aston Villa	42	12	13	17	66	68	37
16	West Bromwich A.	42	13	11	18	53	61	37
17	Charlton Athletic	42	14	9	19	63	80	37
18	Fulham	42	13	11	18	52	68	37
19	Huddersfield Town	42	15	6	21	64	92	36
20	Chelsea	42	12	8	22	53	65	32
21	Sheffield Weds.	42	12	8	22	64	83	32
22	Everton	42	12	8	22	48	86	32

SECOND DIVISION

		P	W	D	L	F	A	Pts
1	Preston North End	42	26	5	11	91	49	57
2	Manchester City	42	19	14	9	89	61	52
3	Cardiff City	42	17	16	9	53	45	50
4	Birmingham City	42	20	9	13	64	53	49
5	Leeds United	42	20	8	14	63	55	48
6	Blackburn Rovers	42	19	8	15	65	66	46
7	Coventry City	42	19	7	16	75	59	45
8	Sheffield United	42	16	12	14	72	62	44
9	Brentford	42	18	8	16	75	74	44
10	Hull City	42	16	11	15	74	70	43
11	Doncaster Rovers	42	15	13	14	64	68	43
12	Southampton	42	15	13	14	66	73	43
13	West Ham United	42	16	10	16	68	69	42
14	Leicester City	42	15	11	16	68	58	41
15	Barnsley	42	15	10	17	74	68	40
16	Queens Park R.	42	15	10	17	71	82	40
17	Notts County	42	13	13	16	61	60	39
18	Swansea Town	42	16	4	22	54	77	36
19	Luton Town	42	9	14	19	57	70	32
20	Bury	42	12	8	22	60	86	32
21	Chesterfield	42	9	12	21	44	69	30
22	Grimsby Town	42	8	12	22	61	95	28

THIRD DIVISION (NORTH)

		P	W	D	L	F	A	Pts
1	Rotherham United	46	31	9	6	103	41	71
2	Mansfield Town	46	26	12	8	78	48	64
3	Carlisle United	46	25	12	9	79	50	62
4	Tranmere Rovers	46	24	11	11	83	62	59
5	Lincoln City	46	25	8	13	89	58	58
6	Bradford Park A.	46	23	8	15	90	72	54
7	Bradford City	46	21	10	15	90	63	52
8	Gateshead	46	21	8	17	84	62	50
9	Crewe Alexandra	46	19	10	17	61	60	48
10	Stockport County	46	20	8	18	63	63	48
11	Rochdale	46	17	11	18	69	62	45
12	Scunthorpe United	46	13	18	15	58	57	44
13	Chester	46	17	9	20	62	64	43
14	Wrexham	46	15	12	19	55	71	42
15	Oldham Athletic	46	16	8	22	73	73	40
16	Hartlepools United	46	16	7	23	64	66	39
17	York City	46	12	15	19	66	77	39
18	Darlington	46	13	13	20	59	77	39
19	Barrow	46	16	6	24	51	76	38
20	Shrewsbury Town	46	15	7	24	43	74	37
21	Southport	46	13	10	23	56	72	36
22	Halifax Town	46	11	12	23	50	69	34
23	Accrington Stanley	46	11	10	25	42	101	32
24	New Brighton	46	11	8	27	40	90	30

THIRD DIVISION (SOUTH)

		P	W	D	L	F	A	Pts
1	Nottingham Forest	46	30	10	6	110	40	70
2	Norwich City	46	25	14	7	82	45	64
3	Reading	46	21	15	10	88	53	57
4	Plymouth Argyle	46	24	9	13	85	55	57
5	Millwall	46	23	10	13	80	57	56
6	Bristol Rovers	46	20	15	11	64	42	55
7	Southend United	46	21	10	15	92	69	52
8	Ipswich Town	46	23	6	17	69	58	52
9	Bournemouth	46	22	7	17	65	57	51
10	Bristol City	46	20	11	15	64	59	51
11	Newport County	46	19	9	18	77	70	47
12	Port Vale	46	16	13	17	60	65	45
13	Brighton & Hove A.	46	13	17	16	71	79	43
14	Exeter City	46	18	6	22	62	85	42
15	Walsall	46	15	10	21	52	62	40
16	Colchester United	46	14	12	20	63	76	40
17	Swindon Town	46	18	4	24	55	67	40
18	Aldershot	46	15	10	21	56	88	40
19	Leyton Orient	46	15	8	23	53	75	38
20	Torquay United	46	14	9	23	64	81	37
21	Northampton Town	46	10	16	20	55	67	36
22	Gillingham	46	13	9	24	69	101	35
23	Watford	46	9	11	26	54	88	29
24	Crystal Palace	46	8	11	27	33	84	27

WE need to time-machine back to May 25 1952 to discover how Bolton warrior Nat Lofthouse got one of the most famous nicknames in football: The Lion of Vienna. The place: the Prater Stadium in Vienna. The match: Austria against England, described as the unofficial championship of Europe. Austria had scored 57 goals in their last 16 matches. England had regained pride and prestige with a sequence of eight games without defeat following a humiliating early exit from the 1950 World Cup.

It was a meeting of two worlds, the old and the new. Austria, with the versatile Ernst 'Clockwork' Ocwirk conducting the team from midfield, were experimenting with a fresh, flowing style of soccer soon to be perfected by the magical Magyars of Hungary. England were still sticking to the effective but old-fashioned 2-3-5 formation, and Walter Winterbottom decided that a counter-attacking policy was the best way to dismantle a defence that had helped Austria to the No 1 rating in Europe.

It was completely against the run of play when England snatched the lead in the twenty-first minute after soaking up non-stop pressure from the Austrians. A penetrating pass by Eddie Baily opened the heart of the Austrian defence and Lofthouse finished off the move with a left-foot volley deep into the net. The cheers of the thousands of British soldiers in the 65,000 crowd were still filling the Prater Stadium when Jack Froggatt conceded a penalty from which Huber side-footed an equaliser. The Portsmouth centre-half quickly made amends with a pass that put Jackie Sewell through to score after he had wrong-footed the Austrian defenders with two exaggerated dummies.

Austria pulled level again just before half-time through centre-forward Dienst, who shrugged off Billy Wright's challenge before powering the ball past goalkeeper Gil Merrick. Then came the storybook climax from Lofthouse.

Eight minutes from the end, with the game deadlocked at 2-2, Tom Finney collected a long throw from goalkeeper Gil Merrick, and released a pass that sent centre-forward Lofthouse clear just inside the Austrian half. He galloped fory-five yards with a pack of defenders snapping at his heels, and collided with oncoming goalkeeper Musil as he released a low shot. He was flat out unconscious and was the only person in the packed stadium who did not see the ball roll over the line for the winning goal.

Lofty, who hit the woodwork in the last minute, said later: 'The Austrian goalkeeper was in two minds and hesitated about coming out and so was a split-second too late to stop me shooting. I went out like a light when we collided, but our trainer Jimmy Trotter told me I had scored when he brought me round with the magic sponge. They tried to say I couldn't go back on, but wild horses couldn't have kept me off the pitch.'

A characteristic lion-hearted challenge from Nat Lofthouse, this time against Uruguay in the 1954 World Cup quarter-finals in Switzerland.

THE LEAGUE CHAMPIONSHIP 1951-52
Hat-trick hero Rowley shoots United to the title

JACK ROWLEY, a thunderboots of a forward with Manchester United, helped himself to four hat-tricks in a season when Matt Busby's team at last shook off their 'second best' reputation in the League. They had finished runners-up in four of the five seasons since the war, and they had to go right down to the wire before celebrating their first championship triumph for forty-one years.

It was Rowley's goal raids that made all the difference. He had scored three hat-tricks by the first week of September, the fastest this had ever been achieved in the First Division. But it was his fourth and final triple strike that had the biggest impact.

This crucial hat-trick came in the last League match of the season against Arsenal, who had reached the FA Cup final at Wembley and were chasing the elusive double. With two games to go, Arsenal and United were level on points and gearing up for a title-deciding showdown on the last Saturday of the League season.

But in their penultimate game injury-ravaged Arsenal were beaten 3-1 by West Bromwich Albion, and it meant they were then faced with a huge mountain to climb at Old Trafford. They needed to beat United 7-0 to take the title on goal difference.

It was Rowley who mercilessly put an end to the impossible dream with a hat-trick as United outgunned the Gunners and cruised to a 6-1 victory and the championship. Arsenal were reduced to ten men through injury midway through the first half, and finished with just nine players on the pitch.

Johnny Carey's commanding captaincy had been a feature of United's march to the title, while Allenby Chilton was a rock and Henry Cockburn a dynamo sparking the team in midfield. Stan Pearson contributed 22 goals, but it was Jack Rowley's 30-goal barrage that was the key factor in clinching the League championship.

'Jack Rowley has been on fire this season,' said manager Matt Busby. 'His confidence is sky-high and he feels he can score any time he gets the ball in the box. He and Stan Pearson are a handful for any defence.'

Relatively speaking, there have never been brothers to challenge the joint goal collections of Jack and the seven-years-younger Arthur Rowley, who during his career scored an all-time record 434 League goals. Jack's final tally was 208, and 182 of those were scored for Manchester United at the highest level.

The championship race finished in complete heartbreak for Arsenal, who on that dramatic last Saturday of the League season were pipped for runners-up place by neighbours Tottenham after they had beaten Chelsea 2-0 at Stamford Bridge. Now the Gunners had the FA Cup left as a consolation target.

THE 1952 FA CUP FINAL
Robledo makes it a chilly Wembley for Arsenal

HERE'S a question that will have you searching your memory: Who was the first foreign-born footballer to score a winning goal in an FA Cup final at Wembley?

The initial temptation will be to come up with the likes of Ricky Villa and Eric Cantona. But you have to go back much farther for the answer, when every corner of an English field was not full of foreign footballers.

Here's a clue: He played against England in the 1950 World Cup finals. His name, as many Geordie old-timers will tell you, is George Robledo.

George (real name Jorge) was six when he moved from his native Chile in 1932 with his two-years-younger brother Ted (Eduardo) to live in Yorkshire with their English mother and Chilean father. He started his playing career as an amateur with Huddersfield while working as a miner before he and Ted were signed by Barnsley.

Ted was a solid wing-half, but it was George who took the eye with his pace and finishing power. Newcastle were so impressed that they paid a joint fee of £26,500 for the brothers in 1949. George had refused to move until United also agreed to sign Ted.

The return on their investment from George alone was worth double the money. In 146 League games for Newcastle he scored 82 goals and formed a twin-engined plundering partnership with 'Wor' Jackie Milburn.

It was in his final year with Newcastle – 1951-52 – that he was at his peak. His thirty-ninth and last goal of that memorable season came six minutes from the end of a deadlocked FA Cup final against Arsenal at Wembley.

Arsenal, reduced to ten men because of a crippling injury to Walley Barnes, had hit the Newcastle bar moments earlier with a spectacular overhead kick from Doug Lishman. The Geordies struck back instantly and it was George Robledo who rose to head in a Bobby Mitchell cross off the near post for the only goal of the game.

The goal-scoring move had been started by Ted Robledo, and it was a fitting finale from the brothers to their Newcastle adventure before they returned home to Chile to play for Colo-Colo F.C.

George – speaking Spanish with a heavy Yorkshire accent – later coached the national team, and Ted came back to England for a brief spell with Notts County.

Had George been playing in today's game he would have been in the superstar category. He had Hollywood star looks, a stocky, muscular physique and he was known as a Muddy Marvel because he was so strong and quick on the sort of heavy grounds that were commonplace in the 'forties and 'fifties.

George passed on in 1989, and his brother two years later in mysterious circum-

The Newcastle team that retained the FA Cup in 1952. Back row, left to right:Bobby Cowell, Joe Harvey, Ronnie Simpson, Frank Brennan, Alf McMichael, Ted Robledo. Front: Tommy Walker, Billy Foulkes, Stan Seymour (Director/Manager), Jackie Milburn, George Robledo, Bobby Mitchell.

stances, falling overboard from a ship and drowning. The Robledo name will live on in football folklore, particularly on Tyneside.

For Arsenal, the 1952 FA Cup final was a nightmare, coming so soon after the disappointment of their failure to win the League title. Ray Daniel played with his broken wrist in a cast, Doug Lishman was limping because a cut had turned septic, and Jimmy Logie played despite internal bleeding in a recurring thigh injury. To add to the burden, key defender Walley Barnes limped off after he had twisted his right knee trying to turn on the lush Wembley turf in the opening minutes of the match. He briefly came back on to the pitch but was a limping passenger and finally hobbled off with a ligaments injury that kept him side-lined throughout the following season.

Newcastle's celebrations at winning the Cup for a second successive year were muted because they recognised that ten-man Arsenal had put up a defiant show.

France, Highbury, 3.10.51. Drew 2-2

Les Medley's first goal for England and an own goal saved a mediocre England team from a first home defeat by a foreign side. France were robbed of a deserved victory when Bert Williams made a desperate late save from French centre-forward Jean Grumellon, who gave centre-half Allenby Chilton a nightmare afternoon. Arthur Willis, partnering his Spurs team-mate Alf Ramsey, was one of four players - along with Chilton, Henry Cockburn and Wilf Mannion - who never played for England again. It was a scrappy team performance and England's problems continued in the middle of the defence. France could count themselves unlucky not to have won by a convincing margin, and it was Wolves goalkeeper Bert Williams who saved England from defeat with a succession of Swift-standard saves. *Team: Williams Ramsey Willis Wright* Chilton Cockburn Finney Mannion Milburn Hassall Medley (1) 1 o.g.*

Wales, Ninian Park, 20.10.51. Drew 1-1

Eddie Baily saved England from defeat against a Welsh team in which Ivor Allchurch and Trevor Ford were constantly putting England's defence under pressure. Newcastle right winger Billy Foulkes scored in the third minute with his first shot for Wales in international football. Baily, noted more for his scheming than his scoring, equalised with a rare header following a counter attack generated by a perfect pass from Billy Wright. Ford, the idol of Sunderland, missed two easy chances late in the game to give Wales their first victory over England since the war. Malcolm Barrass was the seventh centre-half tried by the selectors since the defection of Neil Franklin. Tommy Thompson, Aston Villa's diminutive ball-playing inside-right, won the first of two caps. *Team: Williams Ramsey Smith L Wright* Barrass Dickinson Finney Thompson Lofthouse Baily (1) Medley.*

Northern Ireland, Villa Park, 14.11.51. England won 2-0

The selectors experimented by giving inside-forwards Jackie Sewell and Len Phillips their first caps either side of Nat Lofthouse, who scored a goal in each half. Birmingham City goalkeeper Gil Merrick made the short journey to Villa Park for his first of twenty-three caps. He kept a clean sheet, but was lucky in the second-half when a twenty-five yard shot from Barnsley forward Eddie McMorran crashed against the crossbar. Lofthouse's match-clinching goal was gifted to him seven minutes from the end. Goalkeeper Norman Uprichard dropped a harmless cross from Jackie Swell, and Lofty had the simple task of guiding the ball into the ungaurded net. Billy Wright gave a vintage performance. He was the boss both of the defence and the midfield, impressing with his tigerish tackling and precise passing. *Team: Merrick Ramsey Smith L Wright* Barrass Dickinson Finney Sewell Lofthouse (2) Phillips Medley.*

Austria, Wembley, 28.11.51. Drew 2-2

An injury to Tom Finney forced yet another permutation by the selectors, with Glouc-ester cricketer and Arsenal forward Arthur Milton partnering Ivor Broadis on the right wing. Austria, under the baton of the remarkable Ernst 'Clockwork' Ocwirk, took the lead in the forty-seventh minute after a first half of cut-and-thrust football of the highest quality. Ocwirk sent a precision free-kick into the penalty area where Melchior forced it wide of goalkeeper Gil Merrick. England equalised in the seventieth minute when Alf Ramsey scored from the penalty spot after his Spurs team-mate Eddie Baily had been sent sprawling. Six minutes later Ramsey made a goal for Nat Lofthouse with a pin-pointed free-kick which the Bolton centre-forward headed high into the net. Austria, rated one of the best sides in Europe and fresh from becoming the first overseas team to beat Scotland at home, saved the match two minutes from the end with a penalty by Stojaspal. There was some breath-taking attacking movements by both teams, yet all the goals came from set-piece play. Milton was the last player capped by England at cricket and football. *Team: Merrick Ramsey (1, pen) Eckersley Wright* Froggatt J Dickinson Milton Broadis Lofthouse (1) Baily Medley.*

Scotland, Hampden Park, 5.4.52. England won 2-1

Two neatly taken goals by Stan Pearson stretched England's unbeaten run in full inter-nationals at Hampden Park to fifteen years. His first after eight minutes was a superb hooked shot, and his second just before half-time followed a mix-up in Scotland's defence. The Scots screamed that they were robbed of a penalty when Gil Merrick pulled down Lawrie Reilly, and the 134,504 crowd roared with rage when the referee waved play on. Reilly managed to score in the last minute, Scotland's first home goal against England since the war. But it was too late to stop an England victory that gave them a share of the Home Championship with Wales. Blackpool defender Tom Garrett made a sound debut at left-back in place of the injured Bill Eckersley. *Team: Merrick Ramsey Garrett Wright* Froggatt J Dickinson Finney Broadis Lofthouse Pearson (2) Rowley J.*

Italy, Florence, 18.5.52. Drew 1-1

Only Billy Wright and Tom Finney remained of the England team that had conquered Italy 4-0 in Turin in 1948. Ivor Broadis gave England a fourth minute lead that was cancelled out by a spectacular solo effort from Amadei in the sixty-third minute. The idolised centre-forward Piola, who had helped Italy retain the World Cup in 1938, was recalled for a swansong appearance at the age of thirty-nine. It ended on a sad note for him when he missed an easy chance for a winner in front of an empty net. It was the cool heads of Wright and Ramsey that brought England safely through to a draw when the Italians were threatening to run riot in the second half. Goalkeeper Gil Merrick pulled off a series of excellent saves to break the hearts of the Italian forwards. *Team: Merrick Ramsey Garrett Wright* Froggatt J Dickinson Finney Broadis (1) Lofthouse Pearson Elliott.*

Austria, Vienna, 25.5.52. England won 3-2

The match that earned Nat Lofthouse the nickname The Lion of Vienna (see page 47). England skipper Billy Wright said of Lofty's dramatic winning goal against Austria: 'If you were ever in trouble, Nat was the sort of iron man you wanted alongside you. We could only stand and watch his lonely run into the Austrian half and as the goalkeeper came off his line it was obvious there was going to be a collision. But Nat didn't check his stride or take his eye off the ball. He just kept going. It was unbelievable bravery. The courage he showed was typical of him as a man and as a player. The way he insisted on coming back into the match lifted the heart of every Englishman in the stadium. It made us redouble our efforts to keep out the Austrians.' *Team: Merrick Ramsey Eckersley Wright* Froggatt J Dickinson Finney Sewell (1) Lofthouse (2) Baily Elliott.*

Switzerland, Zurich, 28.5.52. England won 3-0

Just three days after his heroics in Vienna, Nat Lofthouse was back in double goal-scoring action for England. The Swiss were beaten by the same combination that had won the match against the Austrians: Jackie Sewell one, Lofty two. West Bromwich Albion's versatile forward Ronnie Allen won the first of his five caps, and gave a lively performance on the right wing. Lofty's two goals were typical crash and bash efforts, while Sewell scored with a delicate lob. Billy Wright was credited with taking over the England caps record from Bob Crompton with this forty-third international appearance (although most record books give Crompton's old record as 41 caps). *Team: Merrick Ramsey Eckersley Wright* Froggatt J Dickinson Allen R Sewell (1) Lofthouse (2) Baily Finney.*

FOOTBALL began to see the light in 1951. It was Arsenal who staged the first official match bathed in floodlights since experiments way back in 1878. They were hosts to the Hapoel club of Tel Aviv in a friendly match at Highbury on 19 September. A crowd of 44,000 saw the Gunners cruise to a 6-1 win. Southampton followed by playing a reserve match under floodlights at The Dell.

Arsenal were always prepared to be trend-setters. When thick smog was forecast before their First Division match against Bolton on 24 November 1951 they erected fluorescent green sightscreens at both ends of the Highbury pitch to make the goals more visible. Arsenal won 4-2, which gave them a warm glow.

Derek Dooley, a galloping centre-forward with Sheffield Wednesday, became the talk of football when banging in 46 goals in 30 Second Division games. He was promoted from the reserves as Wednesday struggled near the bottom of the table, and his rush of goals got them promoted as champions. It was just the start of the Dooley legend.

Admission charges were raised by threepence at the start of the 1951-52 season. Spectators now had to pay one shilling and sixpence (1s 6d ... 7.5p) to stand on First Division terraces watching the likes of Matthews, Finney, Wright, Shackleton and Lofthouse perform.

A stand-off between the Football League and the BBC was ended when the League reversed their decision to ban the broadcast of live wireless match commentaries. But television was still given the cold-shoulder and the BBC were allowed to show only newsreel shots of the 1952 FA Cup final forty-eight hours after the game.

The incredible Con Martin completed the full circle in his career when he returned to his original position as goalkeeper with Aston Villa. Capped in five different positions by Ireland, Martin had defended as a centre-half for Villa and also scored as a centre-forward.

Chester City experienced the highs and lows of football in January 1952. They held mighty Chelsea to a draw in the third round of the FA Cup before going down 3-2 in the replay, after extra-time. A week later they were beaten by Oldham 11-2 in a Third Division North match.

First Division: Manchester United, 57pts. **Runners-up:** Tottenham, 53 pts.
Manchester United record: P42 W23 D11 L8 F95 A52 Pts57
Representative team: Allen; McNulty, Byrne (Aston); Carey (capt.), Chilton, Cockburn; Berry, Downie, Rowley, Pearson, Bond.
Top scorer: Rowley (30).
Manager: Matt Busby.

Second Division: Sheffield Weds, 53pts. **Runners-up:** Cardiff City, 51pts.
Third Division (South): Plymouth, 66pts. **Runners-up:** Reading, 61pts.
Third Division (North): Lincoln City, 69pts. **Runners-up:** Grimsby, 66pts.

FA Cup final: Newcastle United 1, Arsenal 0
Newcastle: Simpson; Cowell, McMichael; Harvey (capt.), Brennan, Robledo E; Walker, Foulkes, Milburn, Robledo G, Mitchell.
Scorer: George Robledo
Arsenal: Swindin; Barnes, Smith; Forbes, Daniel, Mercer (capt.); Cox, Logie, Holton, Lishman, Roper

Top First Division marksman: George Robledo (Newcastle), 33 goals
Top Second Division marksman: Derek Dooley (Sheffield Wednesday), 46 goals (Dooley's goals came in just 30 League games)
Top Third Division North marksman: Andy Graver (Lincoln City), 36 goals
Top Third Division South marksman: Ronnie Blackman (Reading), 39 goals
Footballer of the Year: Billy Wright (Wolves)

Scottish First Division: Hibernian, 45pts. **Runners-up:** Rangers, 41pts.
Top Scottish First Division marksman: Lawrie Reilly (Hibernian), 27 goals
Scottish Cup final: Motherwell 4, Dundee 0
Scottish League Cup final: Dundee 3, Rangers 2

FA Amateur Cup final: Walthamstow Avenue 2, Leyton 1

THE LEAGUE TABLES
Where they finished in 1951-52

FIRST DIVISION

		P	W	D	L	F	A	Pts
1	Manchester United	42	23	11	8	95	52	57
2	Tottenham Hotspur	42	22	9	11	76	51	53
3	Arsenal	42	21	11	10	80	61	53
4	Portsmouth	42	20	8	14	68	58	48
5	Bolton Wanderers	42	19	10	13	65	61	48
6	Aston Villa	42	19	9	14	79	70	47
7	Preston North End	42	17	12	13	74	54	46
8	Newcastle United	42	18	9	15	98	73	45
9	Blackpool	42	18	9	15	64	64	45
10	Charlton Athletic	42	17	10	15	68	63	44
11	Liverpool	42	12	19	11	57	61	43
12	Sunderland	42	15	12	15	70	61	42
13	West Bromwich A.	42	14	13	15	74	77	41
14	Burnley	42	15	10	17	56	63	40
15	Manchester City	42	13	13	16	58	61	39
16	Wolverhampton W.	42	12	14	16	73	73	38
17	Derby County	42	15	7	20	63	80	37
18	Middlesbrough	42	15	6	21	64	88	36
19	Chelsea	42	14	8	20	52	72	36
20	Stoke City	42	12	7	23	49	88	31
21	Huddersfield Town	42	10	8	24	49	82	28
22	Fulham	42	8	11	23	58	77	27

SECOND DIVISION

		P	W	D	L	F	A	Pts
1	Sheffield Weds.	42	21	11	10	100	66	53
2	Cardiff City	42	20	11	11	72	54	51
3	Birmingham City	42	21	9	12	67	56	51
4	Nottingham Forest	42	18	13	11	77	62	49
5	Leicester City	42	19	9	14	78	64	47
6	Leeds United	42	18	11	13	59	57	47
7	Everton	42	17	10	15	64	58	44
8	Luton Town	42	16	12	14	77	78	44
9	Rotherham United	42	17	8	17	73	71	42
10	Brentford	42	15	12	15	54	55	42
11	Sheffield United	42	18	5	19	90	76	41
12	West Ham United	42	15	11	16	67	77	41
13	Southampton	42	15	11	16	61	73	41
14	Blackburn Rovers	42	17	6	19	54	63	40
15	Notts County	42	16	7	19	71	68	39
16	Doncaster Rovers	42	13	12	17	55	60	38
17	Bury	42	15	7	20	67	69	37
18	Hull City	42	13	11	18	60	70	37
19	Swansea Town	42	12	12	18	72	76	36
20	Barnsley	42	11	14	17	59	72	36
21	Coventry City	42	14	6	22	59	82	34
22	Queens Park R.	42	11	12	19	52	81	34

THIRD DIVISION (NORTH)

		P	W	D	L	F	A	Pts
1	Lincoln City	46	30	9	7	121	52	69
2	Grimsby Town	46	29	8	9	96	45	66
3	Stockport County	46	23	13	10	74	40	59
4	Oldham Athletic	46	24	9	13	90	61	57
5	Gateshead	46	21	11	14	66	49	53
6	Mansfield Town	46	22	8	16	73	60	52
7	Carlisle United	46	19	13	14	62	57	51
8	Bradford Park A.	46	19	12	15	74	64	50
9	Hartlepools United	46	21	8	17	71	65	50
10	York City	46	18	13	15	73	52	49
11	Tranmere Rovers	46	21	6	19	76	71	48
12	Barrow	46	17	12	17	57	61	46
13	Chesterfield	46	17	11	18	65	66	45
14	Scunthorpe United	46	14	16	16	65	74	44
15	Bradford City	46	16	10	20	61	68	42
16	Crewe Alexandra	46	17	8	21	63	82	42
17	Southport	46	15	11	20	53	71	41
18	Wrexham	46	15	9	22	63	73	39
19	Chester	46	15	9	22	72	85	39
20	Halifax Town	46	14	7	25	61	97	35
21	Rochdale	46	11	13	22	47	79	35
22	Accrington Stanley	46	10	12	24	61	92	32
23	Darlington	46	11	9	26	64	103	31
24	Workington	46	11	7	28	50	91	29

THIRD DIVISION (SOUTH)

		P	W	D	L	F	A	Pts
1	Plymouth Argyle	46	29	8	9	107	53	66
2	Reading	46	29	3	14	112	60	61
3	Norwich City	46	26	9	11	89	50	61
4	Millwall	46	23	12	11	74	53	58
5	Brighton & Hove A.	46	24	10	12	87	63	58
6	Newport County	46	21	12	13	77	76	54
7	Bristol Rovers	46	20	12	14	89	53	52
8	Northampton Town	46	22	5	19	93	74	49
9	Southend United	46	19	10	17	75	66	48
10	Colchester United	46	17	12	17	56	77	46
11	Torquay United	46	17	10	19	86	98	44
12	Aldershot	46	18	8	20	78	89	44
13	Port Vale	46	14	15	17	50	66	43
14	Bournemouth	46	16	10	20	69	75	42
15	Bristol City	46	15	12	19	58	69	42
16	Swindon Town	46	14	14	18	51	68	42
17	Ipswich Town	46	16	9	21	63	74	41
18	Leyton Orient	46	16	9	21	55	68	41
19	Crystal Palace	46	15	9	22	61	80	39
20	Shrewsbury Town	46	13	10	23	62	86	36
21	Watford	46	13	10	23	57	81	36
22	Gillingham	46	11	13	22	71	81	35
23	Exeter City	46	13	9	24	65	86	35
24	Walsall	46	13	5	28	55	94	31

FOOTBALLING FIFTIES
1952-53: Matthews, the Wizard of Dribble

BLACKPOOL's 1953 FA Cup final against Bolton Wanderers was seen as the last chance for Stanley Matthews to collect the FA Cup winners' medal that had always eluded him during a distinguished 21-year career. Nobody could have guessed that twelve years later he would still be weaving his magic on the First Division stage at the age of fifty.

Matthews, famous across the world of football as the 'Wizard of Dribble', was 38 years old when Blackpool reached the FA Cup final for the third time in five years. They had been runners-up in 1948 and 1951.

The match was televised live and it is estimated that ten million viewers crowded round the country's two million sets, many of them bought for Queen Elizabeth II's Coronation the following month.

What few of the watching millions knew is that Matthews almost missed the game because of problems with a pulled thigh muscle. He had a pain-killing injection on the morning of the match. Could he at last collect a winners' medal? The nation held its breath.

It was Bolton and the Lion Nat Lofthouse who took instant command of the match. Lofty tried a speculative shot after just seventy-five seconds that caught Blackpool's Scottish international goalkeeper George Farm cold and he allowed the ball to slip from his grasp and into the net. It was a goal that spotlighted how brittle form and fortune could be in football. Just a few weeks earlier Farm had played brilliantly against England (and Lofthouse) on the same Wembley turf.

Blackpool skipper and centre-half Harry Johnston was finding Lofthouse hard to pin down, and in the twentieth minute the Bolton bulldozer almost made it 2-0 with a shot that cannoned off a post.

Blackpool's forwards were making little impact on the match, and just as it seemed Bolton were going to dominate a one-side game their left-half Eric Bell pulled a muscle. Bolton had gambled on playing him because the injury – similar to the one troubling Matthews – had caused Bell concern during the build-up to the final.

The gamble failed, and Bell, with no substitutes allowed, was reduced to a limping passenger's role on the left wing. Harold Hassall was pulled back into defence in an emergency reshuffle of the Bolton team. Ten minutes before half-time the unfortunate Hassall could only help a left foot shot from Stan Mortensen into his own net.

Four minutes later Farm was slow to come off his line to a cross from Bobby Langton and Willie Moir dived across him to divert the ball into the net to give Bolton a 2-1 half-time lead.

Stanley Matthews, the Wizard of Dribble. The first footballer to earn a knighthood.

Ten minutes into the second-half the Matthews' Cup-winning dream seemed to have distintegrated when the hobbling Bell, left unmarked by the Blackpool defence, defied the pain from his leg and leapt to head in a cross from Doug Holden to give Bolton what looked to be a victory-clinching 3-1 lead. No team in any of the previous 71 FA Cup finals had managed to come back from being two goals down.

But then, enter stage right the maestro Matthews. For an hour, he had been on a tight rein, almost as if he was saving himself for a final burst. The moment Bolton scored their third goal he rolled up the sleeves of his orange shirt and clapped his hands to attract the attention of his colleagues. It was the signal that he wanted the ball.

Little Ernie Taylor, the orchestrator of the Blackpool attack, responded by sending a stream of passes to Matthews, who for thirty glorious minutes turned on one of the finest individual performances ever seen at Wembley.

He ran the Bolton defence ragged with his slow-slow-quick-quick-slow dribbling, and harassed left-back Ralph Banks made so many turns trying to tame his tormentor that he became a cramp victim.

Matthews sent over a cross in the sixty-eighth minute that his England team-mate Stan Mortensen forced over the over the line, colliding with a post as he collected his second goal of the game. Blackpool 2, Bolton 3.

The suddenly highly motivated Matthews was pushing his play to new dimensions. He continually tricked his way past the luckless Banks, who was totally perplexed by his feints and changes of pace. But time was running out for Blackpool and four scoring chances laid on by Matthews were wasted. With just three minutes to go, Mortensen blasted a deflected free-kick into the net from twenty yards for an equaliser. It completed the one and only FA Cup final hat-trick at Wembley.

Extra time looked inevitable, but Matthews had other ideas. There was one minute left on the watch of referee Mervyn Griffiths when the Maestro dribbled inside Banks yet again. England international centre-half Malcolm Barrass came charging across to try to cover but Matthews dismissed him from his path with a dip of the left shoulder and a shimmy to the right. He took the ball down to the deadball line and then hooked a pass back into the path of South African left winger Bill Perry, who swept it into the net from six yards. The goal was Perry's, but the glory belonged to Matthews and three-goal Mortensen. It should have been called the Stanleys Final.

In a 1960s interview Matthews – by then, Sir Stanley – told me:
'The '53 FA Cup final was my most unforgettable match, but I did not win the game on my own. That's a myth. It was a great team effort. The minute I saw Ralph Banks limping wth cramp I knew there was a weak spot in the Bolton defence that we could exploit. I don't think enough credit has been given to Stan Mortensen. He was a real inspiration with his never-say-die spirit, and I knew that if I could get the ball into the middle I could count on Stan to bulge the net.'

THE LEAGUE CHAMPIONSHIP 1952-53
Mercer and Arsenal in seventh heaven

Along with Stanley Matthews, Joe Mercer was the 'Grand Old Man of Football.' He was three months off his thirty-ninth birthday when he went into what was intended to be the final game of his long-playing career – and what a game! It would decide the League title, and Old Joe could be leading Arsenal to a record seventh championship triumph.

The all-important match was played at Highbury on the Friday evening before what became the Matthews Final, and the opponents were Burnley. On the previous Saturday Arsenal had been beaten 2-0 by Preston at Deepdale. It meant that going into this final game Tom Finney's team were top of the table and poised for their first championship success since their 'Invincibles' team won the first back-to-back inaugural League titles in the 1880s. Only Arsenal could stop them.

Burnley, who had held the Gunners to a 1-1 draw at Turf Moor in December, did their best to give their Lancashire neighbours reason to celebrate by taking an early lead as a heavy downpour turned the Highbury pitch to mud. Arsenal nerves were jangling, but powerhouse wing-half Alex Forbes brought almost a sigh of relief from the 51,000 crowd when he equalised with his very timely first goal of the season.

Doug Lishman and Jimmy Logie then scored a goal each to give Arsenal a 3-1 stranglehold on the game before half-time. Burnley managed to pull a goal back in the second-half but the Gunners, with Mercer playing his heart out in a defensive midfield role, held on for a 3-2 victory.

At the final whistle Arsenal and Preston were level at the top of the First Division table with almost identical statistics. Each had twenty-one wins, twelve draws and nine defeats, but Arsenal's goal average was 1.51 to Preston's 1.41. Arsenal had won a record seventh title by a short head.

There were tears mixed with the cheers as Joe Mercer led his Arsenal team-mates out to take their bow from the East Stand with thousands of supporters jamming the pitch below. Old Joe, famous for saying 'just one more season' announced that he had finally decided to hang up his boots.

'I have had a wonderful career,' he said later, 'first with Everton and then at Arsenal. My spirit is willing but my my old bandy legs feel as if they have had enough. They have served me very well considering Dixie Dean said when we used to share a dressing-room, "Those legs would not last a postman a round."'

But Joe could not let go, and continued to play until a broken leg against Liverpool a year later finally foced his retirement. A great managerial career awaited him.

Northern Ireland, Windsor Park, 4.10.52. Drew 2-2

Nat Lofthouse scored in the first minute and Billy Elliott in the last minute of a dramatic match. Sandwiched in between was the magic of Celtic ball artist Charlie Tully, who scored twice for Ireland. He beat Merrick from 25 yards and then with his specialist inswinging corner-kick after the Irish team had been reduced by injury to ten men (In a game for Celtic against Falkirk Tully netted direct from a corner and was ordered to re-take it because the referee was not ready. He immediately repeated the trick and put the ball in the exact same spot in the net!). Northern Ireland, urged on by a record 60,000 Windsor Park crowd, had two young midfield partners called Danny Blanchflower and Jimmy McIlroy dictating the pace and the pattern of the match. They were on the verge of their first victory over England since 1927 when Elliott silenced the celebrating fans with an equalising header in the desperate closing moments. Billy Wright and Jimmy Dickinson were the match stars for England, steadying the ship with their cool defensive work when the Irish threatened to take a stranglehold on the game. Team manager Walter Winterbottom was furious over the goal that Charlie Tully scored direct from a corner-kick. England had worked at nullifying the Tully corners in training by placing Alf Ramsey on the near post and then centre-half Jack Froggatt directly behind goalkeeper Gil Merrick. The corner from which he scored was curling towards Ramsey, who suddenly ducked under the ball. Gil reached out but only caught thin air as the ball swung into the net. Alf said later that he thought Gil had shouted 'mine', but it had apparently been one of the Irish forwards. The huge crowd went berserk when the ball swung into the back of the net. And no wonder – it was Northern Ireland's first goal in international football for eighteen months! *Team: Merrick Ramsey Eckersley Wright* Froggatt J Dickinson Finney Sewell Lofthouse (1) Baily Elliott (1).*

Wales, Wembley, 12.11.52. England won 5-2

This was the first time Wales had ever played at Wembley, and a Wednesday afternoon crowd of 93,500 paid record gate receipts of £43,000. England were two goals up in the first ten minutes through Tom Finney and Nat Lofthouse. Five minutes later Trevor Ford pulled a goal back for Wales, and was then involved in a collision with Jack Froggatt that led to the England centre-half being carried off. Billy Wright switched

Roy Bentley (right) in action in the 1952-53 season for Chelsea at Stamford Bridge, and challenged by Aston Villa defender Harry Parkes. Bentley scored nine goals in twelve England appearances spread over six years.

to the middle of the defence, with Billy Elliott dropping back from the wing to left-half. Jack Froggatt, whose cousin, Redfern, was making his debut at inside-right, came back on as a passenger on the left wing. Remarkably, it was Jack who scored England's third goal just before half-time with a brave diving header. Roy Bentley made it 4-1 in England's first attack after half-time, with Ford instantly replying for Wales. Nat Lofthouse rounded off the scoring with a shot from twenty-five yards. The significant thing about this match was that it was the first time that Billy Wright played at centre-half for England, but the selectors were blind to the fact that he was the man who could cure their constant problem at the heart of the defence. They continued to experiment with a queue of centre-halves before settling on the Wolves captain as the No 5. *Team: Merrick Ramsey Smith L Wright* Froggatt J (1) Dickinson Finney (1) Froggatt R Lofthouse (2) Bentley (1) Elliott.*

Belgium, Wembley, 26.11.52. England won 5-0

Nat Lofthouse kept up his one-man bombardment with a double strike that took his haul to nine goals in five games. Redfern Froggatt scored his first goal for England, and Burnley winger Billy Elliott netted twice against the outplayed Belgians. The game was played in a driving sleet, and ice patches formed on the famous Wembley turf, making it difficult for defenders to keep their feet. England led 2-0 at the end of a first-half in which they might have had half a dozen goals. The freezing weather kept the Wednesday crowd down to 65,000. Skipper Billy Wright said after the game: 'I have never been colder at Wembley. The sleet made it feel as if you were being continually slapped in the face and it was really stinging. But the team performance warmed us all up. Some of the football we played was as good as any we've produced in my time with England.' *Team: Merrick Ramsey Smith L Wright* Froggatt J Dickinson Finney Bentley Lofthouse (2) Froggatt R (1) Elliott (2).*

Scotland, Wembley, 18.4.53. Drew 2-2

Lawrie 'Last Minute' Reilly equalised for Scotland with the final kick of the match. It was Reilly's second goal in reply to two from Ivor Broadis. The Scots, driven from midfield by Preston's Tommy Docherty and Dundee's Doug Cowie, dominated play for long spells and thoroughly deserved their late equaliser. They played for much of the second-half with only ten men after Rangers left-back Sammy Cox had been injured trying to stop a thrusting run by Tom Finney. Utility player Jack Froggatt, capped by England at centre-half and also as an outside-left, partnered his cousin Redfern on the left wing. Each of the cousins missed simple chances to give England the lead before Broadis (later a respected football journalist) scored what looked like being a winning second goal, at last beating Blackpool goalkeeper George Farm who had been in magnificent form. The following month he would feature in the famous Matthews Final against his England team-mate Nat Lofthouse. There were just thirty seconds left when Lawrie Reilly popped up with one of his typical late goals that so often saved Scotland. This draw meant that it was nineteen years since England had last beaten the Scots on home territory. *Team: Merrick Ramsey Smith L Wright* Barrass Dickinson Finney Broadis (2) Lofthouse Froggatt R Froggatt J.*

Argentina, Buenos Aires, 17.5.53

Abandoned at 0-0 after 23 minutes following a rain storm

The pitch became waterlogged following a cloudburst and British referee Arthur Ellis, up to his ankles in water, had no alternative but to abandon the game. Three days earlier an Argentinian XI had beaten an FA XI 3-1 in an unofficial international watched by a crowd of 120,000 including Juan Peron and his wife, Eva. The selectors had to wait to see if the new left wing partnership of Manchester United team-mates Tommy Taylor and Johnny Berry would work at international level. Referee Arthur Ellis, later to make a name for himself in TV's *It's A Knockout*, was quite a joker. As he signalled for the teams to return to the dressing-rooms, he said to Billy Wright, 'If we stay out any longer we'll need lifeboats!' The pitch just disappeared under a lake of water, and England's kit was so wet the players needed help from the training staff to strip off. *Team: Merrick Ramsey Eckersley Wright* Johnston Dickinson Finney Broadis Lofthouse Taylor T Berry.*

Chile, Santiago, 24.5.53. England won 2-1

Tommy Taylor's first goal for England in the forty-eighth minute was a freak. His intended cross was turned into the net by Chilean goalkeeper Livingstone-Eves, who was the son of a Scot. Nat Lofthouse scored the second decisive goal after one of a dozen thrusting runs by Finney, and three minutes later he headed another Finney cross against the bar. The Chileans scored their only goal seven minutes from the end when a Rojas shot was deflected wide of the diving Gil Merrick. The Chilean press hailed Finney as 'a world beater.' Nat Lofthouse said: 'It's a privilege to play with Tom Finney. He is a fantastic individualist yet always plays for the team. If I were a defender I would hate to have the job of marking him. He has two good feet, has excellent close control, can dribble and accelerates like a Rolls Royce. He is the complete forward.' *Team: Merrick Ramsey Eckersley Wright* Johnston Dickinson Finney Broadis Lofthouse (1) Taylor (1) Berry.*

Uruguay, Montevideo, 31.5.53. England lost 2-1

World champions Uruguay turned on an exhibition against the old masters, and might have trebled their score but for being over elaborate with dazzling approach play. Abbadie gave Uruguay the lead in the twenty-seventh minute, and clever centre-forward Oscar Miguez made it 2-0 on the hour. Nat Lofthouse and Ivor Broadis struck the woodwork and Tommy Taylor scored in the closing moments after an Alf Ramsey shot had been blocked. It was a spirited fight back by England after they had struggled to hold the world champions in a one-sided first half. Miguez, a master of ball control and as crafty as a monkey, led the entire England defence a dance. Billy Wright, winning his fiftieth cap, played him as well as any defender could do, but was often tackling the shadow of a player who three years earlier had played a key role in helping Uruguay win the World Cup. Walter Winterbottom said later: 'Several of our players were ill with food poisoning, but I don't want to use this as an excuse for our defeat. The Uruguyans are exceptiuonally talented, and we discovered just why they are holders of the World Cup. They will be a difficult to beat when they defend the trophy in Europe next year. Miguez in particular took the eye. His control of the ball and positional sense made him a very difficult player to mark. We wcrc not disgraced, but there is no question that the best team won.' *Team: Merrick Ramsey Eckersley Wright* Johnston Dickinson Finney Broadis Lofthouse Taylor T (1) Berry.*

USA, New York City, 8.6.53. England won 6-3

This first full soccer international staged in New York was arranged to mark the Queen's Coronation six days earlier. It was the first international match that England had ever played under floodlights. The freak rain followed England from South America and a storm forced a 24-hour postponement. Then, under the floodlights at the Yankee Stadium, England – with Tom Finney running riot – avenged the 1-0 World Cup defeat with a comfortable victory in front of a 7,271 crowd. England missed a shoal of chances before Ivor Broadis gave them the lead two minutes before half-time. They quickly went 3-0 clear with goals early in the second half from Finney and Lofthouse. The Americans battled back with the help of a dubious penalty, but another goal each from Lofthouse and Finney followed by a sixth goal from Redfern Froggat underlined England's supremacy in a match in which they could and should have reached double figures. At last, Billy Wright, Alf Ramsey, Jimmy Dickinson and Tom Finney exorcised the ghosts that had haunted them ever since England's humiliating 1-0 World Cup defeat by the USA in Brazil in 1950. Wright, in particular, played like a man possessed, determined not to suffer the same embarrassment. The press described England as avenging their World Cup defeat by the United States, but it was empty revenge because it was a pretty meaningless match that attracted very little interest in New York. There was a ghostly atmosphere in the Yankee Stadium with the seven thousands fans 'lost' in that vast arena. Terry Springthorpe was prominent for the Americans. He had played for Wolves in the 1949 FA Cup final and used to share digs with Billy Wright. *Team: Ditchburn Ramsey Eckersley Wright* Johnston Dickinson Finney (2) Broadis (1) Lofthouse (2) Froggatt R (1) Froggatt J*

THE legend of Derek Dooley took the cruellest of all twists in February 1953. He was adding to his reputation as an exceptional and exciting prospect with sixteen goals in twenty-nine First Division games for Sheffield Wednesday to follow the 46 he had banged in during Wednesday's promotion run the previous season. Playing against Preston at Deepdale, he broke a leg when challenging goalkeeper George Thompson for a 50-50 ball. He was taken to Preston Royal Infimrary and was about to be discharged two days later when a cut on the leg became infected. Gangrene had set in and to save his life Dooley had to have the leg amputated. His meteoric career was over at the age of twenty-three. In 61games for the Owls he netted 62 goals. A hero in in Sheffield, he continued to serve first Wednesday and then rivals United in various capacities over the next fifty years.

Nat Lofthouse was among the goals again playing for the Football League against the League of Ireland at Molineux on 24 September 1952. He scored six goals in a row, a record for an inter-League game.

Jimmy Glazzard scored five goals for Huddersfield in their 8-2 defeat of Everton in a Second Division match at Leeds Road. All his goals were headers and all of them were from crosses from winger Vic Metcalfe.

Amateur club Walthamstow Avenue eliminated Wimbledon, Watford and Stockport County in a remarkable FA Cup run before going out to Manchester United after holding them to a 1-1 fourth round draw at Old Trafford. Their giant-killing ended in a 5-2 defeat by United at Highbury. Avenue's star player was Jim Lewis, who in two periods with the club scored 423 goals in 522 appearances. In between he netted 40 goals in 95 games for Chelsea, always retaining his amateur status.

Rangers completed yet another League and Cup double, beating Aberdeen 1-0 in a replayed Scottish Cup final and then three days later pipping Hibs for the title on goal average after a 1-1 draw with Queen of the South at Dumfries. Centre-half George Young played in goal for twenty minutes in the Cup final after an injury to the 'keeper.

Aston Villa full-back Peter Aldis scored with a header against Sunderland that travelled thirty-five yards. It was the only goal he scored in 262 League games for Villa.

1952-53 WHO WON WHAT
All the champions and runners-up

First Division: Arsenal, 54pts. **Runners-up:** Preston, 54 pts.
Arsenal record: P42 W21 D12 L9 F97 A64 Pts54
Representative squad: Kelsey; Wade, Lionel Smith; (from) Shaw, Forbes, Daniel, Mercer (capt.); (from) Milton, Logie, Goring, Holton, Lishman, Roper.
Top scorer: Lishman (22).
Manager: Tom Whittaker.

Second Division: Sheffield United, 60pts. **Runners-up:** Huddersfield, 58pts.
Third Division (South): Bristol Rovers, 64pts. **Runners-up:** Millwall, 62pts.
Third Division (North): Oldham Athletic, 59pts. **Runners-up:** Port Vale, 58pts.

FA Cup final: Blackpool 4, Bolton Wanderers 3
Blackpool: Farm; Shimwell, Garrett; Fenton, Johnston (capt.), Robinson; Matthews, Taylor E, Mortensen, Mudie, Perry. **Scorers:** Mortensen (3), Perry
Bolton: Hanson; Ball, Banks; Wheeler, Barrass, Bell; Holden, Moir (capt.), Lofthouse, Hassall, Langton. **Scorers:** Lofthouse, Moir, Bell

Top First Division marksman: Charlie Wayman (Preston North End), 24 goals
Top Second Division marksman: Arthur Rowley (Leicester City), 39 goals
Top Third Division North marksman: Jimmy Whitehouse (Carlisle United), 29 goals
Top Third Division South marksman: Geoff Bradford (Bristol Rovers), 33 goals
Footballer of the Year: Nat Lofthouse (Bolton)

Scottish First Division: Rangers, 43pts. **Runners-up:** Hibernian, 43pts.
Top Scottish First Division marksmen: Lawrie Reilly (Hibernian), Charlie Fleming (East Fife) 30 goals
Scottish Cup final: Rangers 1, Aberdeen 0 (after a 1-1 draw)
Scottish League Cup final: Dundee 2, Kilmarnock 0

FA Amateur Cup final: Pegasus 6, Harwich & Parkeston 0

THE LEAGUE TABLES
Where they finished in 1952-53

FIRST DIVISION

		P	W	D	L	F	A	Pts
1	Arsenal	42	21	12	9	97	64	54
2	Preston North End	42	21	12	9	85	60	54
3	Wolverhampton W.	42	19	13	10	86	63	51
4	West Bromwich A.	42	21	8	13	66	60	50
5	Charlton Athletic	42	19	11	12	77	63	49
6	Burnley	42	18	12	12	67	52	48
7	Blackpool	42	19	9	14	71	70	47
8	Manchester United	42	18	10	14	69	72	46
9	Sunderland	42	15	13	14	68	82	43
10	Tottenham Hotspur	42	15	11	16	78	69	41
11	Aston Villa	42	14	13	15	63	61	41
12	Cardiff City	42	14	12	16	54	46	40
13	Middlesbrough	42	14	11	17	70	77	39
14	Bolton Wanderers	42	15	9	18	61	69	39
15	Portsmouth	42	14	10	18	74	83	38
16	Newcastle United	42	14	9	19	59	70	37
17	Liverpool	42	14	8	20	61	82	36
18	Sheffield Weds.	42	12	11	19	62	72	35
19	Chelsea	42	12	11	19	56	66	35
20	Manchester City	42	14	7	21	72	87	35
21	Stoke City	42	12	10	20	53	66	34
22	Derby County	42	11	10	21	59	74	32

SECOND DIVISION

		P	W	D	L	F	A	Pts
1	Sheffield United	42	25	10	7	97	55	60
2	Huddersfield Town	42	24	10	8	84	33	58
3	Luton Town	42	22	8	12	84	49	52
4	Plymouth Argyle	42	20	9	13	65	60	49
5	Leicester City	42	18	12	12	89	74	48
6	Birmingham City	42	19	10	13	71	66	48
7	Nottingham Forest	42	18	8	16	77	67	44
8	Fulham	42	17	10	15	81	71	44
9	Blackburn Rovers	42	18	8	16	68	65	44
10	Leeds United	42	14	15	13	71	63	43
11	Swansea Town	42	15	12	15	78	81	42
12	Rotherham United	42	16	9	17	75	74	41
13	Doncaster Rovers	42	12	16	14	58	64	40
14	West Ham United	42	13	13	16	58	60	39
15	Lincoln City	42	11	17	14	64	71	39
16	Everton	42	12	14	16	71	75	38
17	Brentford	42	13	11	18	59	76	37
18	Hull City	42	14	8	20	57	69	36
19	Notts County	42	14	8	20	60	88	36
20	Bury	42	13	9	20	53	81	35
21	Southampton	42	10	13	19	68	85	33
22	Barnsley	42	5	8	29	47	108	18

THIRD DIVISION (NORTH)

		P	W	D	L	F	A	Pts
1	Oldham Athletic	46	22	15	9	77	45	59
2	Port Vale	46	20	18	8	67	35	58
3	Wrexham	46	24	8	14	86	66	56
4	York City	46	20	13	13	60	45	53
5	Grimsby Town	46	21	10	15	75	59	52
6	Southport	46	20	11	15	63	60	51
7	Bradford Park A.	46	19	12	15	75	61	50
8	Gateshead	46	17	15	14	76	60	49
9	Carlisle United	46	18	13	15	82	68	49
10	Crewe Alexandra	46	20	8	18	70	68	48
11	Stockport County	46	17	13	16	82	69	47
12	Chesterfield	46	18	11	17	65	63	47
13	Tranmere Rovers	46	21	5	20	65	63	47
14	Halifax Town	46	16	15	15	68	68	47
15	Scunthorpe United	46	16	14	16	62	56	46
16	Bradford City	46	14	18	14	75	80	46
17	Hartlepools United	46	16	14	16	57	61	46
18	Mansfield Town	46	16	14	16	55	62	46
19	Barrow	46	16	12	18	66	71	44
20	Chester	46	11	15	20	64	85	37
21	Darlington	46	14	6	26	58	96	34
22	Rochdale	46	14	5	27	62	83	33
23	Workington	46	11	10	25	55	91	32
24	Accrington Stanley	46	8	11	27	39	89	27

THIRD DIVISION (SOUTH)

		P	W	D	L	F	A	Pts
1	Bristol Rovers	46	26	12	8	92	46	64
2	Millwall	46	24	14	8	82	44	62
3	Northampton Town	46	26	10	10	109	70	62
4	Norwich City	46	25	10	11	99	55	60
5	Bristol City	46	22	15	9	95	61	59
6	Coventry City	46	19	12	15	77	62	50
7	Brighton & Hove A.	46	19	12	15	81	75	50
8	Southend United	46	18	13	15	69	74	49
9	Bournemouth	46	19	9	18	74	69	47
10	Watford	46	15	17	14	62	63	47
11	Reading	46	19	8	19	69	64	46
12	Torquay United	46	18	9	19	87	88	45
13	Crystal Palace	46	15	13	18	66	82	43
14	Leyton Orient	46	16	10	20	68	73	42
15	Newport County	46	16	10	20	70	82	42
16	Ipswich Town	46	13	15	18	60	69	41
17	Exeter City	46	13	14	19	61	71	40
18	Swindon Town	46	14	12	20	64	79	40
19	Aldershot	46	12	15	19	61	77	39
20	Queens Park R.	46	12	15	19	61	82	39
21	Gillingham	46	12	15	19	55	74	39
22	Colchester United	46	12	14	20	59	76	38
23	Shrewsbury Town	46	12	12	22	68	91	36
24	Walsall	46	7	10	29	56	118	24

ENGLAND had never been beaten in a home international by overseas opposition (apart from a 2-0 set-back at Goodison in 1949 against an Irish team containing nine English-based players). As that proud record stretched back 45 years there was no reason why people with just a surface knowledge of football should have suspected that 1952 Olympic champions Hungary were the team to end the run. But anybody who made a study of how the game was developing abroad – which embraced few in England – would have known that this Hungarian team was something quite special.

The Hungarians, on a run of twenty-nine successive matches without defeat, were professional in everything but name. They were officially soldiers in the Hungarian army, but their parade ground was the football field and the only drills they carried out were designed purely to improve their skills. They were under the command of Major Ferenc Puskas, whose influence on the pitch was so great that he should have held the rank of Field Marshal.

The 'Magical Magyars,' with the portly yet light-footed Puskas plotting their raids with the arrogance of a modern-day Napoleon, had found a way of combining the short passing game of the South Americans with the long-ball technique that had for so many years been a copyright of the British game. They played to a flexible 4-2-4 formation, inter-changing positions and making England's traditional 2-3-5 pattern seem about as outdated as an air balloon at Heathrow.

As Puskas waited in the centre circle for England skipper Billy Wright to join him for the coin tossing he picked up the match ball and juggled it on his left foot, flicked it into the air, caught it on his thigh and then let it run down his shin and back on to the centre spot. There were muted jeers from among the 100,000 spectators who interpreted this as somebody showing off rather than doing what came naturally. Puskas was soon showing that he was much more than just a juggler. It was not the circus that had come to town. It was a football revolution.

The Puskas left foot was on display again within the first minute. He delivered the ball through the heart of the England defence like a dagger thrust, and Nandor Hidegkuti quickly brought it under control and then completely deceived centre-half Harry Johnston with a distracting dummy before rifling the ball high into the net from twenty yards. It was a goal born of sheer genius.

Johnston was one of four Blackpool players in the England team-along with Matthews, Mortensen and Ernie Taylor who six months earlier had featured in one of the greatest of all FA Cup finals. Against Bolton, Johnston had his hands full with Nat

Lofthouse but at least he knew where to find Lofty. He did not have a clue where Hidegkuti was going to pop up next.

The Hungarian wore the No 9 shirt, but was one of a new breed of centre-forwards who liked to lie back in a deep position from where he could navigate a path to goal. Blackpool skipper Johnston, one of the most reliable centre-halves in Britain, was used to playing against robust, English-style centre-forwards who trod on his toes and dug him in the ribs and rarely left the penalty area. He did not know whether to follow Hidegkuti deep into midfield or stay on guard in his usual territory marking nobody. He was so torn by indecision that he finished up giving Hidegkuti the freedom of Wembley.

Johnston got into the game as a creator of a goal in the fifteenth minute after a hair-line offside decision had robbed Hidegkuti a split second before he whipped the ball past advancing goalkeeper Gil Merrick following dazzling approach play by Czibor and Puskas. Johnston boldly raced thirty yards from his own penalty area with the ball at his feet and ended an inspired run with a pinpoint pass to his club-mate Mortensen, who outpaced his marker before transferring the ball to Sewell out on the left. He cut in and beat Groscis with a low, left-foot cross shot.

The 100,000 crowd, bewildered and bemused by the hurricane start Hungary had made, breathed a collective sigh of relief. England, they were convinced, were unbeatable at home and now they would put the cherry shirted invaders in their place.

Thirteen minutes later the scoreline was England 1, Hungary 4, and by then it had dawned on everybody but the most obstinate spectators that England were being exposed to a new world of football that had left the English style of play looking not only old fashioned but also redundant.

Hidegkuti scored Hungary's second goal from close range and then Puskas stepped imperiously on to the scoring stage with what many consider the finest goal ever created at Wembley. Let England skipper Billy Wright, closest to the action, describe it:

'Puskas was in the inside-right position when he received the ball. I thought I was perfectly placed to make a tackle, but as I challenged he pulled the ball back with the sole of his left foot and all in the same movement fired a left foot shot inside Gil Merrick's near post. I tackled thin air and the next day that great reporter Geoffrey Green wrote in The Times *that I was like a fire engine going in the wrong direction for the fire. It was a perfect summary. Puskas had completely hoodwinked me. In all my 105 internationals for England I did not see a better executed goal.'*

Puskas netted goal number four three minutes later when he deftly flicked the ball past Merrick from a free-kick taken by master of the midfield Jozsef Bozsik.

If nothing else England had fighting spirit going for them and 'Blackpool Bomber' Stan Mortensen battled his way through the disciplined Hungarian defence with typical gusto to smash-and-grab a second goal for England just before half-time.

'We can still pull this out of the fire,' Morty said to his club-mate Stanley Matthews as they walked together back to the dressing-rooms. You needed to pin Mortensen to the canvas before he would admit defeat.

Any hope England had of getting back into the game died within ten minutes of the second half when first Bozsik scored with a rising drive, and then hat-trick hero Hidegkuti put the finishing touch to a dazzling succession of passes as the Hungarians reduced the match to something of an exhibition that earned them the nickname the 'Magical Magyars'.

Right-back Alf Ramsey pulled one back for England from the penalty spot after Tottenham schoolmaster George Robb, playing his one and only international match, was pulled down by goalkeeper Grosics. At 6-3, the scoreline flattered England.

The Wembley crowd shook off their disappointment at seeing their heroes humbled to acclaim a Hungarian team that had flourished a standard and style of football never before witnessed at Wembley. They showed the Old Masters the way the game could and should be played.

Gil Merrick, England's goalkeeper who had to pick the ball out of his net thirteen times in two appearances against the Hungarians, said at the close of his playing career: 'Whoever said the Hungarians did not know how to shoot must have been wearing a blindfold. They were the most accurate marksmen I ever faced. Their passing was so accurate and their running off the ball so intelligent that they often seemed to have two players to every one of ours.

Jozsef Bozsik, a member of the Hungarian House of Representatives who played in 100 international matches, recalled: 'The victory at Wembley was the greatest moment in the history of our football. England gave the game to the world and to beat them was like winning at the home of football. We were confident that we could cause a surprise but to score six goals at Wembley where no visiting team had ever won was like a dream come true.'

Ron Greenwood, who was a professional footballer with Chelsea watching from the stand, said: 'It was one of the most exciting days of my life. Tomorrow's world was suddenly opened up to us. It was going to be a long process, but at last it was accepted that we had to start rethinking our tactics and revising the way we approached the game. That defeat for England was the start of a much-needed revolution in our game.'

Noel Cantwell, West Ham left-back and later Manchester United skipper, said: 'As a Republic of Ireland player I could watch the game as a neutral, and my mouth was continually open with amazement at the football displayed by the Hungarians. It was almost like a religious experience, and I immediately became a disciple of the Hungarian way of playing the game. Several of my clubmates at Upton Park including Malcolm Allison and John Bond had a similar flash-of-light experience, and we started to introduce a 4-2-4 formation at Upton Park despite our manager Ted Fenton

Captains Billy Wright and Ferenc Puskas exchange pennants and pleasantries before the England-Hungary match. Billy was big enough to say later: 'That was the closest I got to him all afternoon.'

not understanding quite what we were up to. The Hungarians had taught us there was a better way to play the game.'

Don Revie was another player deeply affected by the Hungarian performance, and he started to push the case to be allowed to play a Hidegkuti-style deep-lying centre-forward role. It later became known at Manchester City as 'the Revie Plan.'

With his stunningly powerful left-foot shot and his ability to be a thought and a deed ahead of most defenders, Ferenc Puskas was the most influential player in that magnificent Hungarian team of the 1950s.

Born in Budapest in 1926, he won eighty-four international caps and scored eighty-five goals before his defection from Hungary following the 1956 Uprising. He was leading marksman in the Hungarian League in 1947, 1950 and 1953 when playing for Honved, the team consisting of players who had been commissioned in the Hungarian army. Puskas had the rank of Major and was nicknamed the 'Galloping Major' following his performance against England at Wembley. But he trotted rather than galloped.

After the Hungarian revolution he added to his reputation as one of the greatest players of all time by becoming a front-line master with Real Madrid where he struck up a devastating partnership with Alfredo di Stefano. Puskas was top Spanish League scorer in 1960, 1961, 1963 and 1964. Pancho – as he was affectionately known in Madrid – played for Spain in three World Cup final matches in 1962 but was then thirty-six and slowed to a stroll by a spreading waistline. At the end of his brilliant and eventful playing career he switched to management and guided Panathinaikos of Athens to the 1971 European Cup final.

Puskas told me during my football reporting days for the *Daily Express*:

'To understand how we felt about the match against England in 1953 you first had to appreciate how highly we regarded English football. Players like Stanley Matthews and Billy Wright were giants in our eyes and we were in awe of playing at Wembley. I played in many hundreds of games during my career but no victory gave me greater pleasure than the 6-3 win against England. I don't think anybody will accuse me of exaggeration when I say we could have scored ten goals. We felt ten feet tall when we walked off at the end because we knew we had given the old masters a lesson. The wonderful thing about it was the sportsmanship showed by the England players, particularly Billy Wright. They accepted their defeat with great dignity, and Billy and I became great friends with huge respect for each other.'

The 1954 World Cup was there for the taking by one of the greatest teams ever to tread on a football pitch. The fact that they failed to lift the trophy brought astonishing drama to the World Cup stage, and that's our next story in this nostalgic journey back into the footballing 'fifties.

ONE of the biggest surprises of the Footballing Fifites is that the Hungarian side of Puskas, Hidegkuti and Co failed to win the 1954 World Cup. They went into the finals as the warmest favourites of all time. Olympic champions – shamateurs rather than amateurs – they had gone four years without a single defeat, including crushing victories over both England and Scotland in home and away matches on their way to the finals in Switzerland.

In their opening matches they beat South Korea 9-0 and then a deliberately under-strength West Germany 8-3. Puskas was wickedly fouled in the match against the Germans, and was limping heavily with an ankle injury at the end. He later claimed the tackle that damaged him had been a brutal attempt to put him out of the tournament.

The concentration and composure of the Hungarians was severely affected by an ugly dressing-room brawl with the Brazilians after an ill-tempered quarter-final that they won 4-2. It became known as the Battle of Berne, with players from both sides trying to kick each other rather than the ball. English referee Arthur Ellis had to call police to try to restore order after he had sent off two players for having a full-scale fist fight. It got even worse after the final whistle, with the Brazilians attacking the Hungarians in their dressing-room. Players from both sides were cut and gashed by broken bottles in the most violent incident in World Cup history.

It had been more like a war than a football match. The game was always overspilling with violence from the moment in the third minute when Hidegkuti had his shorts ripped off him as he lashed a rising shot into the Brazilian net. Five minutes later Hidegkuti centred for Sandor Kocsis to head in a second goal as cascading rain threatened to swamp the ground.

The tackling, particularly by the Brazilians, became reckless and ferocious. Defender Djalma Santos pulled Brazil back into the game with a penalty, but early in the second half Mihaly Lantos restored Hungary's two-goal lead, again from the penalty spot.

Industrous Julinho made it 3-2 with a stunning shot after a weaving run through the Hungarian defence. It was then that the game deteriorated into a wild brawl, and referee Ellis sent off Nilton Santos and Jozsef Bozsik (captain in place of the injured Puskas) for having a stand-up fist fight. It was so out of control that Queensbury boxing rules would have been more appropriate than FIFA laws.

Ellis summoned police to clear the pitch when the Brazilian trainer came on to re-monstrate with him, followed by a posse of Press photographers. There were personal feuds being fought all over the pitch and Brazilian forward Humberto Tozzi fell to his knees pleading and crying when he became the third player to be sent off.

Three minutes from the end Kocsis rose to head his second goal of the game to clinch a 4-2 victory for Hungary. But it did not end there. The fighting continued as the teams left the field at the final whistle, and the battles were taken into the dressing-rooms as police used batons to try to restore some sort of order.

Still minus the injured Puskas, Hungary had a scare in a classic semi-final against Cup-holders Uruguay. They led 2-0 at half-time but the Uruguayans pulled back in the second-half to force extra-time. Juan Hohberg was a coat of paint away from completing a hat-trick for Uruguay before Sandor 'Golden Head' Kocsis scored two of his typical headers to clinch a place for Hungary in the final against a now full-strength West Germany. Shrewd team manager Sepp Herberger had purposely fielded a weakened team against the Hungarians in the qualifying round because he knew that his team would still go through if beaten and he believed it would give the opponents a false sense of confidence and complacency.

The early indications were that Hungary would repeat the thrashing they had given the Germans in the early round. Puskas, less than one hundred per cent fit, and Zoltan Czibor scored goals within ninety seconds of each other before the game was ten minutes old. But it then became clear that the gamble of playing Puskas had back-fired as the 'Galloping Major' became more of a struggling foot soldier. Hungary began to look decidedly shaky under a series of swift counter-attacks, and the Germans pulled level with goals from Max Morlock and Helmut Rahn.

It was the powerful Rahn, a last-minute choice for the German squad, who cut in from the right wing to shoot the ball into Hungary's net for the winning goal six minutes from the end.

Puskas claimed he had scored a dramatic late equaliser. but English referee Bill Ling ruled it out after Welsh linesman Mervyn Griffiths had flagged for off-side.

To the surprise of most people it was German captain Fritz Walter who collected the trophy from the veteran Jules Rimet, retiring President of FIFA.

'I will always swear that my goal near the end should have stood,' Puskas said later. 'I was not off-side when I received the ball, and the linesman made a terrible mistake waving his flag. At first the referee correctly signalled a goal but then changed his mind when he saw the flag. It was the biggest disappointment of my career. And nobody will ever convince me I was not deliberately kicked and badly injured when we played the Germans in the early round. It was a terrible foul and wrecked my World Cup.'

Sepp Herberger, the tactical genius who had come up with the mind-games plan to unhinge Hungary, said: 'Hungary's long run without defeat worked against them. It meant that when they went two goals clear early in the game they thought it was all going to be easy. We had a team of real fighters in such players as Morlock, Mai, Liebrich and Posipal, and our wingers Rahn and Schafer were the sort who could turn a

It's the end of a Hungarian dream as Helmut Rahn scores Germany's winning goal.

game in a flash. In our skipper Fritz Walter we had a player every bit as skilful as any of the Hungarians, who became victims of their complacency.'

Walter was a former paratrooper who refused to fly again after the Second World War because of a nightmare experience when a close friend of his was killed beside him during an air-raid.

He and his brother, Ottmar, were idolised in Kaiserlauten where they developed into a great tandem team, Ottmar doing the scoring and Fritz the scheming.

Fritz was thirty-three when collecting the Jules Rimet trophy, and he carried on playing international football for another four years, leading West Germany in the 1958 finals in Sweden where his midfield authority and controlled passing was again a feature of the tournament as in the 1954 finals.

'Everybody expected Hungary to win the final in 1954, including most German supporters,' he said after hanging up his boots. 'But people did not take into account the great team spirit that we had, and also the fact that we were confident we could match the Hungarians in midfield. This is where most games are won and lost, and we knew we had the energy to wear down the Hungarians.'

Despite their defeat that Hungarian side of the early 1950s will always be remembered as one of the greatest teams ever to grace a football field. The 1954 final was a bridge too far.

THE LEAGUE CHAMPIONSHIP 1953-54
Stan Cullis and his golden Wolves

ALL that glistered on the English soccer scene during the 1950s were the old gold shirts of Wolves as they powered through a startling sequence of success. In nine years from 1952-53 they won the League crown three times including successive Championships, finished out of the first three only once and missed a hat-trick of First Division titles and the FA Cup and League double by just one point in 1959-60.

After two team-building seasons when they flirted with life in the bottom half of the table, Wolves made a spirited challenge for the 1952-53 championship. They finally finished third behind Joe Mercer's Arsenal and Tom Finney's Preston, a race won on goal average by the North London giants. For Wolves, it was just a beginning. The next seven seasons were truly golden years.

Billy Wright, giant-hearted skipper of Wolves and England, was the chief motivator on the pitch for all but the final year of the decade, by which time he had voluntarily climbed off at the top of the mountain. While he was the heart of the team, master tactician Stan Cullis was the brains. Billy provided the drive, Cullis the direction.

I am biased when it comes to Billy Wright because we were close pals, and his widow Joy allowed me the privilege of being his official biographer. It is without apology that I repeat some of the facts from the Billy Wright story here because they are worth retelling for that generation of supporters not lucky enough to have seen how Billy gave his all for club and country. He would always shrug off praise for his part in the Wolves success story and pile the credit on his iron hard but always meticulously fair manager Stan Cullis.

With each of his teams, Cullis famously put a heavy emphasis on fitness and strength, and their overall impression was of muscularity and raw power. Yet there was also a thread of artistry running through the side, and they provided a procession of players for the England team.

The Wolves method of pumping long balls out of defence for their forwards to chase might appear a crude tactic on paper but on the pitch it was mightily effective. There was sneering criticism of their method from so-called purists in the game who dismissed it as 'kick-and-rush.' It was more like a goal rush. In their peak-success years they scored 878 goals and, astonishingly, topped the century mark in the First Division in four consecutive seasons.

The Cullis theory was a simple one. He argued that one long ball, accurately placed in the path of fast-moving attacking players, could do the work of three or four short passes and in half the time. The modern name for it would be route one. There were times when it was not particularly pretty, but it was extremely potent.

Cullis himself had been schooled by Major Frank Buckley, his renowned predecessor as Wolves manager who was a tough disciplinarian and a firm believer in the doctrine of quick and simple attacking football; also of discovering and developing young talent rather than raiding the transfer market. Cullis did not *buy* his teams – he *built* them; and many outstanding Wolves players came off the conveyor belt at Wath Wanderers, the Wolves nursery club in South Yorkshire which was run for them on professional lines by former Molineux winger Mark Crook. Every Wolves team – from the 'cubs' through to the first team – was fashioned around the controversial but successful 'long ball' game.

With Billy Wright as their shining role model, the Wolves youngsters were encouraged to battle for every ball as if their lives depended on it and then to move it into the opposition penalty area as quickly as possible. The biggest sin any Wolves player could commit was to shirk a challenge, and to dwell on the ball instead of releasing it was rated nearly as serious. A player pulling out of a tackle knew he faced the even more unnerving experience of having to explain his action to the awesome Cullis, who considered football to be first and foremost a physical game. He was, remember, out of the 1930s school where barging and charging were a vital and integral part of the game.

To support his 'long ball' theories Cullis made use of the computer-like mind of a statistician called Charles Reep, a football-loving wing commander who was stationed at RAF Bridgnorth close to Wolverhampton. Reep had a system of plotting and recording in detail every move of a football match, and he fed Cullis with facts and figures that strengthened his argument that long, direct passes provided the most efficient and successful method of breaking down a defence. Cullis claimed that if too much time was spent in building up an attack with a series of short passes it gave the opposition time to cover, and allowed fewer opportunities for his forwards to shoot at goal.

Stamina and strength were as valued as skill in Cullis-influenced teams, and pre-season training used to be so punishing that the players ached to play football as a release from the torture of training. They faced the daily challenge of having to tackle a commando-like assault course, culminating with an exhausting sprint up a steep hill in the tangled heathland of Cannock Chase. 'We used to call it Heartbreak Hill,' Billy Wright revealed. 'It was used as a barometer of our fitness.'

This was all designed to get the players fit enough to last a season of physically demanding football. Opponents were quite literally run into the ground by Wolves players whom they could sometimes match for skill but never for energy, drive, and determination.

For all the criticism of the Wolves style – or rather the alleged lack of it – nobody could argue that the Cullis system did not bring startling results. As well as being dominant on the domestic front, the whirlwind Wolves side of the 1950s had some memorable triumphs in unofficial floodlit international thrillers that hastened the inauguration of organised European competition.

The goalkeeping was in the safe hands of the graceful England international Bert 'The Cat' Williams, and later of Malcolm Finlayson, a flying Scot bought from Millwall. Both had bravery to go with their great talent, and could withstand physical challenges from shoulder-charging forwards in an era when goalkeepers had little of the protection given to them by today's 'thou-shalt-not-touch' laws.

Wolves were wall-solid at full back with Eddie Stuart and Bill Shorthouse and then George Showell and Gerry Harris as resolute partners. All were dependable defenders who were strong in the tackle and well drilled in the art (if art is the right word) of hammering huge clearances deep into opposition territory.

These were the days when all teams played two orthodox wingers, so full backs were detailed to full-time defensive duties and 'overlap' had not found a way into the football vocabulary. Wingers did not relish facing Wolves because they had a tradition for producing full backs who tackled like a clap of thunder and took no prisoners.

The real match-winning power emanated from a magnificent half-back line that featured a combination of skipper Billy Wright, Bill Slater, Eddie Clamp, and Ron Flowers, all England internationals, gifted footballers, and with the right mixture of skill and strength. Each of them was capable of putting the emphasis on defence or attack as the situation demanded.

Billy was the kingpin. He made a successful switch to the middle of the defence after winning 59 of his 105 England caps as a robust wing-half. As an indication of their reliability as the backbone of the Wolves team, there were four international matches when the England half-back line read Clamp-Wright-Slater.

With the calculating Cullis insisting on quick release, the ball rarely stayed long in midfield. The chief architect of the attacking movements was Peter Broadbent, a master of ball control and precise passing. He was one of the few players allowed the luxury of dwelling on the ball while he looked for the best place to deposit it with passes that were both accurate and incisive.

Wright, Slater and Ron Flowers shared midfield duties with Broadbent, the intelligent and versatile Slater later replacing Billy as captain and centre-half. Eddie Clamp brought discipline and a competitive edge to the midfield as a powerful right-half who epitomised the Wolves style of play with his driving enthusiasm and vigorous challenges that struck terror into the hearts of opposing inside forwards.

A feature of the Wolves format was the flying wing play of the tiny Johnny Hancocks and the clever Jimmy Mullen. Both were deadly accurate crossers of the ball and Hancocks packed a rocket shot in his schoolboy-size right boot (Legend has it that it was a size-two, but I am assured that it was a five). Norman Deeley later carried on

A picture that captures the sort of challenges that were part and parcel of a goalkeeper's life in the fifties. This is Wolves goalkeeper Malcolm Finlayson punching clear under pressure from Tottenham and England centre-forward Bobby Smith.

the winger tradition and scored two goals in the 1960 FA Cup Final. Waiting in the middle to convert the crosses of the Wolves wingers into goals were powerful forwards of the calibre of Roy Swinbourne, Dennis Wilshaw, Colin Booth, Jim Murray and Bobby Mason. They followed in the footsteps of the idolised Jesse Pye, an enterprising centre-forward in the immediate post-war years at Molineux who plundered 90 goals in 188 League games.

All the forwards who wore the gold shirts during the 1950s followed the Cullis creed of putting industry before invention. While their chief priority was to get the ball into the net they were also expected to hassle and harass any opposing defender in possession so that he was unable to make a comfortable clearance. If any Wolves forward came off at the final whistle feeling less than exhausted, the demanding Cullis would want to know the reason why. Wolves *worked* for their success.

Under the Cullis-Wright axis, Wolves were FA Cup winners in 1949, League Champions in 1953-4, 1957-8 and 1958-9, FA Cup winners again in 1960 (the season after Billy's retirement), and out of the first three in the First Division only three times between 1950 and 1961. In the same period the reserves won the Central League title seven times and the youth team reached three FA Youth Cup Finals. They narrowly missed a hat-trick of championships in 1959-60 when Burnley overhauled them with victory in their final match of the season. By beating Wolves to the title by a point, Burnley stopped them becoming the first team in the 20th century to pull off the League and FA Cup double. Tottenham did it the following season.

In the first fifteen post-war seasons their final positions in the First Division were 3, 5, 6, 2, 14, 16, 3, 1, 2, 3, 6, 1, 1, 2 and 3, and in each of the last four seasons they scored over a hundred League goals, which remains a unique feat. They had one of the most successful seasons ever undertaken by an English club in 1957-58 when they won the League title with a near-record 64 points, the reserves topped the Central League, the third team won the Birmingham and District League, the fourths carried off the Worcester Combination League and Cup, and the youth team won the FA Youth Cup.

Wolves started their success run under Cullis with a 3-1 FA Cup Final victory over Second Division Leicester City at Wembley in 1949. Their triumph followed two epic semi-final battles with the Cup holders, Manchester United. They held on for a 1-1 draw in the first match when reduced to only nine fit men, and then won a classic replay 1-0. Wolves took eventual Cup winners Newcastle to a semi-final replay in 1951, and won the Cup again in 1960 with a comfortable 3-0 victory over Blackburn Rovers at Wembley.

For those of us of a certain age, this golden Wolves era will be best remembered for their pioneering of European club football under floodlights. They mastered the mightiest teams in Europe in a series of unofficial world club championship matches at Molineux. Honved of Budapest – virtually the Hungarian national side that had ripped the heart out of the England team – Moscow Spartak, Moscow Dynamo, and Real Madrid were conquered in so-called 'friendlies' that were played at full throttle because of the enormous international prestige and pride involved.

Wolves concentrated on their domestic world where they battled with Manchester United for the unofficial mantle of England's greatest club side – the Cullis Cubs v the Busby Babes. Billy Wright, for whom I used to 'ghost' a weekly column in the *Daily Express* during his days as Arsenal manager, told me:

'It was the easiest job in the world to captain the Wolves teams of the 1950s. Everybody knew exactly what he had to do. Our success was due to our team understanding and the willingness of everyone to work for each other. Off the pitch, Stan Cullis was an inspiration and demanded and got one hundred per cent effort and enthusiasm from everybody who pulled on a Wolves shirt. He set the highest standards of discipline and responsible behaviour, and made every player aware that it was an honour to wear the old gold of Wolves. Pride and loyalty were important in football in those days, and all the Wolves players and fans of that era were proud to be associated with the club. Stan could be hard and sometimes strict to the point of harsh, but his heart was in the right place and you were only in trouble with him if you gave less than your best. You could almost warm your hands on the club spirit, and it used to be a joy to meet up with the lads for matches and training. We were on first-name terms with many fans, and used to drink tea and chat to them in a local café called the Copper Kettle. There was no 'them' and 'us'. We were one big, happy family, and I felt honoured to be the captain.'

Sir Matt Busby, who was creating his own miracles with Manchester United, went on record near the close of his career with this assessment of the team that provided his greatest opposition: 'Wolves in those days stood for everything that was good about British football. They played with great power, spirit and style. Their performances against top-class continental teams gave everybody in the game over here a lift. Stan Cullis moulded his teams in his own image. They were honest, straightforward, uncomplicated, and full of zest and determination.'

A young ex-professional footballer started out with ambitions to be a manager the same season that Cullis took over at Wolves. His name Bill Shankly, and he said later: 'There was not a manager in the league who was not impressed and influenced by what Stan achieved at Molineux. I never tried to copy the style of football Wolves played with my teams, but I did take note of how fitness was all important in his scheme of things. You never saw any of my players less than fit, and what I copied from the Cullis way of doing things was to always make it quick and simple.'

This is how mastermind Stan Cullis summed up his team and his triumphs: 'The

Bill Shankly in his last season as a player at Preston and soon to be influenced by the startling success of the Stan Cullis Wolves.

whole style of play in my time as manager was geared towards keeping the ball in the opponents' penalty area for as long as possible. We had the players to make our plan work. It was really exhilarating. There were critics of the way we played, but I have not the slightest doubt that the entertainment value of our matches was higher than at any time in my long experience of the game. We gave the spectators goals and excitement, and we managed to win all the trophies that mattered. My one regret is that the directors saw fit to dismiss me when I still had much to give to the club. I'd given them a yardstick by which they could measure my achievements, and when we had the dip in fortunes that happens to all teams at some time they quickly removed me. They took away my job, but could never take away my memories. They were unforgettable years.'

THE 1954 FA CUP FINAL
Finney fails to do a Matthews at Wembley

THROUGHOUT the 'forties and 'fifties two names went together like bacon and eggs ... Matthews and Finney. All neutral fans were hoping that Preston Plumber Tom could 'do a Matthews' and collect an FA Cup winners' medal at Wembley in 1954. On the eve of the final he was named Footballer of the Year.

Preston's opponents were West Bromwich Albion, who reached Wembley by eliminating the season's shock side Port Vale 2-1 in the semi-final. Vale were the first Third Division side to reach the semi-final stages since Millwall back in 1937, and along the way they collected the scalps of Cup holders Blackpool and First Division Cardiff. Norwich City also emerged as giantkillers, humbling Arsenal at Carrow Road in the fourth round.

But it was First Division giants Preston and West Brom who survived to battle it out in the final, and all attention was on Tom Finney, the first gentleman of the game who had become a legend with the Deepdale club without ever winning a major domestic honour.

West Brom had finished runners up to Wolves in the First Division, with Preston down in eleventh place. It was, however, Preston who went to Wembley as favourites because of the Finney factor.

Albion's canny manager Vic Buckingham had a plan to shut out Finney that worked to perfection. Three players were detailed to blanket mark him each time he got the ball so that they were able to force him to run into a cul de sac. They also cut out the service of Preston's power-propelled right-half Tommy Docherty.

West Brom emerged 3-2 victors, which on paper suggests it was an exciting final. But on the pitch there was too much attention to defence to make it anything approaching a classic.

Ronnie Allen, a neat well-organised centre-forward playing almost in Hidegkuti style, gave West Brom the lead after twenty-one minutes, with Preston hitting an instant equaliser when Angus Morrison headed in a Docherty cross.

Preston centre-forward Charlie Wayman looked yards offside when he was allowed to race unchallenged to score Preston's second goal early in the second-half. The West Brom equaliser in the sixty-third minute was equally controversial. Few agreed that Tommy Docherty had fouled Ray Barlow, but the referee awarded a penalty from which Ronnie Allen scored.

Extra-time seemed a certainty until Frank Griffin settled it with an angled shot inside the far post with referee Arthur Luty moments away from blowing the final whistle.

Wales, Ninian Park, 10.10.53. England won 4-1

Dennis Wilshaw celebrated his first England cap with two goals, and Nat Lofthouse netted twice for the second successive match. All of England's goals came in the ten minutes either side of the half-time interval after Wales had taken a deserved twenty-third minute lead through Ivor Allchurch. Wales played for much of the game with left-back Alf Sherwood a passenger on the wing after he had been concussed in the thirty-second minute. Giant Leeds centre-forward John Charles might have had a hat-trick but for a succession of superb saves by England goalkeeper Gil Merrick. Albert Quixall, literally worth his weight in gold when sold by Sheffield Wednesday to Manchester United for £45,000 in 1958, made his England debut at inside-right at the age of twenty. Wales were unlucky not to have salvaged a draw from a game they often dominated. As in 1949-50, the Home Championship was used to determine Great Britain's qualifiers for the World Cup finals. There were more than 60,000 fans packed into Ninian Park, all witness to the fact that England were hugely flattered with the size of the victory. This was the beginning of the rise of the greatest Welsh football team in their history, with John Charles and Ivor Allchurch laying the foundations to their memorable careers. *Team: Merrick Garrett Eckersley Wright* Johnston Dickinson Finney Quixall Lofthouse (2) Wilshaw (2) Mullen.*

Rest of Europe, Wembley, 21.10.53. Drew 4-4

An Alf Ramsey penalty in the last minute gave England a draw in a showpiece match to mark the Football Association's 90th birthday. England trailed three times against the European all-stars in a Wednesday afternoon match at Wembley Stadium that provided a feast of football for the 97,000 spectators. Some forty-six years later FIFA saw fit to downgrade the game to non-international status, but the Football Association awarded Billy Wright a cap and it stays in the English record books as a full international. That is good news for talented Charlton defender Derek Ufton, a solid batsman and understudy at Kent to wicket-keeper Godfrey Evans, who won his only cap in the game. England took the game very seriously because there was a lot of pride and prestige at stake. Considering they had only been together for a couple of days, the Rest of Europe side played some magnificent football. The pick of the players was Ladislav Kubala, who had been the first of the outstanding Hungarians to switch his football allegiance to Spain. Ask anybody from Barcelona or Budapest and they will tell you that he was in the class of Puskas. He had wonderful ball control and the ability to make space for himself with clever changes of pace. A naturally gifted genius, Kubala became a Hungarian exile just before the rise of their greatest of all teams. Just imagine how good they would have been had he still been available for selection! Kubala AND Puskas to mark. The mind boggles! *Team: Merrick Ramsey (1, pen), Eckersley Wright* Ufton Dickinson Matthews Mortensen (1) Quixall Mullen (2)..*

Rest of Europe: Zeman (Austria), Navarro (Spain), Hanappi (Austria), Cajkovski (Yugoslavia), Posipal (West Germany, Ocwirk (Austria), Boniperti (Italy 2), Kubala (Hungary2, 1pen), Nordahl (Sweden), Vukas (Yugoslavia), Zebec (Yugoslavia).

Northern Ireland, Goodison Park, 11.11.53. England won 3-1

Harold Hassall, playing alongside his Bolton team-mate Nat Lofthouse, scored the first of his two goals in just thirty seconds to mark his international recall after two years. It was Hassall's fifth and last cap. Doncaster Rovers forward Eddie McMorran equalised for the Irish nine minutes after half-time, and they started to play with a new confidence and increased pace that had England's defence stretched. Stanley Matthews turned the game England's way with a typical mazy run on the hour before passing to Billy Wright, who set up a simple second goal for Hassall. It was Lofthouse who clinched victory for England fifteen minutes later when he headed in a Jimmy Mullen cross, colliding with goalkeeper Smyth as he powered the ball into the net. Lofthouse limped off and Smyth was carried off with a broken nose. West Bromwich Albion right-back Stan Rickaby played in his one and only England match in place of the injured Alf Ramsey. *Team: Merrick Ricakby Eckersley Wright* Johnston Dickinson Matthews Quixall Lofthouse (1) Hassall (2) Mullen.*

Hungary, Wembley, 25.11.53. England lost 6-3

The match that changed the face of English football (see pages 70-74). The fall-out from the defeat claimed some famous scalps. For full-back partners Alf Ramsey (32 caps) and Bill Eckersley (17), centre-half Harry Johnston (10) and Stan Mortensen (25) it was their last appearance in an England shirt, and Ernie Taylor and George Robb were dropped after this one game. It was the London press that campaigned for Tottenham schoolteacher Robb to be included instead of Tom Finney, who at the end of the season was the Football Writers' Association Footballer of the Year! *Team: Merrick Ramsey (1, pen) Eckersley Wright* Johnston Dickinson Matthews Taylor E Mortensen (1) Sewell (1) Robb.*

Scotland, Hampden Park, 3.4.54. England won 4-2

The amateur committee of England selectors (some would say the blind leading the bland) made eight changes to the team taken apart by Hungary. Johnny Nicholls had good reason to remember his debut. It was his 23rd birthday and he celebrated with England's second goal, a flying header from a Tom Finney cross. Playing alongside his West Bromwich team-mate Ronnie Allen, he was one of four debutants, along with Ron Staniforth, Harry Clarke and Manchester United left-back Roger Byrne, who was to prove himself one of the finest players ever to wear the No 3 shirt. Clarke, 31-year-old centre-half, followed Ditchburn, Ramsey, Willis, Nicholson and Medley as members of the Spurs 'push-and-run' team who were capped after the age of thirty-plus. Roared on by a vast Hampden crowd of 134,554, Scotland took the lead in the seventh minute through Blackpool's Allan Brown. Ivor Broadis equalised eight minutes later after penetrating approach work by Wright and Finney. It was the same combination of Wright and Finney that set up England's second goal by Nicholls five minutes into the second half. Headed goals by Allen and Jimmy Mullen wrapped up the game for England and guaranteed them going to the World Cup finals as Home Champions. Scotland scored a strange second goal in the last minute when a wind-assisted cross from Willie Ormond suddenly swirled into the net. *Team: Merrick Staniforth Byrne R Wright* Clarke H Dickinson Finney Broadis (1) Allen R (1) Nicholls (1) Mullen (1).*

Yugoslavia, Belgrade, 16.5.54. England lost 1-0

Syd Owen, veteran Luton Town defender, was the eleventh centre-half tried since the defection of Neil Franklin to the outlawed Colombian league. England concentrated on a deep defence and a counter-attacking policy, and almost got away with a draw. Jimmy Mullen, Ronnie Allen and Johnny Nicholls had shots saved during breakaway raids, but the Yugoslavs were generally in control. They were always the sharper side and deserved their winning goal three minutes from the end when a 35-yard free-kick was deflected by Owen into the path of Mitic, who scored from six yards. This was Tom Finney's fiftieth international, and England wanted so much to get at least a draw to mark the occasion. Tom was arguably the finest player to wear the England shirt in the early post-war years. Stanley Matthews was the people's favourite, but most of the professionals would have given Tom the nod just ahead of Stanley because there was so much to his all-round game. The defeat in Yugoslavia did little to help England's confidence as they went on to Budapest for the return match with Hungary. Readers of a nervous disposition might want to skip the next match summary! *Team: Merrick Staniforth Byrne R Wright* Owen Dickinson Finney Broadis Allen R Nicholls Mullen.*

Hungary, Budapest, 23.5.54. England lost 7-1

This was the biggest defeat in England's 90-year football history (and continues to be so to this day). Just four of the England team had survived from the 6-3 slaughter at Wembley in November: Merrick, Wright, Dickinson and Finney. Fulham centre-forward Bedford Jezzard made a best-forgotten debut, while the unfortunate Peter Harris was winning his second and last cap after a gap of five years. His first cap came in the 2-0 home defeat by the Republic of Ireland in 1949. Puskas and Kocsis scored two goals each. The Hungarians, leading 3-0 at half-time, were six goals clear and cantering before Ivor Broadis opened the scoring for England. Hungary immediately replied with their seventh goal, scored by Puskas from a pass by Hidegkuti. Hungary's scorers were Puskas (2), Kocsis (2), Lantos, Toth and Hidegkuti. *Team: Merrick Staniforth Byrne R Wright* Owen Dickinson Harris P Sewell Jezzard Broadis (1) Finney.*

Belgium, World Cup, Basle, 17.6.54. Drew 4-4 after extra-time

A Jimmy Dickinson own goal during extra-time gave Belgium a draw in a helter-skelter match full of defensive blunders as England made an eventful start to their challenge for the World Cup. A goal down in five minutes, England produced some enterprising and energetic football and deserved their 2-1 half-time lead from goals by Ivor Broadis and Nat Lofthouse. The Lofthouse goal was a cracker, a spectacular diving header to send a Tom Finney cross powering into the net. When Broadis added a third goal early in the second half it looked odds on an England victory. Then defensive lapses let the Belgians in for two soft goals that took the game into extra-time. Lofty made it 4-3 in the opening moments of extra-time, and England seemed destined for full points when Jimmy Dickinson turned an intended headed clearance into his own net. Billy Wright took over at centre-half in the closing stages as Syd Owen limped to a passenger's role on the wing. *Team: Merrick Staniforth Byrne R Wright* Owen Dickinson Matthews Broadis (2) Lofthouse (2) Taylor T Finney.*

Switzerland, World Cup, Berne, 20.6.54. England won 2-0

Wolves left wing partners Dennis Wilshaw and Jimmy Mullen scored the goals, and their club captain Billy Wright started his first match as England's centre-half. Bill McGarry gave a solid debut performance in Wright's old position at right-half against the host nation and in searing-hot conditions that sapped the energy of the players. Mullen scored the first goal three minutes before half-time to silence a capacity 60,000 crowd. Wilshaw clinched the victory with a superb individual goal midway through the second-half, cleverly evading three Swiss defenders before steering a firm shot into the

Nat Lofthouse scores with a spectacular diving header against Belgium, one of two goals the Bolton lionheart collected in the 4-4 World Cup draw in Basle.

net. Syd Owen's injury had accidentally solved England's on-going centre-half crisis. Billy Wright slotted smoothly into the position as naturally as if born to the job. *Team: Merrick Staniforth Byrne R McGarry Wright* Dickinson Finney Broadis Taylor T Wilshaw (1) Mullen (1).*

Uruguay, World Cup, Basle, 26.6.54. England lost 4-2

Two mistakes by goalkeeper Gil Merrick let defending world champions Uruguay in for goals that turned this quarter-final match in their favour after Nat Lofthouse and Tom Finney had each scored to give England hope of causing an upset. Shuffling Stanley Matthews, the undisputed man of the match, hit a post and had a shot pushed off target before Uruguay clinched victory with their fourth goal in the eighty-fourth minute when Merrick failed to save a speculative shot from Ambrois. It was shell-shocked Merrick's final match for England. He had let in thirty goals in his last ten games after conceding only fifteen in his first thirteen internationals. The Uruguayans had beaten Scotland 7-0 in a qualifying round match, but were never allowed to show that sort of superiority by an England team that performed with pride and purpose. *Team: Merrick Staniforth Byrne R McGarry Wright* Dickinson Matthews Broadis Lofthouse (1) Wilshaw Finney (1).*

WE cannot let the 1954 World Cup finals go without mentioning one of the most incredible matches ever played. Austria were 3-0 down after twenty-three minutes of their quarter-final against host team Switzerland in Lausanne. Ten minutes later they were 5-3 up! By half-time their lead was down to 5-4, and they had missed a penalty. Austria eventually won 7-5, with all twelve goals coming in the space of just 49 minutes of playing time. The Swiss came up with an unusual reason for some eccentric play by goalkeeper Eugene Parlier on a blistering-hot day. It was announced after the match that Parlier had been suffering from sunstroke.

Scotland suddenly became the team without a manager when Andy Beattie announced his resignation after the Scots had gone down 1-0 to Austria in their opening match in the 1954 finals. Beattie felt that he was not being allowed to manage by the Scottish selectors. Scotland lost their next game to Uruguay 7-0 in scorching conditions, and wise-cracking right-half Tommy Docherty said: 'We were given such a run-around that we came off the pitch at the end with sun-burned tongues.'

Port Vale's FA Cup run to the semi-finals took the headlines, but their League form was equally impressive. Managed by a great character in Freddie Steele, they topped the Third Division North table by eleven points and set new records for the fewest goals conceded (21). the most games with a clean sheet (30) and a division record for fewest defeats (3).

Jimmy 'Old Bones' Delaney completed a unique medals collection when he won a Cup winners' medal with Derry City in Northrn Ireland. It made a full house to go with his Scottish Cup medal with Celtic in 1937 and an FA Cup winners' medal with Manchester United at Wembley in 1948.

Celtic, who had not won the Scottish championship since 1938 and the Scottish Cup only once since the war, achieved the double under the driving leadership of veteran centre-half Jock Stein. He was to become the new motivating power at Parkhead. Scot Symon was named as successor to the long-serving Bill Struth at Rangers.

Wolves beat Racing Club of Buenos Aires 3-1 in a friendly at Molineux in March. Now the club were considering a series of floodlit friendlies against top opposition.

1953-54 WHO WON WHAT
All the champions and runners-up

First Division: Wolves, 57pts. **Runners-up:** West Bromwich Albion, 53 pts.
Wolves record: P42 W25 D7 L10 F96 A56 Pts57
Representative team: Williams; Short, Pritchard; Slater, Shorthouse, Wright (capt.); Hancocks, Broadbent, Swinbourne, Wilshaw, Mullen.
Top scorer: Hancocks (25).
Manager: Stan Cullis.

Second Division: Leicester City, 56pts. **Runners-up:** Everton, 56pts.
Third Division (South): Ipswich Town, 64pts. **Runners-up:** Brighton, 61pts.
Third Division (North): Port Vale, 69pts. **Runners-up:** Barnsley, 58pts.

FA Cup final: West Bromwich Albion 3, Preston North End 2
West Brom: Sanders; Kennedy, Millard (capt.); Dudley, Dugdale, Barlow; Griffin, Ryan, Allen, Nicholls, Lee. **Scorers:** Allen (2, 1 pen.), Griffin
Preston: Thompson; Cunningham, Walton; Docherty, Marston, Forbes; Finney (capt.), Foster, Wayman, Baxter, Morrison. **Scorers:** Morrison, Wayman

Top First Division marksmen: Jimmy Glazzard (Huddersfield), Johnny Nicholls (West Brom), 29 goals
Footballer of the Year: Tom Finney (Preston)

Scottish First Division: Celtic, 43 pts. **Runners-up:** Hearts, 38 pts
Scottish Cup final: Celtic 2, Aberdeen 1
Scottish League Cup final: East Fife 3, Partick Thistle 2

FA Amateur Cup final: Crook Town 1, Bishop Auckland 0

World Cup final: West Germany 3, Hungary 2 (Berne, attendance: 60,000)
West Germany: Turek, Posipal, Kohlmeyer, Eckel, Liebrich, Mai, Rahn, Morlock, O. Walter, F. Walter (capt.), Schafer. **Scorers:** Morlock, Rahn (2)
Hungary: Grosics, Buzansky, Lantos, Bozsik, Lorant, Zakarias, Czibor, Kocsis, Hidegkuti, Puskas (capt.), Toth. **Scorers:** Puskas, Czibor
Referee: Bill Ling (England)
Third place: Austria 3, Uruguay 1
Leading scorer: Sandor Kocsis (Hungary) 11 goals in 5 games

THE LEAGUE TABLES
Where they finished in 1953-54

FIRST DIVISION

		P	W	D	L	F	A	Pts
1	Wolverhampton W.	42	25	7	10	96	56	57
2	West Bromwich A.	42	22	9	11	86	63	53
3	Huddersfield Town	42	20	11	11	78	61	51
4	Manchester United	42	18	12	12	73	58	48
5	Bolton Wanderers	42	18	12	12	75	60	48
6	Blackpool	42	19	10	13	80	69	48
7	Burnley	42	21	4	17	78	67	46
8	Chelsea	42	16	12	14	74	68	44
9	Charlton Athletic	42	19	6	17	75	77	44
10	Cardiff City	42	18	8	16	51	71	44
11	Preston North End	42	19	5	18	87	58	43
12	Arsenal	42	15	13	14	75	73	43
13	Aston Villa	42	16	9	17	70	68	41
14	Portsmouth	42	14	11	17	81	89	39
15	Newcastle United	42	14	10	18	72	77	38
16	Tottenham Hotspur	42	16	5	21	65	76	37
17	Manchester City	42	14	9	19	62	77	37
18	Sunderland	42	14	8	20	81	89	36
19	Sheffield Weds.	42	15	6	21	70	91	36
20	Sheffield United	42	11	11	20	69	90	33
21	Middlesbrough	42	10	10	22	60	91	30
22	Liverpool	42	9	10	23	68	97	28

SECOND DIVISION

		P	W	D	L	F	A	Pts
1	Leicester City	42	23	10	9	97	60	56
2	Everton	42	20	16	6	92	58	56
3	Blackburn Rovers	42	23	9	10	86	50	55
4	Nottingham Forest	42	20	12	10	86	59	52
5	Rotherham United	42	21	7	14	80	67	49
6	Luton Town	42	18	12	12	64	59	48
7	Birmingham City	42	18	11	13	78	58	47
8	Fulham	42	17	10	15	98	85	44
9	Bristol Rovers	42	14	16	12	64	58	44
10	Leeds United	42	15	13	14	89	81	43
11	Stoke City	42	12	17	13	71	60	41
12	Doncaster Rovers	42	16	9	17	59	63	41
13	West Ham United	42	15	9	18	67	69	39
14	Notts County	42	13	13	16	54	74	39
15	Hull City	42	16	6	20	64	66	38
16	Lincoln City	42	14	9	19	65	83	37
17	Bury	42	11	14	17	54	72	36
18	Derby County	42	12	11	19	64	82	34
19	Plymouth Argyle	42	9	16	17	65	82	34
20	Swansea Town	42	13	8	21	58	82	34
21	Brentford	42	10	11	21	40	78	31
22	Oldham Athletic	42	8	9	25	40	89	25

THIRD DIVISION (NORTH)

		P	W	D	L	F	A	Pts
1	Port Vale	46	26	17	3	74	21	69
2	Barnsley	46	24	10	12	77	57	58
3	Scunthorpe United	46	21	15	10	77	56	57
4	Gateshead	46	21	13	12	74	55	55
5	Bradford City	46	22	9	15	60	55	53
6	Chesterfield	46	19	14	13	76	64	52
7	Mansfield Town	46	20	11	15	88	67	51
8	Wrexham	46	21	9	16	81	68	51
9	Bradford Park A.	46	18	14	14	77	68	50
10	Stockport County	46	18	11	17	77	67	47
11	Southport	46	17	12	17	63	60	46
12	Barrow	46	16	12	18	72	71	44
13	Carlisle United	46	14	15	17	83	71	43
14	Tranmere Rovers	46	18	7	21	59	70	43
15	Accrington Stanley	46	16	10	20	66	74	42
16	Crewe Alexandra	46	14	13	19	49	67	41
17	Grimsby Town	46	16	9	21	51	77	41
18	Hartlepools United	46	13	14	19	59	65	40
19	Rochdale	46	15	10	21	59	77	40
20	Workington	46	13	14	19	59	80	40
21	Darlington	46	12	14	20	50	71	38
22	York City	46	12	13	21	64	86	37
23	Halifax Town	46	12	10	24	44	73	34
24	Chester	46	11	10	25	48	67	32

THIRD DIVISION (SOUTH)

		P	W	D	L	F	A	Pts
1	Ipswich Town	46	27	10	9	82	51	64
2	Brighton & Hove A.	46	26	9	11	86	61	61
3	Bristol City	46	25	6	15	88	66	56
4	Watford	46	21	10	15	85	69	52
5	Northampton Town	46	20	11	15	82	55	51
6	Southampton	46	22	7	17	76	63	51
7	Norwich City	46	20	11	15	73	66	51
8	Reading	46	20	9	17	86	73	49
9	Exeter City	46	20	8	18	68	58	48
10	Gillingham	46	19	10	17	61	66	48
11	Leyton Orient	46	18	11	17	79	73	47
12	Millwall	46	19	9	18	74	77	47
13	Torquay United	46	17	12	17	81	88	46
14	Coventry City	46	18	9	19	61	56	45
15	Newport County	46	19	6	21	61	81	44
16	Southend United	46	18	7	21	69	71	43
17	Aldershot	46	17	9	20	74	86	43
18	Queens Park R.	46	16	10	20	60	68	42
=19	Bournemouth	46	16	8	22	67	70	40
=19	Swindon Town	46	15	10	21	67	70	40
21	Shrewsbury Town	46	14	12	20	65	76	40
22	Crystal Palace	46	14	12	20	60	86	40
23	Colchester United	46	10	10	26	50	78	30
24	Walsall	46	9	8	29	40	87	26

LONG long before the arrival of Roman Abramovich and Jose Mourinho, Chelsea had been the target for jokes by music-hall comedians. This is a typical one that 'fifties 'Cheeky Chappie' Max Miller used to tell: 'Here, have you seen the cock up the architect has made when designing the new stand at Stamford Bridge? It's facing the pitch.'

When Ted Drake, former England , Southampton and Arsenal centre-forward hero, took over as manager in 1952 he vowed he was going to change the image of the club. The first thing he did was to order the removal of the Chelsea Pensioner from the club badge.

'I don't want to hear anybody referring to us as Pensioners,' he said in his heavy Hampshire accent. 'And I suggest comedians look elsewhere for their material. I want this to be a football club to be proud of, not to be laughed at.'

Yet even he would have laughed if somebody had suggested that within three years of taking over Chelsea would be League champions in a division dominated by the likes of major clubs Manchester United, Arsenal, Wolves and Tottenham.

Drake locked up the manager's office, donned a tracksuit and spent most of his time at the training ground where he expanded the youth and scouting programme. He had served his managerial apprenticeship at Reading and used his knowledge of the lower divisions to sign value-for-money players he knew would come to Chelsea hungry for football rather than the bright lights of the nearby West End.

'Ted was the hardest man I ever played for,' said goalkeeper Chic Thomson. 'He used to take the training sessions and God help anybody who shirked. He used to almost kill us, but it was all for our own good and we all became fit as fiddles and could sail through the matches. There was certainly a touch of the Fergie about him, and he could take the paint off the walls with his half-time talks. In one of the matches our other goalkeeper, Bill Robertson, threw the ball out to Ken Armstrong, who slipped and miskicked and the ball ended up in the back of our net. Ted put up a big notice in the dressing room saying, "Goalkeepers will not, I repeat NOT throw the ball." Unfortunately, I forgot this and did it in a practice match the following Tuesday. I was immediately relegated to an early bath and dropped from the team the next Saturday. He was a fearsome man, but you had to respect him. He had been there and done that as a player, and he instilled the highest possible standards into his team.'

Around established stars Ken Armstrong, John Harris, Stan Willemse and Eric Parsons, Drake built a new-look Chelsea team that included imports from the lower leagues: John McNicholl, Les Stubbs, Stan Wicks, John and Peter Sillett, and from Crewe an exceptional teenage prospect in Frank Blunstone. Drake even brought in amateur players Derek Saunders and Jim Lewis from Walthamstow Avenue and Seamus O'Connell, a cattle farmer who used to travel from Carlisle when required to play.

O'Connell experienced an astonishing debut for Chelsea in October 1954. He scored a hat-trick against Manchester United at Stamford Bridge ... but finished on the losing side. United won a see-sawing game 6-5. This was during a run of six games in which Chelsea picked up just two points. Hardly championship form.

From a mid-table position at Christmas, Chelsea started a charge that was to take them to the title in one of the lowest points scoring seasons of all time.

By Easter Chelsea were four points clear of defending champions Wolves at the top of the table. Stan Cullis brought his team to Stamford Bridge for a crunch match that drew an attendance of 75,000.

The game was goalless with fifteen minutes to go when Wolves skipper Billy Wright fisted a shot off the goal-line. At first the referee waved play on, but was finally persuaded to award a penalty after protests from the Chelsea players and a discussion with a linesman. Peter Sillett thumped home the spot-kick for a vital victory.

Chelsea clinched the championship in their Jubilee year in the penultimate game of the season, beating Sheffield Wednesday 3-0 on St George's Day.

Roy Bentley, missing only one game and scoring 21 goals, was a motivational captain, and he summed up the title triumph by saying: 'Now the comedians will have to look elsewhere for their jokes.'

Eric Parsons and Derek Saunders both played every one of the 42 games, while centre-half Ron Greenwood earned a championship medal with twenty-one appearances.

On the last Saturday of the season Chelsea played at Old Trafford. Matt Busby sent instructions for them to wait in their dressing-room until they were summoned. When Chelsea finally came out on to the pitch they found the United players forming an avenue, and they applauded them all the way to the centre-circle.

As title holders Chelsea were poised to become pioneers in Europe. They were drawn to play Swedish champions Djurgarden in the new European Cup, but pulled out on the instructions of the Football League.

Chelsea's players were each given a free suit as a bonus for winning the championship, except the amateurs. They had to make do with a framed illuminated address marking their part in the triumph. Walthamstow Avenue hero Jim Lewis hung his in the loo for the next fifty years.

The year after winning the championship Chelsea slumped to sixteenth, but Ted Drake kept telling everybody that the future was bright. His youth building plans were starting to bear fruit and among the youngsters who would turn Chelsea into Drake's Ducklings were players of the calibre of Jimmy Greaves and Bobby Tambling.

THE 1955 FA CUP FINAL
Hat-trick for Magpies as jinx strikes City

MUCH of the attention before the 1955 final had been on Don Revie's role with Manchester City. He had been so impressed by Nandor Hidegkuti's performance as a withdrawn centre-forward for Hungary in the annihalation of England that he had decided to adopt the style with City. It became famous as 'the Revie Plan.' It had worked so well for him that on the eve of the final he was presented with the Footballer of the Year award, the only individual prize available in the 1950s and the original concept of the Football Writers' Association.

But Newcastle had a plan of their own, and it was simply to frustrate Revie's runs from deep positions by springing the off-side trap at every opportunity. City were never allowed to get into any sort of rhythm after the Geordies had taken a first-minute lead through a magnificent header by Jackie Milburn.

Their balance was completely disrupted when right-back Jimmy Meadows limped out of the game after twenty minutes with a knee injury. The Wembley injury jinx had struck again, and it was almost eerie the way Meadows was sidelined. He had twisted his knee and damaged ligaments trying to stop a jinking run by Newcastle's elusive winger Bobby Mitchell. In 1952 in exactly the same area of the pitch and in exactly the same minute of the match Arsenal full back Walley Barnes had suffered a twisted knee trying to mark the same player.

Big-hearted Bobby Johnstone dived to head an equaliser for the ten men of City in the last minute of the second-half, but they were flattened by two Newcastle goals in the first fifteen minutes after the interval. The mercurial Mitchell cut inside and shot under Bert Trautmann's despairing dive from a narrow angle, and then Mitchell placed the ball perfectly for George Hannah to run on to the ball and score from twelve yards.

It completed a record-setting afternoon for Newcastle. They became the first team to win the FA Cup three times in five seasons, their sixth victory meant they equalled the Cup-winning aggregate records of Blackburn Rovers and Aston Villa, and they became the first club to compete in ten finals. On top of all that, Milburn's goal was clocked at forty-five seconds, the fastest ever recorded at Wembley.

Not for the first or last time the subject of substitutes was aired in the newspapers. It was not only Meadows who was injured, but Newcastle were reduced to nine fit men when Milburn and Len White hobbled through much of the second-half. But it would be another ten years before substitutes became part of the game.

Don Revie said, prophetically: 'It surely makes sense to have substitutes for injured players. Now we have to pick ourselves up and try to come back again next year.'

AWAY from their growing dominance on the domestic stage, Wolves were building an international reputation with their pioneering of European club football under floodlights. They mastered the mightiest teams in Europe in a series of unofficial world club championships at Molineux that were staged so successfully that they accelerated the move towards organised European competitions. These midweek evening games , alleged friendlies, were played with total commitment because of the enormous international prestige and pride involved. The matches were screened live on television – a rarity in those days – and the exciting exploits of Wolves captured the nation's interest and imagination.

Wolves, reaching the absolute peak of their power, triumphed against all-comers in what proved a trail blazer for European inter-club competitions. The influential French sports newspaper, *L'Equipe*, noticed that English newspapers were calling Wolves the kings of Europe, and they proposed a proper competition to decide just who were the champions of Europe.

Typical of our blinkered, insular football hierarchy, the European Cup kicked off in 1955-56 without English involvement. The Football League and FA Cup competitions were seen as the be-all-and-end-all, and European football was considered beneath the country that gave organised football to the world. After all the visionary ground work of Wolves, English clubs were banned from competing in Europe. It was the 'Euro' controversy of the 'fifties.

The Wolves game that grabbed most attention was against Honved of Budapest on 13 December 1954. Honved were virtually the Hungarian national team that had hammered thirteen goals against the full England side in two meetings during the previous fourteen months. Could Wolves do what England failed to do and conquer Ferenc Puskas and Co? Sixty thousand fans packed into the Molineux ground and armchair viewers at home waited for the answer.

After throwing bouquets to the crowd, the Hungarians started to deflower the Wolves defence which was under the direction of England skipper Billy Wright. Honved might easily have scored three goals in the opening ten minutes as they skipped lightly over the muddy Molineux turf to test goalkeeper Bert 'The Cat' Williams. A goal seemed inevitable and it came in the eleventh minute when Puskas floated over a free-kick for Kocsis to power the ball past Williams to add to the belief that he was the true 'head man' of football.

Three minutes later goal-taker Kocsis turned goal-maker with a defence-splitting

William Ambrose Wright, first footballer in the world to win 100 international caps.

pass to Machos, who drove the ball firmly past the oncoming Williams. These two knife thrusts would have been enough to kill off most sides, but Wolves – characterising the iron will of their demanding manager Stan Cullis – were never a team of quitters. The match settled into a fascinating duel between two worlds: the short passing game of the Hungarians against the thumping long-ball tactics of Wolves. With the pitch becoming heavier and muddier by the minute, it was the Wolves strategy that began to pay dividends and despite going off at half-time two goals in arrears there were definite signs of the game beginning to swing in favour of the Midlanders.

They started a second-half revival movement that had Honved stretched to breaking point. Tiny England winger Johnny Hancocks used his schoolboy-size right boot to hammer a forty-ninth minute penalty into the net after he had been bundled off the ball by Kovaks.

Captain Wright, with nightmare memories of Hungary's thirteen goals against England as his motivation for revenge, was giving a Herculean performance in the middle of the defence, and he drove his forwards to new peaks of effort as Wolves set up camp in the Honved half.

After half a dozen chances had been made and missed, Wolves finally snatched an equaliser in the seventy-sixth minute when Bill Slater and Denis Wilshaw combined to create an opening for centre-forward Roy Swinbourne who nodded the ball wide of Farago's despairing dive.

Honved were suddenly almost visibly drained of spirit and energy, and all resistance was knocked out of them two minutes later when Wilshaw and Swinbourne again got their act together, this time Swinbourne volleying in a centre for the winning goal.

Stan Cullis, the Wolves manager who was the master of Molineux, said: 'It was without any question the most exciting match I ever saw. Even when we were two goals down at half-time I was convinced we could win, and I simply told the lads to keep plugging away. It was a magnificent team performance.'

Dennis Wilshaw, who later in the season scored four goals for England against Scotland at Wembley, said: 'There has never been a match quite like it for atmosphere and excitement. The newspapers were calling us the club champions of the world, and I don't think anybody who saw our victory against Honved would have argued.'

Ferenc Puskas commented: 'Billy Wright is a good friend of mine as well as a respected opponent. I told him after the match that he should be proud to be captain of such an outstanding team. We have not come up against a better club side. Wolves do not have a single weakness.'

This is how Billy summed it up: 'The win against Honved went some way to making up for the hammerings against Hungary. It was one of the greatest nights of my club football career. To give a team of Honved's calibre a two-goal lead and then beat them 3-2 was like something out of a fairy story.'

ENGLAND FOOTBALL DIARY
Summary of their 1954-55 matches

Northern Ireland, Windsor Park, 2.10.54. England won 2-0

Don Revie and Johnny Haynes got their first taste of international football together and scored a goal each. There were five other new caps in a team that had been completely re-modelled following the quarter-final exit from the World Cup: Ray Wood, Bill Foulkes, Johnny Wheeler, Ray Barlow and Brian Pilkington, who played in place of the injured Tom Finney. Foulkes, Wheeler, Barlow and Pilkington were not capped again after this victory. The Irish worked desperately hard in a bid for their first victory over England since 1927, but were sunk by two goals inside two minutes late in the second half. Haynes exchanged a one-two pass with Revie before shooting wide of Portsmouth goalkeeper Norman Uprichard. Within a minute it was 2-0, Revie running on to a pass from Haynes and steering the ball low into the net. Haynes was just nineteen, and already looked an assured and confident player who could hit accurate forty yard passes with either foot. But the powers-that-be decided he was too young to trust with the role of midfield general, and he was dropped along with Don Revie and six other players. *Team: Wood Foulkes Byrne R Wheeler Wright* Barlow Matthews Revie (1) Lofthouse Haynes (1) Pilkington.*

Wales, Wembley, 10.11.54. England won 3-2

Roy Bentley, at last forgiven for his part in the 1950 World Cup humiliation against the United States, celebrated his recall by sinking Wales with a hat-trick. Two of his goals came from headers at the far post after he had exchanged passes with Matthews. John Charles, leading the Welsh attack with fire and flair, scored twice to bring the scores level at 2-2 before Bentley completed his hat-trick two minutes from the end of a thrilling match played on a rain-saturated Wembley surface. Bentley's Chelsea team-mate Frank Blunstone made his England debut on the left wing and Bill Slater played alongside his Wolves skipper Billy Wright in his first international match. The duel between John Charles and Billy Wright was worth the admission money on its own. Two great and talented competitors locked in a struggle for supremacy. Charles won on points, but it would have been a knockout against any other England centre-half that the selectors had tried since the Neil Franklin fiasco. Wright managed to shut the big man out for most of the match, but he took the two chances that came his way in dynamic style. *Team: Wood Staniforth Byrne R Phillips Wright* Slater Matthews Bentley (3) Allen R Shackleton Blunstone.*

West Germany, Wembley, 1.12.54. England won 3-1

The 100,000 crowd for this Wednesday afternoon match against the world champions broke the Wembley receipts record by paying £51,716 to watch a classic encounter. With Stanley Matthews running the German defenders into dizzy disarray, England took the lead in the twenty-seventh minute when Roy Bentley headed in a pin-pointed centre from the Maestro. Ronnie Allen made it 2-0 three minutes after half-time following neat combination work between Finney and Len Shackleton. The Germans pulled back to 2-1 through Beck before Shackleton, the Clown Prince, clinched a memorable victory in the eightieth minute with an impudent chip shot as the goalkeeper came racing towards him. Shack had thrilled the crowd throughout the match with his tricks, but he was too much an individualist for the taste of the selectors and never played for England again after a paltry five caps. It remains a mystery to many people why he did not win a cupboardful of caps. He just refused to conform. Shack upset the selectors with a book published in 1955 in which a chapter headed 'The Average Director's Knowledge of Football' was left completely blank. With his ability, he should have won dozens of caps but he just could not bring himself to toe the line. At least he could say he went out at the very top, because his brilliant goal made sure that England toppled the new world champions. The Germans included only three of the team that won the trophy in Switzerland as they started rebuilding ready for their defence of the World Cup. *Team: Williams   Staniforth   Byrne R   Phillips   Wright*   Slater   Matthews   Bentley (1)   Allen R (1)   Shackleton (1)   Finney.*

A QUICK TRUE TALE OF THE EXPECTED FROM SHACK

Shack became a respected football writer after his retirement, and reminiscing in the press box one day he regaled us with a story that captures the times in which he played:

> *'After scoring one of my finest ever goals to help England beat world champions Germany I was handed a third-class rail ticket for the overnight sleeper back to Sunderland. I said to the Bowler Hat handing me the ticket, "Couldn't you raise enough money for a first-class ticket?" The FA official said that all the first-class tickets had been sold. When I got to Kings Cross I had no trouble transferring to first-class because there was plenty of space, and I was happy to pay the five pounds difference out of my own pocket. By the time I'd paid tax and expenses, I was left with just £20 out of my £50 match fee. The Wembley receipts for the match were over £50,000, but we footballers who had drawn the crowd and the money were considered third-class citizens by those blinkered fools who ran the FA.'*

Shack was one of the most skilful footballers England ever produced. Think Gazza with a brain. Five England caps? What a joke they played on the Clown Prince.

Len Shackleton, the Clown Prince of football.

Scotland, Wembley, 2.4.55. England won 7-2

Stanley Matthews was the engineer and Dennis Wilshaw the executioner in this an-nihilation of the Scots. Wilshaw's four goals included the first hat-trick by an England player against Scotland. Duncan Edwards, the human powerhouse from Manchester United, was, at 18 years 183 days, the youngest England player of the 20th century. Chelsea right-half Ken Armstrong collected his only cap, and later emigrated to New Zealand for whom he won thirteen caps. This was England's first victory over Scotland at Wembley since 1934. Wilshaw started his goal rush in the first minute, and two goals from Nat Lofthouse and one from Don Revie gave England a commanding 4-1 lead at half-time. Scotland caved in as Wilshaw snatched three goals in thirteen minutes in the last third of the match. Tommy Docherty, who ran himself into the ground for the Scots, got a little reward for all his work when he scored with a late free-kick. The talk afterwards was of the dynamic performance from Duncan Edwards, who looked the complete player in his debut. *Team: Williams Meadows Byrne R Armstrong Wright* Edwards Matthews Revie (1) Lofthouse (2) Wilshaw (4) Blunstone.*

France, Paris, 15.5.55. England lost 1-0

Peter Sillett, making his debut at right-back, conceded the thirty-sixth minute penalty from which the great Raymond Kopa scored the winning goal for France. Just a month earlier Sillett's penalty goal against Wolves had virtually clinched the League championship for Chelsea, and forced Wolves into settling for runners-up place. Ron Flowers, making his debut alongside his Wolves skipper Billy Wright, had to wait three years for his second cap and then won forty in a row – an unbroken sequence beaten only by Billy's seventy consecutive appearances. The nearest England came to scoring was when Frank Blunstone was unceremoniously pulled down as he shaped to shoot. England appeals for a penalty were dismissed, while the German referee had no hesitation in awarding the penalty to France for a less obvious foul by Sillett. *Team: Williams Sillett P Byrne R Flowers Wright* Edwards Matthews Revie Lofthouse Wilshaw Blunstone.*

Spain, Madrid, 18.5.55. Drew 1-1

In a bad-tempered match Nat Lofthouse had his shirt ripped off his back in the first-half, and played throughout the second half with a numberless shirt. Even Stanley Matthews was drawn into the roughhouse, and conceded a free-kick with a tackle, the first time anybody could recall him committing a foul. Roy Bentley scored from a Lofthouse pass in the thirty-eighth minute and Spain equalised in the sixty-fifth minute following a mistake by Duncan Edwards that was as rare as a foul by Matthews. The trouble flared after Lofthouse had been rugby tackled to the ground when on a run towards the penalty area. There were so many personal feuds going on after this that the game lost all of its rhythm. *Team: Williams Sillett P Byrne R Dickinson Wright* Edwards Matthews Bentley (1) Lofthouse Quixall Wilshaw.*

Portugal, Oporto, 22.5.55. England lost 3-1

England were disjointed from the moment Nat Lofthouse went off injured with the score at 1-1. Albert Quixall came on as substitute in what was his final England appearance. It was also Roy Bentley's last match for England after twelve appearances in three different shirts over a period of six years. His nineteenth minute goal could not save England from their first defeat by Portugal. Defensive errors let the Portuguese in for two late goals and a famous victory. Stanley Matthews and Billy Wright were the only players on the pitch who had featured in the 10-0 slaughter of Portugal in Lisbon eight years earlier. *Team: Williams Sillett Byrne Dickinson Wright* Edwards Matthews Bentley (1) Lofthouse (Quixall) Wilshaw Blunstone.*

FACTS, STATS AND TRIVIA
The winners and losers of 1954-55

TOMMY BRIGGS scored a Second Division record seven goals as Blackburn beat Bristol Rovers 8-3 at Ewood Park on 5 February 1955. In the same season Rovers thumped Middlesbrough 9-0, Doncaster 7-2 and netted five goals against West Ham (twice) and Derby. They scored 114 goals in the League, but leaked 79 and finished sixth in the table.

Birmingham City won the Second Division title on goal average after a three-way tie at the top with Luton and Rotherham. Back-to-back victories against Port Vale (7-2) and Liverpool (9-1) clinched their promotion as champions.

Wales played two pairs of brothers when they beat Northern Ireland 3-2 in Belfast. John and Mel Charles and Len and Ivor Allchurch made it a relatively successful match, with Big John scoring all the Welsh goals.

Stan Milburn and Jack Froggatt were credited with half an own goal each for Leicester against Chelsea. They both tried to kick the ball clear at the same time, connected together and it skidded off their boots into their own net.

Managerless York City were the shock side of the FA Cup. They eliminated Blackpool and Tottenham, and then took Newcastle United to a semi-final replay as they just failed to become the first Third Division club to reach an FA Cup final. Stoke City needed five matches to beat Bury in the third round, and Doncaster overcame Aston Villa in their fifth meeting in the fourth round.

Supporters were up in arms when the Football League announced that minimum admission prices were going up from 1s 9d to two shillings (10p). Attendances were falling, and the growing popularity of television was blamed.

Aberdeen won the Scottish championship, Hearts the League Cup and Clyde the Scottish Cup, leaving the two Old Firm clubs Celtic and Rangers empty-handed.

A proposal for a European Cup competition to be introduced was narrowly defeated at a meeting of UEFA clubs in Vienna in March 1954. But influential French sports paper L'Equipe stepped up their campaign for a European Cup when English newspapers declared that 'Wolves are the kings of Europe.'

First Division: Chelsea, 52pts. **Runners-up:** Wolves, 48 pts.

Chelsea record: P42 W20 D12 L10 F81 A57 Pts52

Representative team: Robertson (Thomson); Harris (Peter Sillett), Willemse; Armstrong, Greenwood (Wicks), Saunders; (from) Parsons, McNichol, Bentley (capt.), Stubbs, Blunstone, Lewis, O'Connell (Peter Brabrook made three appearances).

Top scorer: Bentley (21).

Manager: Ted Drake.

Second Division: Birmingham City, 54pts. **Runners-up:** Luton Town, 54pts.

Third Division (South): Bristol City, 70pts. **Runners-up:** Leyton Orient, 61pts.

Third Division (North): Barnsley, 65pts. **Runners-up:** Accrington, 61pts.

FA Cup final: Newcastle United 3, Manchester City 1

Newcastle: Simpson; Cowell, Batty; Scoular (capt.), Stokoe, Casey; White, Milburn, Keeble, Hannah, Mitchell. Scorers: Milburn, Mitchell, Hannah

Manchester City: Trautmann; Meadows, Little; Barnes, Ewing, Paul (capt.); Spurdle, Hayes, Revie, Johnstone, Fagan. **Scorer:** Johnstone

---

Top First Division marksman: Ronnie Allen (West Bromwich Albion), 27 goals

Top Second Division marksman: Tommy Briggs (Blackburn Rovers), 33 goals

Top Third Division North marksman: Arthur Bottom (York City), 30 goals

Top Third Division South marksman: Ernie Morgan (Gillingham), 31 goals

Footballer of the Year: Don Revie (Manchester City)

Scottish First Division: Aberdeen, 49pts. **Runners-up:** Celtic, 46pts.

Top Scottish First Division marksman: Willie Bauld (Hearts), 21 goals

Scottish Cup final: Clyde 1, Celtic 0 (after a 1-1 draw)

Scottish League Cup final: Hearts 4, Motherwell 2

FA Amateur Cup final: Bishop Auckland 2, Hendon 0

THE LEAGUE TABLES
Where they finished in 1954-55

FIRST DIVISION

		P	W	D	L	F	A	Pts
1	Chelsea	42	20	12	10	81	57	52
2	Wolverhampton W.	42	19	10	13	89	70	48
3	Portsmouth	42	18	12	12	74	62	48
4	Sunderland	42	15	18	9	64	54	48
5	Manchester United	42	20	7	15	84	74	47
6	Aston Villa	42	20	7	15	72	73	47
7	Manchester City	42	18	10	14	76	69	46
8	Newcastle United	42	17	9	16	89	77	43
9	Arsenal	42	17	9	16	69	63	43
10	Burnley	42	17	9	16	51	48	43
11	Everton	42	16	10	16	62	68	42
12	Huddersfield Town	42	14	13	15	63	68	41
13	Sheffield United	42	17	7	18	70	86	41
14	Preston North End	42	16	8	18	83	64	40
15	Charlton Athletic	42	15	10	17	76	75	40
16	Tottenham Hotspur	42	16	8	18	72	73	40
17	West Bromwich A.	42	16	8	18	76	96	40
18	Bolton Wanderers	42	13	13	16	62	69	39
19	Blackpool	42	14	10	18	60	64	38
20	Cardiff City	42	13	11	18	62	76	37
21	Leicester City	42	12	11	19	74	86	35
22	Sheffield Weds.	42	8	10	24	63	100	26

SECOND DIVISION

		P	W	D	L	F	A	Pts
1	Birmingham City	42	22	10	10	92	47	54
2	Luton Town	42	23	8	11	88	53	54
3	Rotherham United	42	25	4	13	94	64	54
4	Leeds United	42	23	7	12	70	53	53
5	Stoke City	42	21	10	11	69	46	52
6	Blackburn Rovers	42	22	6	14	114	79	50
7	Notts County	42	21	6	15	74	71	48
8	West Ham United	42	18	10	14	74	70	46
9	Bristol Rovers	42	19	7	16	75	70	45
10	Swansea Town	42	17	9	16	86	83	43
11	Liverpool	42	16	10	16	92	96	42
12	Middlesbrough	42	18	6	18	73	82	42
13	Bury	42	15	11	16	77	72	41
14	Fulham	42	14	11	17	76	79	39
15	Nottingham Forest	42	16	7	19	58	62	39
16	Lincoln City	42	13	10	19	68	79	36
17	Port Vale	42	12	11	19	48	71	35
18	Doncaster Rovers	42	14	7	21	58	95	35
19	Hull City	42	12	10	20	44	69	34
20	Plymouth Argyle	42	12	7	23	57	82	31
21	Ipswich Town	42	11	6	25	57	92	28
22	Derby County	42	7	9	26	53	82	23

THIRD DIVISION (NORTH)

		P	W	D	L	F	A	Pts
1	Barnsley	46	30	5	11	86	46	65
2	Accrington Stanley	46	25	11	10	96	67	61
3	Scunthorpe United	46	23	12	11	81	53	58
4	York City	46	24	10	12	92	63	58
5	Hartlepools United	46	25	5	16	64	49	55
6	Chesterfield	46	24	6	16	81	70	54
7	Gateshead	46	20	12	14	65	69	52
8	Workington	46	18	14	14	68	55	50
9	Stockport County	46	18	12	16	84	70	48
10	Oldham Athletic	46	19	10	17	74	68	48
11	Southport	46	16	16	14	47	44	48
12	Rochdale	46	17	14	15	69	66	48
13	Mansfield Town	46	18	9	19	65	71	45
14	Halifax Town	46	15	13	18	63	67	43
15	Darlington	46	14	14	18	62	73	42
16	Bradford Park A.	46	15	11	20	56	70	41
17	Barrow	46	17	6	23	70	89	40
18	Wrexham	46	13	12	21	65	77	38
19	Tranmere Rovers	46	13	11	22	55	70	37
20	Carlisle United	46	15	6	25	78	89	36
21	Bradford City	46	13	10	23	47	55	36
22	Crewe Alexandra	46	10	14	22	68	91	34
23	Grimsby Town	46	13	8	25	47	78	34
24	Chester	46	12	9	25	44	77	33

THIRD DIVISION (SOUTH)

		P	W	D	L	F	A	Pts
1	Bristol City	46	30	10	6	101	47	70
2	Leyton Orient	46	26	9	11	89	47	61
3	Southampton	46	24	11	11	75	51	59
4	Gillingham	46	20	15	11	77	66	55
5	Millwall	46	20	11	15	72	68	51
6	Brighton & Hove A.	46	20	10	16	76	63	50
7	Watford	46	18	14	14	71	62	50
8	Torquay United	46	18	12	16	82	82	48
9	Coventry City	46	18	11	17	67	59	47
10	Southend United	46	17	12	17	83	80	46
11	Brentford	46	16	14	16	82	82	46
12	Norwich City	46	18	10	18	60	60	46
13	Northampton Town	46	19	8	19	73	81	46
14	Aldershot	46	16	13	17	75	71	45
15	Queens Park R.	46	15	14	17	69	75	44
16	Shrewsbury Town	46	16	10	20	70	78	42
17	Bournemouth	46	12	18	16	57	65	42
18	Reading	46	13	15	18	65	73	41
19	Newport County	46	11	16	19	60	73	38
20	Crystal Palace	46	11	16	19	52	80	38
21	Swindon Town	46	11	15	20	46	64	37
22	Exeter City	46	11	15	20	47	73	37
23	Walsall	46	10	14	22	75	86	34
24	Colchester United	46	9	13	24	53	91	31

THE birth of the Busby Babes was not an easy one. They started the run to their first League championship in this 1955-56 season in stuttering style, drawing their first two games and losing to neighbours Manchester City, Sheffield United, Everton and Bolton before the winter programme. But from December they hit a hot patch that melted away doubts about manager Matt Busby's decision to put his faith at the feet of untried youngsters.

For more than four years Busby had been quietly cultivating a youth squad of outstanding talent, bringing them up with good Manchester United habits of putting skilled football first and then mixing it with hard graft; this in an era when many other teams were putting power and energy first, ahead of individual skills.

Only Roger Byrne and Johnny Berry survived from the team that had won the League title four years earlier. There were just three imports from other clubs, and the rest of the squad consisted of home-grown talent.

'We had all grown up together as boy footballers,' Roger Byrne explained when asked for the secret of the success of the team in that first season. 'The Manchester United way was the only way we knew.'

After the uncertain start to the season United eventually won the championship in a canter. They lost only three more League games and were unbeaten at home with eighteen wins and three draws. At the end they were a staggering eleven points clear of their nearest challengers Blackpool. This, don't forget, in an age when there were just two points for a win. Ominously for the rest of the chasing clubs, the average age of the side was just twenty-three, one of youngest championship-winning sides in League history. It was hard to see how they were not going to dominate domestic football for the next five or more years.

Their success bred some jealousy and not everybody applauded some of the natural swagger and arrogance that emanated from a team still finding its way and sometimes showing off when they began to realise just how good they were. It was shortly after the Munich disaster that Burnley's outspoken chairman Bob Lord was moved to describe them as 'a bunch of Teddy Boys,' which was about the most insulting thing he could say at a time when the Teddy Boy culture was bringing terror to some city streets.

But father figure Busby and his faithful and thoughtful righthand man Jimmy Murphy kept the youngsters on as tight a rein as necessary, occasionally allowing them to express themselves in a way that did not always win approval but which brought great satisfaction to players who were still maturing.

The Old Trafford squad was bursting with young talent, but even among all the gems two players stood out as 24-carat gold prospects. Duncan Edwards, the young giant from Dudley, had already forced his way into the England team at eighteen years of age and was proving himself a colossus in defence and attack. 'He was simply the greatest all-round player I had ever seen in my life,' said his team-mate and future United manager Wilf McGuinness. 'He could tackle like a train, had a bullet shot in both feet and could drill a 40 yard pass right to the perfect spot. On top of all that he was a lovely bloke who could play and take a joke with the best of them.'

Then there was the young, pale-faced Bobby Charlton, who was launched on his League career against Charlton Athletic at the age of eighteen in 1956. He scored two spectacular goals to signpost that here was an extraordinary talent. Bobby lived up to everything that he promised.

It was one of the few imports – Tommy Taylor – who took the eye in the Busby Babes attack. He had joined United from Barnsley for what was then a British record fee of just under £30,000 in March 1953, and soon after he won the first of his nineteen England caps. He had real class and quality and can be bracketed with Tommy Lawton and Nat Lofthouse as the best of England's post-war, old-style centre-forwards. He had excellent positional sense, was strong, determined and difficult to knock off the ball in an age when forwards took a real buffeting from defenders not paralysed by the fear of yellow and red cards.

One of the most impressive features of Taylor's game was his magnificent heading ability, and few centre-halves could get the better of him in aerial duels. He formed a perfect tandem team with the darting Dennis Viollet, and together they fed on the service of flying wingers Johnny Berry and David Pegg, with youngsters of the calibre of Albert Scanlon, Ken Morgans and – from the 1956-57 season – Bobby Charlton continually challenging for places in the formdiable United firing line.

Operating just behind Taylor and Viollet was 'the Quiet Irishman' Liam (Billy) Whelan, who passed precisely and finished with great accuracy when tip toeing through to join the front men from his midfield post, where he was the middle man between the highly skilled Eddie 'Snake-hips' Colman and the colossus Duncan Edwards.

Matt Busby said at the end of the 1955-56 season:

'This team has reached a maturity beyond its years much earlier than I anticipated. Goodness knows what they can achieve when they have experience to go with their ability. What pleases me most of all is that they all play for each other. There are no stars among them. We are being advised by the Football League not to get involved in the new European Cup competition, but I am very keen to see these youngsters tested against the best in Europe. It is the sort of internaional competition that will bring the best out of them and help them become even better players.'

'Now where I can I find a space for our NEXT trophy?' Master manager Matt Busby does a little tidying in the Old Trafford boardroom, with the League championship trophy prominent on top of the cabinet.

THE 1956 FA CUP FINAL
Ex-PoW Trautmann plays with a broken neck

THE astonishing Bert Trautmann story could not have been dreamt up by a Hollywood scriptwriter with an over-active imagination; or even by a Downing Street spin doctor. Let me give you a potted version:

It is the winter of 1945 and British troops are launching an offensive in the last months of the Second World War. They capture a German soldier in Belgium who just days earlier had escaped from a Russian prisoner-of-war camp. The ragged-uniformed soldier tells his new captors in good English: 'I would much rather be with you than the Soviets.'

He identifies himself as Private First Class Bernhard Trautmann of the Bremen regiment. His name is written down as Bert. He looks the stereotypical German, just over six feet tall, corn coloured hair and light blue eyes.

Shipped back to a relaxed British prisoner-of-war camp in Lancashire, 22-year-old Trautmann starts to play football with his fellow prisoners. He had been an outstanding all-round athlete in his hometown of Bremen, and was a specialist centre-half.

When nobody will volunteer to go in goal, Bert fills the position and is soon diving around making saves like a real natural goalkeeper.

At the end of the war he is still held prisoner to help rebuild bomb-shattered Britain. He starts playing in local matches and is spotted by the semi-professional club St Helens Town. Bert falls in love and marries an English girl.

There is huge controversy when Manchester City sign him from St Helens in 1949 to take over from the legendary Frank Swift, and complaints flood in from Manchester's large Jewish community. Trautmann meets local Rabbi Altman, who announces after interrogating him: 'He is a decent fellow, unconnected with any German crimes. I give him my blessing to play for Manchester City.'

Many City fans of a certain age will tell you that Trautmann became an even better goalkeeper than Swift over the next 554 League and FA Cup games.

He will always be remembered for the 1956 Final at Wembley when he played on despite a shooting pain in his neck after a late dive at the feet of Birmingham City forward Peter Murphy.

After collecting his winners' medal, Bert went to hospital where an x-ray revealed he had broken his neck. He was in plaster for several months, but returned to play for another seven years before becoming a successful businessman.

He later lived in retirement in Spain warmed by memories of an astonishing life, and a playing career with Manchester City that lifted him into the land of legend alongside

The moment of agony. This was the 75th minute save Bert Trautmann made at the feet of Birmingham forward Peter Murphy that left him nursing a broken neck.

the fabulous Frank Swift, who was tragically to lose his life while travelling with the Busby Babes as a newspaper reporter.

For Manchester City the 1956 FA Cup final brought swift consolation for their defeat by Newcastle the previous year. It was a personal triumph for Don Revie, whose Hungarian-style deep-lying role completely flummoxed the Birmingham defence. It was 'the Revie Plan' that failed in 1955 but this time worked to perfection after a despondent Don had been called in from the dungeon of reserve team football.

As if scripted, it was Revie who started the move that led to Manchester taking the lead after just three minutes through Joe Hayes. Twelve minutes later Birmingham pulled level when Noel Kinsey rammed the ball past Trautmann.

With Revie pulling the strings, Manchester were always in control and goals from Jack Dyson in the 65th minute and Bobby Johnstone five minutes later finished off the Midlands challenge. Johnstone became the first man to score in successive Wembley finals, and so clinched victory in a match that will always be remembered for the amazing bravery of Bert Trautmann.

I bumped into Bert a few years after he retired and he told me: 'I still look out for City's results before any other club. Whenever I come back to Manchester I feel that I have returned home.'

Home is where the heart is, and the unforgettable Bert Trautmann's heart will always be with Manchester City. There are those who believe he was even better than Peter Schmeichel. Swift, Schmeichel or Trautmann? Discuss.

THE EUROPEAN CUP 1955-56
Start of the Real thing

THE European Cup – which would eventually grow in to today's Champions League – got off the ground in the 1955-56 season, minus any contribution from English clubs. Wolves were the team that had done most to motivate French journalist and ex-player Gabriel Hanot to campaign for the competition to be launched. But the small-minded Football League bosses did not share the vision and persuaded English champions Chelsea that the competition was a (Stamford) bridge too far.

Scotland were more switched on to what was so obviously a great step forward for the game, and Hibernian carried the British flag to the semi-finals where they went down to French champions Reims. In the other semi-final Real Madrid squeezed out AC Milan with a 5-4 aggregate victory.

The first European Cup final was a match and occasion that lived up to the high hopes for the competition. It was played at the Parc des Princes in Paris on 13 June 1956, and Reims and Real Madrid produced a classic. England had an input to the match in the shape of referee Arthur Ellis, who said later: 'It was like being in another world. The football was just unbelievable. I thought to myself, "If this is Eurpean football I can't get enough of it."'

Reims, parading the great Raymond Kopa in attack, got off to a dream start and were two-nil up inside ten minutes through Leblond and Templin. Then the Argentinian-born maestro Alfredo di Stefano stepped imperiously on to the stage with a goal that has rarely been bettered in all the European Cup finals since this pioneering opening match. He beat two men in midfield before releasing the ball to his partner Ramon Marsal, and then almost sauntered into the penalty area to take the return pass and steer a precision-placed shot into the net. It was sheer perfection.

Di Stefano, playing as a withdrawn centre-forward, was dictating the pace and the pattern of the match, and influenced an equaliser by Hector Rial in the thirtieth minute. Michel Hidalgo, who would later manage France, restored the Reims lead in the sixty-second minute, but Real came back five minutes later with a beautifully fashioned goal by Marco Marquitos after some exquisite left wing work by Paco Gento.

The 38,0000 crowd was being treated to a football feast which reached its climax with a thrilling winning goal by Hector Rial in the seventy-ninth minute. Real Madrid 4, Reims 3. This was just the beginning of the Real dominance of what was to become the premier cup competition. It would dwarf all other tournaments in the years ahead. And here at the start English clubs were just spectators. Our football authorites were men with myopic vision.

The man holding the European Cup after the first final in 1956 is arguably the greatest player ever to compete for it ... Alfredo di Stefano, who scored more than 500 goals for Real Madrid including 49 in 58 European Cup ties.

Denmark, Copenhagen, 2.10.55. England won 5-1

Luton goalkeeper Ron Baynham, Birmingham City right-back Jeff Hall and Bristol Rovers inside-left Geoff Bradford all made debuts. Bradford, a consistent force with Rovers in the Second Division and winning his only cap, scored the fifth and final goal eight minutes from the end after two goals from Don Revie (including a penalty) and the usual brace from Lofthouse had floored the Danes. Hall and Byrne were to partner each other at full-back for seventeen successive matches, with only one defeat. This match was played on a Sunday in front of the King and Queen of Denmark to coincide with a British Trades Fair. So as not to weaken club sides for the previous day's League programme, the squad was chosen on a one club, one man basis. In eight instances the players were paired off from the Saturday games so that their clubs were equally weakened. Don Revie had just started experimenting with his Hidegkuti-style deep-lying centre-forward role with Manchester City, but he played as an orthodox inside-right alongside Nat Lofthouse in this match and the pair of them together were always too much of a handful for the Danish defenders. *Team: Baynham Hall Byrne R McGarry Wright* Dickinson Milburn Revie (2, 1 pen) Lofthouse (2) Bradford (1) Finney.*

Wales, Ninian Park, 22.10.55. England lost 2-1

Wales conquered England for the first time since 1938 thanks to a headed winning goal from young Swansea winger Cliff Jones, whose Uncle Bryn had scored one of the four goals that beat England exactly seventeen years to the day earlier. England's high-powered attack floundered against a Welsh defence in which the Charles brothers, John and Mel, played side by side. The game was virtually settled in a two minute spell just before half-time. Derek Tapscott took advantage of hesitancy in the England defence to shoot Wales into the lead, and then Cliff Jones made it 2-0 with a stunning header from a Roy Paul cross. Cliff always described it as his greatest ever goal. The only time England got the ball into the net was when John Charles, trying to clear his lines in the fifty-first minute, turned the ball past brilliant Arsenal goalkeeper Jack Kelsey for a spectacular own goal. England nearly grabbed a draw they hardly deserved when Tom Finney ran on to a neat back heel of Don Revie and thumped a shot against the Welsh crossbar. *Team: Williams Hall Byrne R McGarry Wright* Dickinson Matthews Revie Lofthouse Wilshaw Finney.(1 og)*

Northern Ireland, Wembley, 2.11.55. England won 3-0

Fulham clubmates Johnny Haynes and Bedford Jezzard played alongside each other for the only time in an England international. Haynes, partnering Tom Finney on the right wing, played farther upfield than usual to confuse his marker, Danny Blanchflower, and it was mainly because of his probing passes that England won comfortably with two goals from Dennis Wilshaw and another from Finney. Jezzard's career was prematurely ended a year later by an ankle injury. South African-born Bill Perry came into the attack in place of his Blackpool team-mate Stanley Matthews, and Ronnie Clayton won the first of his thirty-five caps. This was Northern Ireland's first appearance at Wembley, and the only time they threatened to mark the occasion with a goal was when Charlie Tully had a point-blank shot superbly saved by goalkeeper Ron Baynham in the second half. *Team: Baynham Hall Byrne R Clayton Wright* Dickinson Finney (1) Haynes Jezzard Wilshaw (2) Perry.*

Spain, Wembley, 30.11.55. England won 4-1

The Wembley floodlights were switched on for the first time in an international match fifteen minutes from the end of a game in which Spain were always in the dark. Finney missed from the penalty spot in the fifth minute, but then made amends by laying on one goal and scoring another. John Atyeo, the schoolteacher from Bristol City, put the finishing touch to a magnificent seven-man passing movement in the fifteenth minute, and sixty seconds later South African-born Bill Perry scored the first of his two goals. Finney and Perry made it 4-0 in the second-half before the Spaniards snatched a consolation goal ten minutes from the end when Arieta beat goalkeeper Ron Baynham with a close-range header. *Team: Baynham Hall Byrne R Clayton Wright* Dickinson Finney (1) Atyeo (1) Lofthouse Haynes Perry (2).*

Scotland, Hampden Park, 14.4.56. Drew 1-1

Johnny Haynes silenced the Hampden Roar with a last-minute equaliser, shooting the ball past goalkeeper Tommy Younger after Manchester United team-mates Roger Byrne and Tommy Taylor had created the opening. Reg Matthews, making his debut in front of a 134,000 crowd while a Third Division goalkeeper with Coventry City, pulled off a string of magnificent saves and was only beaten on the hour by a mis-hit shot from Aberdeen's Graham Leggat. The last-gasp equaliser from man-of-the-match Haynes stopped Scotland from registering their first victory over the Auld Enemy at Hampden Park since 1937. *Team: Matthews R Hall Byrne R Dickinson Wright* Edwards Finney Taylor T Lofthouse Haynes (1) Perry.*

Brazil, Wembley, 9.5.56. England won 4-2

It was billed as the 'Old World meets the New' and Brazil arrived with many of the players who two years later were to win the World Cup in such dazzling fashion. England got off to a flying start under the Wembley Stadium floodlights with Tommy Taylor and Colin Grainger scoring inside the first five minutes. The Brazilians fought back to 2-2, and then John Atyeo and Roger Bryne each had a penalty saved by goalkeeper Gilmar. The penalty misses sandwiched a second goal by Taylor, made for him by a Stanley Matthews at his magical best against one of the all-time great left-backs, Nilton Santos. Matthews had been recalled by England at the age of forty-one, and he played like a twenty-one-year-old. There was a farcical second-half hold up following a dispute over a quickly taken free-kick by Johnny Haynes. The ball was caught by Nilton Santos and the Brazilians staged a walk-off protest when the referee awarded a penalty. By the time peace was restored it was little wonder that Atyeo failed with the spot-kick. Colin Grainger crowned a memorable debut with a second goal five minutes from the end of an extraordinary match. Cool and commanding at all times, Billy Wright kept his head when all about were losing theirs. He acted as a peacemaker when the talented but temperamental Brazilians threatened a mass walk off. It was a real captain's performance, a mix of diplomacy and sportsmanship. The Maestro Matthews was really wound up for this match because the Brazilians had stressed in the pre-match build-up that there was not a player in the world who could get the better of their exceptional full-back Nilton Santos. But as good a player as Santos was, he could not get near 'the Wizard of Dribble' who was in untouchable form. At the end Nilton was sporting enough to say, 'Mister Matthews, you are the king.' *Team: Matthews R Hall Byrne Clayton Wright* Edwards Matthews S Atyeo Taylor (2) Haynes Grainger (2).*

Sweden, Solna, 16.5.56. Drew 0-0

England were lucky to escape with a draw in a match ruined by a near-gale force wind. Goalkeeper Reg Matthews made three stunning saves to stop the Swedes from getting the victory their superior approach play deserved. It was the first goalless draw in which England had been involved since the game in Denmark in 1948. In conditions that would have sent a yachtsman racing for the shelter of any port, Wright managed to stop England from sinking with a cultured performance in the middle of the defence. The wind was so strong that it was almost impossible to measure a pass. Players would push a pass upfield for the forwards and invariably it would get caught by the wind and be taken for a goal-kick. It was a frustrating and fruitless game for everybody. *Team: R. Matthews Hall Byrne Clayton Wright* Edwards Berry Atyeo Taylor T Haynes Grainger.*

Finland, Helsinki, 20.5.56. England won 5-1

Nat Lofthouse came on as a substitute for the injured Tommy Taylor a minute before half-time, and for the twelfth time in an England shirt he scored two goals. It lifted his haul to twenty-nine goals, one more than the previous England record set by Steve Bloomer before the First World War and equalling the haul of Vivian Woodward (a disputed record because most observers gave one of his goals as an own goal). Gordon Astall, playing in place of the unavailable Stanley Matthews, scored on his debut. England were leading 3-0 when Taylor limped off following a collision with the Finnish goalkeeper. The record-breaking goal by Lotfhouse in the eighty-second minute was a freak effort, the ball rolling over the goal-line between two defenders who left the clearance duties to each other. *Team: Wood   Hall   Byrne   Clayton   Wright*   Edwards   Astall (1)   Haynes (1)   Taylor T (Lofthouse 2)   Wilshaw (1)   Grainger.*

West Germany, Berlin, 26.5.56. England won 3-1

This match is remembered as the finest ever played on the international stage by Duncan Edwards, who was fresh from helping Manchester United win the League championship. He strode the pitch as if he owned it, scoring a scorcher of a goal from twenty yards in the twentieth minute and dominating the entire game both in defence and midfield. Nearly half the 100,000 crowd in the stadium designed by Adolf Hitler were soldiers from the British-occupied zone of Berlin. They staged a delighted pitch invasion when second-half goals from Johnny Haynes and Colin Grainger clinched victory. Fritz Walter, the outstanding German skipper, scored a fine individual goal for the team he had led to the World Cup two years earlier. The name of Duncan Edwards was on the lips of everybody who saw this match. He was phenomenal. The English fans had started calling him 'Boom Boom' because of the sheer power of his shooting and the energy that he poured into every game. There have been few individual performances to match what he produced in Germany that day. He tackled like a lion, attacked at every opportunity and topped it all off with a cracker of a goal. He was still only twenty, and was already a world-class player. Many of the thousands of British soldiers in the crowd surrounded him at the final whistle and carried him off. England had beaten the world champions in their own back yard. Billy Wright, England skipper, said after his then record 105 England appearances: 'Of all the matches I played for England this one stands out above most in my memory. We beat the world champions in their own back yard, and Duncan Edwards underlined that he was as good as any player in the world, and the mind boggled at the thought of what he could achieve in the years ahead. If there has been a better all-round player at that age then I had not had the pleasure of seeing him.' *Team: Matthews R   Hall   Byrne   Clayton   Wright*   Edwards (1)   Astall   Haynes (1)   Taylor T   Wilshaw   Grainger (1).*

ARSENAL were coasting to victory with a 4-0 lead against Blackpool at Highbury on December 17 1955 when Gunners full-back Dennis Evans thought he heard the final whistle. He was in possession at the time and turned and lashed the ball into the Arsenal net. The phantom whistle had come from somebody in the crowd behind the goal. Arsenal 4, Blackpool 1.

Floodlit history was made on 28 November 1955 when Carlise and Darlington decided their deadlocked FA Cup tie at neutral Newcastle. The second-round replay was the first non-friendly match staged under floodlights. Three months later Portsmouth and Newcastle United went into the record books when they played the first League match under floodlights at Fratton Park on 22 February 1956. The Magpies won 2-0.

Something unusual happened in September 1955. Tranmere centre-half Harold Bell missed a match. He had been an ever-present in the Tranmere defence for a League record 401 consecutive matches, starting his astonishing run at the beginning of the 1946-47 season.

Derby County suffered possibly the most embarrassing giant-killing defeat in the history of the FA Cup when they were beaten 6-1 in the second round by non-League Boston ... at home at the Baseball ground! Boston were packed with seven ex-Derby players.

Accrington Stanley fielded an all-Scots teams in several of their Third Division North matches. All but four of the nineteen players in their squad were born in Scotland.

Uefa launched the Inter-Cities Fairs Cup, a tournament that was linked to cities holding industrial fairs and trade shows. The first one took three years t complete and was eventually won by Barcelona, who beat a London select side 8-2 on aggregate in 1958. The Fairs Cup eventually became the Uefa Cup.

Hearts beat Celtic 3-1 in the Scottish Cup final to win the first trophy for the first time since 1906. Rangers lifted the League championship, and Aberdeen the League Cup.

Hibernian announced they had made a £25,000 profit from their bid for the inaugural European Cup and a run to the semi-finals. Now even English clubs were sitting up and taking notice of this new kid on the block.

First Division: Manchester United, 60pts. Runners-up: Blackpool, 49 pts.
Manchester United record: P42 W25 D10 L7 F83 A51 Pts60
Representative team: Wood; Foulkes, Byrne (capt.); Colman, Jones, Edwards; (from)
Berry, Whelan, Taylor, Viollet, Pegg, Doherty, Blanchflower J.
Top scorer: Taylor (25).
Manager: Matt Busby.

Second Division: Sheffield Wednesday, 55pts. Runners-up: Leeds United, 52pts.
Third Division (South): Leyton Orient, 66pts. Runners-up: Brighton, 65pts.
Third Division (North): Grimsby Town, 68pts. Runners-up: Derby County, 63pts.

FA Cup final: Manchester City 3, Birmingham City 1
Manchester City: Trautmann; Leivers, Little; Barnes, Ewing, Paul (capt.); Johnstone,
Hayes, Revie, Dyson, Clarke. Scorers: Hayes, Dyson, Johnstone
Birmingham: Merrick; Hall, Green; Newman, Smith, Boyd (capt.); Astall, Kinsey,
Brown, Murphy, Govan. Scorer: Kinsey

Top First Division marksman: Nat Lofthouse (Bolton Wanderers), 33 goals
Top Second Division marksman: Willie Gardiner (Leicester City), 34 goals
Top Third Division North marksman: Bob Crosbie (Grimsby Town), 36 goals
Top Third Division South marksman: Sammy Collins (Torquay), 40 goals
Footballer of the Year: Bert Trautmann (Manchester City)
First European Footballer of the Year: Stanley Matthews (Blackpool)

Scottish First Division: Rangers, 52pts. Runners-up: Aberdeen, 46pts.
Scottish Cup final: Hearts 3, Celtic 1
Scottish League Cup final: Aberdeen 2, St Mirren 1

FA Amateur Cup final: Bishop Auckland 4, Corinthian Casuals 1 (extra-time)

First European Cup final: Real Madrid 4, Stade de Reims 3 (Paris)
Real Madrid: Alonso; Atienza, Lesmes; Munoz (capt.), Marquitos, Zarraga; Joseito,
Marsal, Di Stefano, Rial, Gento. Scorers: Di Stefano, Rial (2), Marquitos
Stade de Reims: Jacquet; Zimny, Giraudo; Leblond, Jonquet (capt.), Siatka; Hidalgo,
Glovacki, Kopa, Bliard, Templin. Scorers: Leblond, Templin, Hidalgo

THE LEAGUE TABLES
Where they finished in 1955-56

FIRST DIVISION

		P	W	D	L	F	A	Pts
1	Manchester United	42	25	10	7	83	51	60
2	Blackpool	42	20	9	13	86	62	49
3	Wolverhampton W.	42	20	9	13	89	65	49
4	Manchester City	42	18	10	14	82	69	46
5	Arsenal	42	18	10	14	60	61	46
6	Birmingham City	42	18	9	15	75	57	45
7	Burnley	42	18	8	16	64	54	44
8	Bolton Wanderers	42	18	7	17	71	58	43
9	Sunderland	42	17	9	16	80	95	43
10	Luton Town	42	17	8	17	66	64	42
11	Newcastle United	42	17	7	18	85	70	41
12	Portsmouth	42	16	9	17	78	85	41
13	West Bromwich A.	42	18	5	19	58	70	41
14	Charlton Athletic	42	17	6	19	75	81	40
15	Everton	42	15	10	17	55	69	40
16	Chelsea	42	14	11	17	64	77	39
17	Cardiff City	42	15	9	18	55	69	39
18	Tottenham Hotspur	42	15	7	20	61	71	37
19	Preston North End	42	14	8	20	73	72	36
20	Aston Villa	42	11	13	18	52	69	35
21	Huddersfield Town	42	14	7	21	54	83	35
22	Sheffield United	42	12	9	21	63	77	33

SECOND DIVISION

		P	W	D	L	F	A	Pts
1	Sheffield Weds.	42	21	13	8	101	62	55
2	Leeds United	42	23	6	13	80	60	52
3	Liverpool	42	21	6	15	85	63	48
4	Blackburn Rovers	42	21	6	15	84	65	48
5	Leicester City	42	21	6	15	94	78	48
6	Bristol Rovers	42	21	6	15	84	70	48
7	Nottingham Forest	42	19	9	14	68	63	47
8	Lincoln City	42	18	10	14	79	65	46
9	Fulham	42	20	6	16	89	79	46
10	Swansea Town	42	20	6	16	83	81	46
11	Bristol City	42	19	7	16	80	64	45
12	Port Vale	42	16	13	13	60	58	45
13	Stoke City	42	20	4	18	71	62	44
14	Middlesbrough	42	16	8	18	76	78	40
15	Bury	42	16	8	18	86	90	40
16	West Ham United	42	14	11	17	74	69	39
17	Doncaster Rovers	42	12	11	19	69	96	35
18	Barnsley	42	11	12	19	47	84	34
19	Rotherham United	42	12	9	21	56	75	33
20	Notts County	42	11	9	22	55	82	31
21	Plymouth Argyle	42	10	8	24	54	87	28
22	Hull City	42	10	6	26	53	97	26

THIRD DIVISION (NORTH)

		P	W	D	L	F	A	Pts
1	Grimsby Town	46	31	6	9	76	29	68
2	Derby County	46	28	7	11	110	55	63
3	Accrington Stanley	46	25	9	12	92	57	59
4	Hartlepools United	46	26	5	15	81	60	57
5	Southport	46	23	11	12	66	53	57
6	Chesterfield	46	25	4	17	94	66	54
7	Stockport County	46	21	9	16	90	61	51
8	Bradford City	46	18	13	15	78	64	49
9	Scunthorpe United	46	20	8	18	75	63	48
10	Workington	46	19	9	18	75	63	47
11	York City	46	19	9	18	85	72	47
12	Rochdale	46	17	13	16	66	84	47
13	Gateshead	46	17	11	18	77	84	45
14	Wrexham	46	16	10	20	66	73	42
15	Darlington	46	16	9	21	60	73	41
16	Tranmere Rovers	46	16	9	21	59	84	41
17	Chester	46	13	14	19	52	82	40
18	Mansfield Town	46	14	11	21	84	81	39
19	Halifax Town	46	14	11	21	66	76	39
20	Oldham Athletic	46	10	18	18	76	86	38
21	Carlisle United	46	15	8	23	71	95	38
22	Barrow	46	12	9	25	61	83	33
23	Bradford Park A.	46	13	7	26	61	122	33
24	Crewe Alexandra	46	9	10	27	50	105	28

THIRD DIVISION (SOUTH)

		P	W	D	L	F	A	Pts
1	Leyton Orient	46	29	8	9	106	49	66
2	Brighton & Hove A.	46	29	7	10	112	50	65
3	Ipswich Town	46	25	14	7	106	60	64
4	Southend United	46	21	11	14	88	80	53
5	Torquay United	46	20	12	14	86	63	52
6	Brentford	46	19	14	13	69	66	52
7	Norwich City	46	19	13	14	86	82	51
8	Coventry City	46	20	9	17	73	60	49
9	Bournemouth	46	19	10	17	63	51	48
10	Gillingham	46	19	10	17	69	71	48
11	Northampton Town	46	20	7	19	67	71	47
12	Colchester United	46	18	11	17	76	81	47
13	Shrewsbury Town	46	17	12	17	69	66	46
14	Southampton	46	18	8	20	91	81	44
15	Aldershot	46	12	16	18	70	90	40
16	Exeter City	46	15	10	21	58	77	40
17	Reading	46	15	9	22	70	79	39
18	Queens Park R.	46	14	11	21	64	86	39
19	Newport County	46	15	9	22	58	79	39
20	Walsall	46	15	8	23	68	84	38
21	Watford	46	13	11	22	52	85	37
22	Millwall	46	15	6	25	83	100	36
23	Crystal Palace	46	12	10	24	54	83	34
24	Swindon Town	46	8	14	24	34	78	30

MANCHESTER United journeyed to Wembley in May 1957 scorching-hot favourites to become the first team of the 20th Century to complete the League and FA Cup double. They had just retained the First Division championship trophy with eight points to spare over their closest rivals and were now expected to add the FA Cup to their collection. The team standing between the Busby Babes and history were Aston Villa, a club with an even finer pedigree than United. But Villa had been living on the memories of what their ancestors had achieved and few people gave them a prayer of beating all-conquering United.

Villa had lived dangerously on the way to Wembley. They were taken to replays by Luton in the third round, Burnley in the sixth round and by West Bromwich Albion in the semi-final. Each time it was a late goal by Irish winger Peter McParland that rescued them from defeat. It was hardly the sort of form to suggest that Villa could disunite a United team that had plundered 103 goals on the way to retaining the League title.

On the eve of the final the FA big wigs discussed the possibility of introducing substitutes in the case of injury. This was under pressure from the newspaper columnists who pointed out how many of the big occasion finals had been wrecked by a team being reduced to ten men because of injury. But after long deliberations the blazered brigade decided that tinkering with the rules was not a good thing for the game and rejected the proposal.

The Wembley showpiece game was just six minutes old when the FA officials were presented with concrete evidence that they had made a mistake in kicking out the substitutes idea. United goalkeeper Ray Wood was carried off with a fractured cheekbone following a collision with flying winger Peter McParland, who cut in and scored so many goals that he was nicknamed Mac the Knife. United were forced to shuffle their side, with centre-half Jackie Blanchflower taking over in goal and Duncan Edwards switching to a central defensive position. Even with ten men the Busby Babes were difficult to master and they restricted the Villa forwards to long-range shots that Blanchflower handled with care.

Ray Wood rejoined the game for the second half, providing nuisance value for United as a right winger. Just as United were beginning to find a rhythm and dictate the play Villa snatched the lead. It was McParland, branded a villain by the United fans, who became a Villa hero when he headed in a floating centre from skipper Johnny Dixon. Five minutes later McParland struck again, this time hammering the loose ball into the net after Dixon's shot had crashed against the crossbar with the gallant Blanch-

Seconds after the collision that wrecked the 1957 FA Cup final. Peter McParland sits looking dazed, while goalkeeper Ray Wood is nursing a fractured cheek bone. The Irishman was villified by United fans for what they considered an unnecessary challenge, but Peter has also insisted it was a complete accident.

flower beaten. Lesser sides would have conceded defeat, but United raised their pace and pushed Villa back under an avalanche of attacks. Their one reward was a headed goal by Tommy Taylor from a Duncan Edwards corner in the eighty-third minute. The final whistle signalled that the double would have to wait for another day and another team.

Matt Busby said: 'Losing our goalkeeper so early in the match was too great a blow, but I was proud of the way the team battled right up until the end. I honestly felt we were going to at least force a replay until their second goal. That was the one that took the carpet from under our feet. But this team will be back ...'

Pat Saward, Villa's Irish international left-half, said: 'Everybody dismissed us as having no chance against United, but I had a feeling our name was on the Cup after all the narrow escapes we had on our way to Wembley. And it must have been worth a bet that Peter McParland would score. He has always been the man for the big occasion. It was sad that Ray Wood had to go off injured, but we had to dismiss that from our minds. Wembley is no place to start showing sympathy.'

For years afterwards McParland was villified by United supporters, who blamed him for Ray Wood's injury. 'Our victory at Wembley should have been one of the great days of my life,' he said after his retirement, 'but the whole day was ruined by my collision with Ray Wood. The United fans never allowed me to forget it. In those days you could challenge a goalkeeper and it was a complete accident when Ray was injured.'

THE LEAGUE CHAMPIONSHIP 1956-57
United torpedo the Tottenham challenge

IF any one match epitomised Manchester United's determination to retain the League title it was their top-of-the-table clash with Tottenham at White Hart Lane on 24 November 1956. Just three days earlier United had clinched a place in the European Cup quarter-finals with a goalless draw in Dortmund. They were still tired after their trip, and waiting for them in North London were their closest rivals for the precious League trophy.

This was the Tottenham between the push-and-run and double sides, and featured the goalkeeping prowess of Ted Ditchburn, the midfield panache of Danny Blanchflower, the trickery of 'Tom Thumb' forward Tommy Harmer, the direct wing runs of Terry Medwin and George Robb, and the triple stiking power of Dave Dunmore, Bobby Smith and Alfie Stokes. Bill Nicholson was coach, with Jimmy Anderson managing the side.

Spurs came roaring out of the blocks at United and were two goals clear inside eight minutes through a Harmer penalty and a goal by outside-left Robb.

This was when the Busby Babes showed that they were not just a team of creative young masters. They could also roll up their sleeves and battle. Skipper Roger Byrne showed the way with a long dribble out of defence before powering in a shot that rattled the Tottenham crossbar. It was a flashback to his early days as a roaming winger. Duncan Edwards collected the rebound and hammered it against a post.

Right winger Johnny Berry pulled United back into the game with an instant goal in the opening moments of the second-half, and three minutes from the end little Eddie Colman found a gap in the Tottenham defence and drilled the ball into the net for an equaliser.

It was a cracking game that brought loud and prolonged applause from the spectators long after the final whistle.

If United had lost, they would have given impetus to the Tottenham championship challenge. But they showed they could fight back, and they eventually ran away with the title for the second successive season. The Babes clinched the championship with a remarkable ten day spell in April. On the 13th they won 2-0 at Luton, scuppered Burnley 3-1 at Turf Moor on Good Friday, hammered Sunderland 4-0 the next day and, fielding seven reserves, beat Burnley 2-0 at Old Trafford. By then the title was already wrapped up, with Tottenham and Preston both eight points adrift.

United were stretched on three fronts, just failing to pull off the elusive League and Cup double and going all the way to the semis in their first tilt at the European Cup.

THE EUROPEAN CUP 1956-57
Ten out of ten for Busby's stand on Europe

DESPITE the Football League trying to stop them, Manchester United went ahead and launched England's first challenge for the European Cup in 1956-57. It was a decision that brought the English game to the brink of civil war. United accepted the invitation to take part from the Football Association, members of Uefa. This brought the FA to verbal blows with the blinkered Football League bosses who insisted that 'the participation of our champions in the European Cup is not in the best interests of the English game.'

The 'Little Englanders' were ignored, and United went ahead, mainly because it was what strong-minded manager Matt Busby wanted. United's opening match was against Belgian champions Anderlecht. They won 2-0 in the first away leg, with goals by Dennis Viollet and Tommy Taylor after the Belgians had missed a penalty.

The second leg was staged at Maine Road because the Old Trafford floodlights were still being installed. The lights went out for Anderlecht who were squashed 10-0, with Dennis Viollet (4), Tommy Taylor (3), Billy Whelan (2) and Johnny Berry sharing the goals. David Pegg failed to get on the scoresheet but was rated the man of the match because he had a foot in six of the goals.

United beat Borussia Dortmund 3-2 on aggregate in the second round, all the goals coming at Maine Road. Bilbao was the next stop on the United journey into the unknown, and they suffered their first defeat when they went down 5-3 in Arctic conditions. Before they were able to fly home, United players had to help shovel snow off the runway so that their chartered plane could take off. Nobody was to know it then, but it was an eerie portent of horrific things to come.

Winning the return leg at Maine Road 3-0, United set up a semi-final with Cup holders Real Madrid. They were chasing the League and Cup double on the domestic front, and were soundly beaten 3-1 in the first leg in Madrid.

The Old Trafford floodlights were switched on for the second leg, and United performed creditably to hold the multi-talented Real team to a 2-2 draw, going out of the competition 5-3 on aggregate.

'A great experienced side beat a great inexperienced side,' was the Busby summing up. 'But we'll be back. European competition has to be the way forward. Some people have called me a visionary, others a reactionary and some think I am a stubborn and awkward bugger. But I just know what's right for the future of our football.'

Real Madrid retained the trophy with a comfortable 2-0 victory over Fiorentina at the Bernabeu.

Northern Ireland, Windsor Park, 6.10.56. Drew 1-1

A rare goal from Stanley Matthews (his eleventh and last in international football) after just two minutes gave England a dream start, but they were hustled out of their stride by an Irish team motivated by a dazzling performance from skipper Danny Blanchflower. Jimmy McIlroy equalised after ten minutes when goalkeeper Reg Matthews palmed a long throw from Peter McParland into his path. McIlroy was faced with an open goal five minutes from the end but hit a post. If he had found the net, it would have given Northern Ireland their first home win over England since 1927. There was a lot of good-natured ribbing of Stanley Matthews over his goal. His last goal for England had been eight years earlier, also against Northern Ireland and also at Windsor Park. Jackie Blanchflower, Danny's brother and always a quick wit, asked: 'Why does he always pick on us?' Danny himself came into the dressing-room after the match and told Stanley that he had been a schoolboy spectator in short trousers when he scored his last goal. 'You'll have a long beard by the time I score the next one,' said Stanley, with that poker-faced humour of his. *Team: Matthews R Hall Byrne Clayton Wright* Edwards Matthews S (1) Revie Taylor Wilshaw Grainger*

Wales, Wembley, 14.11.56. England won 3-1

This Home Championship match was wrecked by an injury to Welsh goalkeeper Jack Kelsey, who was carried off after being knocked out diving at the feet of Tom Finney. The incident came while the Welsh supporters were celebrating an eighth minute goal from John Charles, who rose above Billy Wright's challenge to head in an Ivor Allchurch corner. Right-back Alf Sherwood took over in the Welsh goal, and from then on England were dominant despite the stirring efforts of John Charles to turn the tide. Second-half goals from Johnny Haynes, debutant Johnny Brooks and the versatile Tom Finney at centre-forward gave England an undistinguished victory. This was England's seventh successive win at Wembley. The injury to goalkeeper Jack Kelsey robbed Wales of their rhythm. They also had Mel Charles as a hobbling passenger for much of the match, and England were handicapped by injuries to Colin Grainger and Johnny Haynes. It would have made sense to at least allow substitute goalkeepers, but the powers-that-be refused to follow the lead of the Continental clubs who were using substitutes more and more. *Team: Ditchburn Hall Byrne Clayton Wright* Dickinson Matthews Brooks (1) Finney (1) Haynes (1) Grainger.*

Yugoslavia, Wembley, 28.11.56. England won 3-0

Johnny Haynes was heavily tackled by Yugoslav right-back Belin in the thirtieth minute, and was unable to continue. It had been agreed beforehand that substitutes would be allowed in the case of injury and Tommy Taylor came on in place of the limping Fulham player. England had taken a thirteenth minute lead when Johnny Brooks fired the ball high into the net after taking a neat pass from Haynes. England dominated throughout the second half and Taylor scored twice, while his Manchester United team-mate Roger Byrne had a penalty saved by world-class Yugoslav goalkeeper Vladimir Beara. Stanley Matthews ran the Yugoslav left-back into such a state of confusion that he finally resorted to rugby tackling him in a bid to stop his dribbling runs. *Team: Ditchburn Hall Byrne Clayton Wright* Dickinson Matthews Brooks (1) Finney Haynes (Taylor 2) Blunstone.*

Denmark, Molineux, 5.12.56. England won 5-2

England's World Cup campaign got under way with this convincing victory over Denmark on Billy Wright's home ground of Molineux. The match was distinguished by a hat-trick from Tommy Taylor and two spectacular goals from his Manchester United team-mate Duncan Edwards, who played at inside-left in place of the injured Johnny Haynes. Edwards scored with two booming long-range shots, had another shot wondrously saved and nearly uprooted a post with another thunderbolt from a free-kick. England had been drawn in a three team group with Denmark and the Republic of Ireland, and this convincing performance underlined why they were rated among the favourites for the World Cup. *Team: Ditchburn Hall Byrne Clayton Wright* Dickinson Matthews Brooks Taylor (3) Edwards (2) Finney.*

Scotland, Wembley, 6.4.57. England won 2-1

Duncan Edwards snatched victory for England six minutes from the end with a blistering twenty-five yard shot. The Scots had got off to a flying start when Sheffield United goalkeeper Alan Hodgkinson had to pick the ball out of his net just a minute into his debut. He was beaten by a snap shot from Clyde winger Tommy Ring. Derek Kevan, making his debut in place of Johnny Haynes, equalised in the sixty-second minute with a diving header from a Colin Grainger cross. Tommy Docherty was the pick of the Scottish players, shutting out his Preston team-mate Tommy Thompson, who was winning his first cap for six years. The winning goal was set up by Matthews, who squared the ball into the path of Edwards. He hit a fierce first-time shot wide of goalkeeper Tommy Younger. *Team: Hodgkinson Hall Byrne Clayton Wright* Edwards (1) Matthews Thompson T Finney Kevan (1) Grainger.*

Republic of Ireland, Wembley, 8.5.57. England won 5-1

A second successive Tommy Taylor hat-trick – all his goals coming in the first-half – and two from John Atyeo unhinged a gallant Irish team in this second of England's four World Cup qualifying matches. The final scoreline flattered England, who were often under pressure from Irish forwards who showed great skill on the ball but poor finishing. *Team: Hodgkinson Hall Byrne Clayton Wright* Edwards Matthews Atyeo (2) Taylor (3) Haynes Finney.*

Denmark, Copenhagen, 15.5.57. England won 4-1

This World Cup qualifier was to prove the international swansong of 'Mr Football' Stanley Matthews, who was retired from the world stage at the age of forty-two and twenty-two years after the first of his fifty-four caps. Many thought he had been put out to grass too early. Denmark took the lead in the twenty-fifth minute, with Johnny Haynes equalising just before half-time. It was not until the final fifteen minutes that England got on top against a brave Danish team. Tommy Taylor scored twice to take his haul in four matches to ten goals. Taylor's double strike came either side of a seventy-fifth minute goal by John Atyeo, who rose at the far post to head in a Johnny Haynes centre. This was, sadly, to be the last match in which full-backs Jeff Hall and Roger Byrne partnered each other. Jeff contracted polio and died on 4 April 1959. Born in Scunthorpe on 7 September 1929, he started as an amateur with Bradford Park Avenue before becoming a regular in Birmingham City's defence. He would have had, statistically, the best individual England record of any player but for the 2-1 defeat by Wales in 1955. In 17 matches he was on the beaten side only once. England won twelve of the games and drew four. Roger Byrne was his partner in every game. *Team: Hodgkinson Hall Byrne Clayton Wright* Edwards Matthews Atyeo (1) Taylor (2) Haynes (1) Finney.*

Republic of Ireland, Dalymount Park, 19.5.57. Drew 1-1

England, needing a point to qualify for the World Cup finals, were rocked by a third minute goal from winger Alf Ringstead. From then on England struggled to make any impact against an inspired Irish defence in which Bournemouth goalkeeper Tommy Godwin and Millwall centre-half Charlie Hurley were outstanding. The game was into its last minute when Tom Finney fired over a cross for John Atyeo to head an equaliser that gave relieved England a passport to Sweden. David Pegg, who came in for the injured Stanley Matthews, won his only cap before becoming one of the victims of the Munich air crash. Atyeo's goal saved England a lot of embarrassment. The selectors rewarded the Bristol City idol by never selecting him again! *Team: Hodgkinson Hall Byrne Clayton Wright* Edwards Finney Atyeo (1) Taylor Haynes Pegg.*

JUVENTUS signed John Charles from Leeds in April 1957 for £70,000, which doubled the British transfer record. 'King John' was paid a £10,000 signing-on fee and £60-a-week basic wages, which was four times what he could earn in the Football League. It proved a bargain buy for the Italians. In return they got a player who was equally at home at centre-forward or centre-half and was, arguably, the greatest all-rounder ever produced in Britain. Nicknamed the Gentle Giant, he became an idol in Italy. There were fears of a mass exodous of English players to Italy, and the PFA stepped up their campaign for a lifting of the maximum wage.

Aston Villa's triumphant FA Cup winners were accused of being disrespectful to the Queen when collecting their medals from Her Majesty. They were all chewing gum as they walked up the 39 steps to the Royal Box.

Ticket touts outside Wembley were getting a record £10 for tickets that had a face value of three shillings and sixpence (17.5p).

Scunthorpe fans warmly reflected on a 2-1 victory against Crewe on 19 September 1956. They did not have a single victory in their next thirty matches, an unwanted Football League record.

Bournemouth winger Reg Cutler caught the post in spectacular style during a fourth round FA Cup tie against mighty Wolves at Dean Court. He hit it so hard that the goal collapsed and the game was held up for repairs. Then Cutler found the net to give the Cherries a shock victory. They then eliminated Tottenham in the fifth round before going down 2-1 to Manchester United in the quarter-finals.

Neville Coleman scored seven goals for Stoke City in their 8-0 thumping of Lincoln on 23 February 1957, equalling the two year old Second Division record set by Tommy Briggs for Blackburn Rovers.

For the first time since 1931-32, all four table topping teams scored more than 100 League goals during the season – League champions Manchester United (103), Leicester City 109 in the Second, Alf Ramsey's Ipswich Town 101 in the Third Division South, and Derby County 111 in winning the Third Division North title.

First Division: Manchester United, 64pts. Runners-up: Tottenham, 56 pts.
Manchester United record: P42 W28 D8 L6 F103 A54 Pts64
Representative team: Wood; Foulkes, Byrne (capt.); Colman, Jones, Edwards; Berry, Whelan, Taylor, Viollet, Pegg. Also: Blanchflower J. (11), Charlton (14), McGuinness (13). Top scorer: Whelan (26).
Manager: Matt Busby.

Second Division: Leicester City, 61pts. Runners-up: Nottingham Forest, 54pts
Third Division (South): Ipswich, 59pts. Runners-up: Torquay, 59pts
Third Division (North): Derby County, 63pts. Runners-up: Hartlepools, 59pts.

FA Cup final: Aston Villa 2, Manchester United 1
Aston Villa: Sims; Lynn, Aldis; Crowther, Dugdale, Saward; Smith, Sewell, Myerscough, Dixon (capt.), McParland. Scorer: McParland (2)
Manchester United: Wood; Foulkes, Byrne (capt.); Colman, Blanchflower J, Edwards; Berry, Whelan, Taylor T, Charlton, Pegg. Scorer: Taylor

Top First Division marksman: John Charles (Leeds) 38 goals
Top Second Division marksman: Arthur Rowley (Leicester City), 44 goals
Top Third Division North marksman: Ray Straw (Derby County), 37 goals
Top Third Division South marksman: Ted Phillips (Ipswich Town), 41 goals
Footballer of the Year: Tom Finney (Preston)
European Footballer of the Year: Alfredo di Stefano (Real Madrid)

Scottish First Division: Rangers, 55pts. Runners-up: Hearts, 53pts.
Scottish Cup final: Falkirk 2, Kilmarnock 1 (after a 1-1 draw)
Scottish League Cup final: Celtic 3, Partick Thistle 0 (after a 0-0 draw)

FA Amateur Cup final: Bishop Auckland 3, Wycombe Wanderers 1

European Cup final: Real Madrid 2, Fiorentina 0 (Madrid)
Real Madrid: Alonso; Torres, Lesmes; Munoz (capt.), Marquitos, Zarraga; Kopa, Mateos, Di Stefano, Rial, Gento. Scorers: Di Stefano (pen.), Gento
Fiorentina: Sarti; Magnini, Cervato (capt.); Scaramucci, Orzan, Segato; Julinho, Gratton, Virgili, Montuori, Bizzarri.

THE LEAGUE TABLES
Where they finished in 1956-57

FIRST DIVISION

		P	W	D	L	F	A	Pts
1	Manchester United	42	28	8	6	103	54	64
2	Tottenham Hotspur	42	22	12	8	104	56	56
3	Preston North End	42	23	10	9	84	56	56
4	Blackpool	42	22	9	11	93	65	53
5	Arsenal	42	21	8	13	85	69	50
6	Wolverhampton W.	42	20	8	14	94	70	48
7	Burnley	42	18	10	14	56	50	46
8	Leeds United	42	15	14	13	72	63	44
9	Bolton Wanderers	42	16	12	14	65	65	44
10	Aston Villa	42	14	15	13	65	55	43
11	West Bromwich A.	42	14	14	14	59	61	42
12	Chelsea	42	13	13	16	73	73	39
13	Birmingham City	42	15	9	18	69	69	39
14	Sheffield Weds.	42	16	6	20	82	88	38
15	Everton	42	14	10	18	61	79	38
16	Luton Town	42	14	9	19	58	76	37
17	Newcastle United	42	14	8	20	67	87	36
18	Manchester City	42	13	9	20	78	88	35
19	Portsmouth	42	10	13	19	62	92	33
20	Sunderland	42	12	8	22	67	88	32
21	Cardiff City	42	10	9	23	53	88	29
22	Charlton Athletic	42	9	4	29	62	120	22

SECOND DIVISION

		P	W	D	L	F	A	Pts
1	Leicester City	42	25	11	6	109	67	61
2	Nottingham Forest	42	22	10	10	94	55	54
3	Liverpool	42	21	11	10	82	54	53
4	Blackburn Rovers	42	21	10	11	83	75	52
5	Stoke City	42	20	8	14	83	58	48
6	Middlesbrough	42	19	10	13	84	60	48
7	Sheffield United	42	19	8	15	87	76	46
8	West Ham United	42	19	8	15	59	63	46
9	Bristol Rovers	42	18	9	15	81	67	45
10	Swansea Town	42	19	7	16	90	90	45
11	Fulham	42	19	4	19	84	76	42
12	Huddersfield Town	42	18	6	18	68	74	42
13	Bristol City	42	16	9	17	74	79	41
14	Doncaster Rovers	42	15	10	17	77	77	40
15	Leyton Orient	42	15	10	17	66	84	40
16	Grimsby Town	42	17	5	20	61	62	39
17	Rotherham United	42	13	11	18	74	75	37
18	Lincoln City	42	14	6	22	54	80	34
19	Barnsley	42	12	10	20	59	89	34
20	Notts County	42	9	12	21	58	86	30
21	Bury	42	8	9	25	60	96	25
22	Port Vale	42	8	6	28	57	101	22

THIRD DIVISION (NORTH)

		P	W	D	L	F	A	Pts
1	Derby County	46	26	11	9	111	53	63
2	Hartlepools United	46	25	9	12	90	63	59
3	Accrington Stanley	46	25	8	13	95	64	58
4	Workington	46	24	10	12	93	63	58
5	Stockport County	46	23	8	15	91	75	54
6	Chesterfield	46	22	9	15	96	79	53
7	York City	46	21	10	15	75	61	52
8	Hull City	46	21	10	15	84	69	52
9	Bradford City	46	22	8	16	78	68	52
10	Barrow	46	21	9	16	76	62	51
11	Halifax Town	46	21	7	18	65	70	49
12	Wrexham	46	19	10	17	97	74	48
13	Rochdale	46	18	12	16	65	65	48
14	Scunthorpe United	46	15	15	16	71	69	45
15	Carlisle United	46	16	13	17	76	85	45
16	Mansfield Town	46	17	10	19	91	90	44
17	Gateshead	46	17	10	19	72	90	44
18	Darlington	46	17	8	21	82	95	42
19	Oldham Athletic	46	12	15	19	66	74	39
20	Bradford Park A.	46	16	3	27	66	93	35
21	Chester	46	10	13	23	55	84	33
22	Southport	46	10	12	24	52	94	32
23	Tranmere Rovers	46	7	13	26	51	91	27
24	Crewe Alexandra	46	6	9	31	43	110	21

THIRD DIVISION (SOUTH)

		P	W	D	L	F	A	Pts
1	Ipswich Town	46	25	9	12	101	54	59
2	Torquay United	46	24	11	11	89	64	59
3	Colchester United	46	22	14	10	84	56	58
4	Southampton	46	22	10	14	76	52	54
5	Bournemouth	46	19	14	13	88	62	52
6	Brighton & Hove A.	46	19	14	13	86	65	52
7	Southend United	46	18	12	16	73	65	48
8	Brentford	46	16	16	14	78	76	48
9	Shrewsbury Town	46	15	18	13	72	79	48
10	Queens Park R.	46	18	11	17	61	60	47
11	Watford	46	18	10	18	72	75	46
12	Newport County	46	16	13	17	65	62	45
13	Reading	46	18	9	19	80	81	45
14	Northampton Town	46	18	9	19	66	73	45
15	Walsall	46	16	12	18	80	74	44
16	Coventry City	46	16	12	18	74	84	44
17	Millwall	46	16	12	18	64	84	44
18	Plymouth Argyle	46	16	11	19	68	73	43
19	Aldershot	46	15	12	19	79	92	42
20	Crystal Palace	46	11	18	17	62	75	40
21	Exeter City	46	12	13	21	61	79	37
22	Gillingham	46	12	13	21	54	85	37
23	Swindon Town	46	15	6	25	66	96	36
24	Norwich City	46	8	15	23	61	94	31

HOW best to cover one of the most tragic events in the history of football that cast a dark shadow over what had been the fabulous 'fifties? Everybody in the game and the millions who followed football from the terraces reeled with shock when news broke of the plane crash at Munich on 6 February 1958 that virtually wiped out the great Manchester United team, known to all as the Busby Babes.

As the *Footballing Fifties* monument to the memory of that outstanding United side, I am spotlighting the very last game that the Busby Babes played on English soil. It was a First Division match against Arsenal at Highbury on 1 February 1958. There has never been a game quite like it.

A crowd of 63,578 gathered at Highbury to watch Arsenal play United, who were bidding to become the first post-war team to complete a hat-trick of League championships. They also had their sights set on the European Cup, and four days after this Saturday showdown with the Gunners they were scheduled to play Red Star in a quarter-final second leg tie in Belgrade.

Arsenal and the Busby Babes produced a game of football that deserves to be captured in oils rather than words.

It looked all over bar the shooting and the shouting at half-time, with United leading 3-0 from goals by midfield giant Duncan Edwards, young blond inside-forward Bobby Charlton and England centre-forward Tommy Taylor.

But, remarkably, Arsenal pulled level early in the second-half with three goals in three minutes. David Herd – soon to be a United player – scored the first, and Jimmy Bloomfield netted twice in sixty seconds.

The Busby Babes took a deep breath, and came straight back at Arsenal. Dennis Viollet headed in a Charlton cross, and then with twenty minutes to go Tommy Taylor scored an exquisite solo goal from the tightest of angles to make it 5-3.

Arsenal were down but not quite out. They clawed back another goal through Derek Tapscott before the final whistle signalled the end of a classic encounter that was cheered and applauded non-stop for ten minutes by the lucky thousands who had witnessed it.

The players of both sides knew they had taken part in something special, and they left the field arm in arm. Little did anybody know that the match was to serve as an obituary for one of the greatest teams ever to set foot on a football pitch.

Dave Bowen was Gunners captain that day and it was his inspiring leadership that triggered the Arsenal fight back. He said later: 'I just cannot describe the shock I felt

A faded but poignant photograph of the greatest of the Busby Babes Duncan Edwards, pictured at the age of 15 with an England schoolboy international cap on his head and with, so it was predicted, a fabulous future at his feet.

when I heard the news of the plane disaster. It was just five days after one of the most incredible games in which I had ever played. It was just too much to take in that all those wonderful United players had been taken from us. The tragedy made that match at Highbury all the more meaningful. Goodness knows who Up There writes the script, but there was definitely something different, something almost weird about the game. The image has always remained in my mind of those wonderful United footballers playing football that had a certain charm about it. Even when you were on the receiving end, you almost felt like applauding. They were simply magnificent, and in what was to prove their last League game we were inspired to almost match them.' For the record, the teams that day:

Arsenal: Kelsey; Stan Charlton, Evans; Ward, Fotheringham, Bowen; Groves, Tapscott, Herd, Bloomfield, Nutt.

Man United: Gregg; Foulkes, Byrne; Colman, Jones, Edwards; Morgans, Bobby Charlton, Taylor, Viollet, Scanlon.

Five days later the Busby Babes were no more. Twenty-four hours after a 3-3 draw in Belgrade had taken them into the European Cup semi-finals, the team's BEA Elizabethan airliner stopped off in Munich for refuelling. The plane crashed on take-off on the snow-bound Munich airfield at the cost of the lives of eight of the United players: Geoff Bent, Roger Byrne, Eddie Colman, Duncan Edwards, Mark Jones, David Pegg, Tommy Taylor and Liam Whelan.

Bobby Charlton and Matt Busby were among those who survived the crash.

It all gave extra significance to that remarkable match at Highbury. It should serve as an epitaph to the spirit in which the Busby Babes always played their football.

Would the Busby Babes have beaten Fergie's Fliers? Those of us who were around in the 'fifties to see the birth (and, sadly, the death) of the Busby Babes would argue that they were the best of the procession of great teams to come off the Old Trafford conveyor belt.

Last word to the Grand Master of Old Trafford, Sir Matt Busby. He said after United had won the European Cup on an emotion-charged night at Wembley in 1968:

'There is no just telling how good that 1950s team could have become. They were still several years short of maturity when they were torn from us. Goodness knows what peaks they would have reached. Some of the football they produced leading up to Munich was just unbelievable, certainly as good as anything I had seen from a club side in all my years in the game. Before the disaster happened I could see ten years ahead; ten years at the top with nothing to stop us. After it I had two choices. I could lie down and hide behind what had happened, or I could pick myself up and accept the challenge. Once I looked at it like that I knew there was only one thing to do. I owed it to the memory of those fine young men who perished in Munich. They were and will always remain very, very special.'

THE LEAGUE CHAMPIONSHIP 1957-58
Wolves juggernaut flattens all-comers

IT's impossible to write about the 1957-58 Football League championship race without reference to the Busby Babes tragedy. United were making a strong bid to win a third successive title when their dreams died in the snows of Munich. By then Wolves had emerged as their most likely successors as champions, and an emphatic 3-1 victory over United at Molineux on 28 September 1957 underlined their desire, determination and their ability to regain the crown.

Ironically, Wolves were scheduled to play United in a crunch match at Old Trafford on 8 February. It was a week that became etched into the memory of Billy Wright, whose thirty-fourth birthday was on 6 February 1958. This is how he remembered that awful time in my official biography of the Wolves and England skipper:

'How can I ever forget that terrible day! I was feeling nice and chirpy as I made my way back from training on the bus. I had a little Ford by then, but used to lend it to my landlady's son, Arthur Colley, so that he could drive to work. Arthur and I shared the same birthday – February 6. So that morning we had had our usual routine of singing "Happy Birthday" to each other, and I left the Colley house with a smile on my face.

'I was sitting day dreaming on the bus after our training session during which we had discussed tactics for our vital match against United at Old Trafford on the Saturday. Suddenly I was aware of a billboard outside a newsagent's that screamed, "Man United Air Crash!" I jumped off at the next stop and bought the Wolverhampton Express & Star. *The stop press story was a first report that the Manchester United plane had crashed on take-off. It said that many were feared dead, but at that stage there were no names. Over the course of next couple of hours we slowly learned the horrible facts. As well as the players, many of my good friends among the football writers had perished. I remember them so well – Alf Clarke, Don Davies, George Follows, Tom Jackson, Archie Ledbrooke, Henry Rose, Eric Thompson and my dear old England buddy Frank Swift, who was travelling as a reporter for the* News of the World. *Along with everybody else, I spent the next twenty-four hours almost permanently weeping over the cruel loss of so many friends and colleagues.*

'If there could be such a thing as good news from an incident like this, we heard that young Bobby Charlton had escaped unhurt and that Sir Matt Busby and Duncan Edwards were injured but likely to live. So it was more tears two weeks later when that young giant Duncan finally lost his battle for life. That hurt more

than anything, because he represented the future of our game. Big Dunc, as we called him, was at least three years short of his peak, and he could already be rated in the "genius" bracket. It was all so tragic, and away from the personal sadness there was the wider repercussions that our national football team had been dealt a mortal blow. Yes, you could say that was a birthday I would rather forget.'

A measure of the effect the crash had on the England football team can be found in the statistics. From beating world champions West Germany at Wembley in 1954, England had won sixteen and drawn eight of twenty-five internationals. After Munich and up to Billy's 105th and final game, England won just six and drew six of twenty international matches.

You do not need to be a football expert to realise that this record would have been greatly improved had Roger Byrne, Duncan Edwards and Tommy Taylor been available for selection. Their loss meant that England had been weakened in every department, defence, midfield and attack. No team in the world could have afforded to lose three such key players and still have hoped to make an impressive impact in the World Cup finals that were scheduled for the summer just five months after the Munich disaster.

On the domestic front, Billy Wright eventually led Wolves to the first of two successive League championships. They scored 103 goals, and conceded just 47. No team had a better defensive record, and only Manchester City scored more. They found the net 104 times and managed to let in 100 goals at the wrong end!

The Wolves juggernaut rumbled into full power after a stuttering start to the season. They lost their opening match 1-0 against Everton at Goodison and in their fifth game went down 1-3 at Luton. They then went a sequence of 18 First Division matches unbeaten and were setting a pace that few could match.

Wolves won the championship at fortress Molineux where they were beaten only once, a 1-2 defeat by Arsenal on Easter Saturday just twenty-four hours after winning 2-0 at Highbury. Jim Murray emerged as their leading goal scorer with a haul of 29 First Division goals. Darting winger Norman Deeley contributed 23 goals and Peter Broadbent weighed in with 17 despite having midfield scheming as his main responsibility.

They finally won the title with five points to spare over runners-up Preston. Tottenham were another eight points adrift in third place, with Manchester United understandably falling away to ninth in the table.

Manager Stan Cullis summed up: 'All the joy of our success is tinged with great regret over what happened in Munich. My good friend and respected rival Matt Busby has been in my thoughts and prayers ever since the crash, and it is wonderful to know that he is going to be fit and well enough to attend the FA Cup final at Wembley. That in itself is a miracle for which we are thankful.'

THE 1958 FA CUP FINAL
Tears and sympathy but no win for United

MANCHESTER UNITED reached the 1958 FA Cup final on a sea of emotion. They could have sailed there on the tears that had been shed after the Munich disaster. Waiting for them was a Bolton Wanderers team under the powerhouse leadership of Nat 'The Lion of Vienna' Lofthouse. There could hardly have been a person outside Bolton who wanted anything but a United victory.

Lofty and his team-mates had given tears and sympathy, but the flourished fist of the Bolton skipper to his team-mates as they prepared to kick off graphically illustrated that the goodwill ended with the first whistle.

The biggest cheer of the afternoon greeted the appearance of Matt Busby as a spectator. It was his first public appearance since he had survived the air crash three months earlier.

Busby's knowledgeable assistant Jimmy Murphy had temporarily taken over the reins. He missed the Belgrade trip because he was busy with his duties as part-time manager of the Welsh international side.

In the wake of Munich, Murphy got special permission to bring in Cup-tied Stan Crowther and Ernie Taylor, and stitched together a makeshift team built around Munich survivors Harry Gregg, Bill Foulkes, Dennis Viollett and twenty-year-old Bobby Charlton, on to whose shoulders all United's future hopes had now been transferred.

Charlton, with his shock of blond hair making him easily recogniseable, ran himself into the ground in a bid to motivate his United team-mates, but they lacked rhythm from the moment Nat Lofthouse lashed the ball into the net after barely three minutes of what was a frantic rather than fluent match.

If any game exposed the differences between football in the 'fifties and today's much more gentle exercise then it was this final. Lofthouse led the Bolton attack with a brute force that would just not be tolerated today. United goalkeeper Harry Gregg always had half an eye on him when taking possession of the ball, because he knew that within a split second of collecting it Lofty would be coming at him like a human battering ram.

Lofthouse did not disappoint Gregg in the fifty-fifth minute. As the Irish goalkeeper parried a Dennis Stevens shot Lofty hit him like a steam train and put man and ball into the back of the net. Today, it would probably have got Lofthouse sent to the Tower. But this violent treatment was considered within the laws by the referee, and Bolton – a team that cost just £110 in signing-on fees – had clinched the FA Cup. A sad statistic for United: it was the first time a team had lost two successive finals at Wembley.

Nat Lofthouse prepares to deliver the old-fashiond shoulder charge against Manchester United goalkeeper Harry Gregg in the 1958 FA Cup final at Wembley. It was considered part and parcel of the game in the fifties, but even believers in football being a game of physical contact considered that Lofty had gone beyond the laws when he rammed Gregg and the ball into the back of the net for Bolton's match-winning second goal.

A MAN TO REMEMBER
The submariner Taylor-made for Wembley

HERE's a question for collectors of football trivia. Which player appeared for both Manchester United, Newcastle United AND Blackpool in FA Cup finals at Wembley in the 1950s? Those of a certain age will dig into the cellar of their mind and come up with a vintage memory of Ernie Taylor. They will smile as they conjure up his image because he was such a wonderfully entertaining player. Sunderland-born Ernie was a shrimp of a footballer, barely 5ft 4in tall and less than nine stone wet through. But, boy, could he make that ball talk. I caught up with him long after he had hung up his size four boots and before he passed on in 1985, and I excavated these three memories of his FA Cup final appearances:

1951: 'I played for Newcastle against Blackpool when 'Wor' Jackie Milburn scored two goals, the second from my back-heeled pass. When they later agreed to sell me to Blackpool for twenty-five thousand quid, skipper Joe Harvey went to the board and pleaded with them not to let me go. He said I made the team tick. "Yes," I said to Joe, "I am like a ticking bomb and that's why they want me out!"

1953: 'They always call it the Matthews final after we had come back from 3-1 down against Bolton to win 4-3, when it should be the Stanleys final. Just before Stan Mortensen took his free-kick to complete his hat-trick, I said to him, "Bet you a tanner you miss." As the ball hit the back of the net, he said, "Sixpence you owe me, Ern!"

1958: 'You could wash your face in the tears of Man United fans that day. Jimmy Murphy got special dispensation to buy me from Blackpool just days after the Munich air crash. Bolton beat us 2-0 in the final after Nat Lofthouse had committed grievous bodily harm on our goalkeeper Harry Gregg. But no complaints. That was the way the game was played then.'

Ernie, who had been a submariner in the war ('They picked me for the subs because I took up so little room'), had one other game at Wembley that I decided not to mention to him. He got his one and only England cap in the November 1953 game against a bunch of alleged amateurs parading as Hungary. The Magical Magyars, propelled by Puskas and with a hat-trick from Hidegkuti, murdered England 6-3 and Ernie's international career was over almost before it had started.

The cheeky genius, who patrolled the midfield like a little Napoleon, deserved a cupboardful of caps. He once told Bobby Charlton: 'When I look up, all I want to see is your arse disappearing up field. Give me something to aim at.'

Ernie wound down his career with his hometown club Sunderland. The most he ever earned was twenty pounds a week. Today he would be worth his weight in gold.

A MATCH TO REMEMBER
A scorching Summers day in December

TAKE my word for it, there has never been a game quite like the one played at The Valley on 21 December 1957. Charlton Athletic were at home to Huddersfield Town, a club managed by Bill Shankly, who was two years away from starting to build his legend at Liverpool. Now fasten your safety belts for an action replay of one of the most extraordinary games in the history of the Beautiful Game.

Charlton were reduced to ten men early in the first-half when their skipper and England international centre-half Derek Ufton was carried off with a broken collar bone. Huddersfield were 2-0 in the lead at half-time, and cantering.

Within seven minutes of the second-half Huddersfield had rocketed 5-1 into the lead, with the one Charlton goal coming from the right boot of veteran left winger Johnny Summers. Huddersfield started to stroll around with the air of a team that, understandably, considered they had the game won. After all, they were easily dismantling a defence missing its best player and which had conceded 120 goals when being relegated from the First Division the previous season.

With just thirty minutes to go, it would need one of the comebacks of the century for Charlton to save the game. Now for the Summers day.

He scored a second goal with a right foot shot, and a minute later set up team-mate John Ryan for another goal. Charlton 3, Huddersfield 5. During the next ten minutes Summers added three more goals – all with his right foot – to take his tally to five, and the score to Charlton 6, Huddersfield 5.

Amazing? You ain't seen nuttin' yet. In the eighty-eighth minute, shell-shocked Huddersfield gathered themselves for one more charge and snatched an equaliser.

Johnny Summers had one more trick left up his sleeve. He dashed down the left wing and sent a last-minute pass into the path of Ryan, who hammered it into the net. Charlton 7, Huddersfield 6.

No pressman had the courage to tell Huddersfield manager Shanks that this was the first time in Football League history that a team had scored six goals and finished on the losing side. For once in his life, Shankly was speechless.

Summers, a chirpy Cockney who had travelled the football roundabout with Fulham, Norwich and Millwall, said: 'I wore these boots for the first time today, and I've never scored a goal with my right foot before. Today I got all five with my right.'

Within a couple of years, lovely Johnny Summers was cut down by cancer. Suddenly it was winter … but those lucky to have been at The Valley on that astonishing day in December 1957 will always be warmed by the memory of a special Summers day.

THE EUROPEAN CUP 1957-58
A South American carnival in Belgium

THE show had to go on after the heartache of Munich, and Manchester United bravely agreed to go ahead with their European Cup semi-final against AC Milan. Five days after the disappointment of their defeat in the FA Cup final at Wembley United won the first leg 2-1 at Old Trafford, Ernie Taylor scoring a late winner from the penalty spot.

United had to go into the second leg in Milan without key forward Bobby Charlton, who was on England international duty. The European adventure, never to be forgotten because of Munich, ended with 4-0 thumping in the San Siro Stadium.

Imperious Cup holders Real Madrid were waiting for Milan in the final at Belgium's Heysel Syadium, and confident they were about to complete a hat-trick of triumphs.

Milan had go down the Real path of importing overseas players, a trait that English clubs frowned on. Indeed, there were those who said it would never ever happen in England.

Real had now bought the redoubtable Uruguayan centre-half Santamaria to shore up the middle of their defence, and facing him for Milan was his countryman Schiaffino. The Italians also had a stylish Swede in Nils Liedholm and Argentinian goal poacher Grillo.

For almost an hour in the final Real and Milan sparred like heavy-hitting boxers searching for an opening but holding back their main punch. Then suddenly the game erupted with goals. Schiaffino scored in the fifty-ninth minute and the graceful di Stefano equalised for Real. Grillo made it 2-1 for Milan in the seventy-ninth minute, and just sixty seconds later Rial made it 2-2. The South Americans were having a football carnvival in Europe.

The game went into extra-time, and first Cucchiaroni hit the Real crossbar before Gento struck a shot against the Milan bar. The final and winning goal was made in Spain. Early in the second period of extra-time Gento danced through the Milan defence like Stanley Matthews on speed and beat goalkeeper Soldan with a shot from the tightest of angles.

While the South Americans dominated the scoring stage before Gento's spectacular winner, it was Sweden's Nils Liedholm who was considered the man of the match. He pulled the strings for Milan, showing the tactical nous that would one day see him rated as a coach of extraordinary motivating powers.

Rangers had carried Scotland's challenge through the qualifying round by beating St Etienne 4-3 on aggregate before going down to AC Milan 6-1 on aggregate.

THE 1958 WORLD CUP
Pele and the ball-juggling boys of Brazil

THE 1958 World Cup finals in Brazil brought to the soccer stage the young man who over the next fifteen years would establish himself as a legend, possibly the greatest player ever to lace up a pair of boots. Enter Edson Arantes do Nascimento, who would forever more be known acrosss planet football as simply Pele.

Since the first World Cup finals in 1930 Brazil had been exhibitionists extraordinary, who were continually tripped up by their suspect temperament whenever the major prize was within shooting distance. Critics sneered that they were jugglers who became clowns when the pressure was at its peak. In the 1958 World Cup they set out with steely determination to prove they could win as well as entertain.

The brilliant Brazilians beat host nation Sweden 5-2 in a memorable final in Stockholm. The Swedes took a 1-0 lead in the fourth minute through Nils Liedholm, who was showcasing his push-and-walk football in Italy with AC Milan, the club where he would eventually be the visionary coach.

This was the first time Brazil had been behind in the tournament. They hit back with purpose, giving full rein to their 'samba soccer' on a rain-sodden surface. Vava equalised in the ninth minute and scored again in the thirtieth minute, both goals created by the ball-playing Garrincha.

Ten minutes into the second half, the young prodigy Pele produced a moment of magic that signalled that here was a glittering talent for all to enjoy for years to come. Positioned with his back to the goal at the heart of the Swedish penalty area, he caught a high, dropping ball on his thigh. In the time it takes a cobra to strike he hooked the ball over his head and whirled round close-marking centre-half Gustavsson to meet it on the volley and send it powering into the net. It was all over in the blinking of an eye and press box reporters reached for new superlatives to describe a goal in a million. This was pure poetry from Pele.

Mario Zagalo, destined to manage the 1970 World Cup winning team, beat two defenders before shooting Brazil's fourth goal in the seventy-seventh minute. In the hectic closing stages Agne Simonsson reduced the lead before Pele put the finishing touch with a deftly headed goal from Zagalo's centre.

Brazil had unveiled a new formation to international football: 4-2-4, a variation on the system the Hungarians had introduced in the immediate post-war years. They illuminated a tournament in which Wales and Northern Ireland did the United Kingdom proud by reaching the quarter-finals. Scotland went out as bottom club in their pool, while England lost a play-off to Russia.

This is Pele at seventeen. It is one of the earliest of the million-plus photographs that have since been taken of the King of football.

Wales may have fared even better but for an injury to the magnificent John Charles. Equally brilliant whether at centre-half or centre-forward, the former Leeds United star was arguably the greatest of all British footballers. But he is rarely included in 'Top 10' lists because he spent his peak years with Juventus, where he was hero worshipped as Il Buono Gigante, the Gentle Giant. John had cost a then record £65,000 when joining Juventus from Leeds in April 1957. If he were playing at his peak today, his transfer fee would have cleared, in one go, the huge debts accumulated by Leeds. It was only after his death in February 2004 that Big John was given the domestic acclaim he deserved as a true master of the game.

Pele had made a World Cup scoring debut against Wales – minus Charles, a goal that put them out of the tournament. It was one of 139 goals he scored that year, and by the time he had hung up his shooting boots his total stood at a mind-boggling 1,281 goals in 1,363 matches. He was summoned into the team along with Garrincha after England had become the only team to hold the Brazilians to a goalless draw. This was due mainly to the clever defensive tactics worked out by Bill Nicholson, soon to be Spurs manager and working in Sweden as Walter Winterbottom's right-hand man.

The England selectors came in for unmerciful media criticism for a series of blunders. They took a squad of only twenty players, when twenty-two were allowed. Among the players left behind were Stanley Matthews, Nat Lofthouse, and two young goal-scoring machines called Jimmy Greaves and Brian Clough. They included Bobby Charlton in the squad after he had scored spectacular goals against Scotland and Portugal in his first two international appearances within just a few weeks of the Munich air disaster. Then, for some unfathomable reason, they did not select him for any World Cup games.

While it was Pele who got most of the headlines after his hat-trick against France in the semi-final and his two goals in the final, Brazil had an even more fascinating character in Garrincha. There has never been another footballer in the same mould as Garrincha, a nickname meaning 'Little Bird.' Born Manoel Francisco dos Santos in the mountain village of Pau Grande in 1933, he was a cripple at birth. An operation left one leg shorter than the other and both legs were so bowed you could have run a pig through them. After the operation he had what were virtually two left feet, and he used to wear two left boots when playing. This helped him confuse defenders, and when there was a ball at his feet he could be the most bewildering winger on earth.

He was such an individualist that even Brazilian coaches, with their preaching of freedom of expression, were petrified of his independent spirit. It was only following a deputation of his team-mates who had pleaded on his behalf that he was included for his 1958 World Cup debut after being left on the sidelines for the first two games.

Garrincha's contribution to the World Cup victories of 1958 and 1962 was greater than anybody's. He tried to motivate the Brazilians again in 1966 but a cartilage operation and injuries collected in a car smash had robbed him of much of his unique magic. He

Garrincha deceives Tottenham's Mel Hopkins in his World Cup debut in 1958.

won sixty-eight caps while playing for Botafogo, Corinthians and Flamengo, and got as much publicity for his wild off the pitch lifestyle as his extraordinary performances with the ball at his odd feet.

Northern Ireland were, along with Wales, the surprise team of the tournament. Inspired by manager Peter Doherty and with Danny Blanchflower and Jimmy McIlroy pulling the strings in midfield, they battled through to the quarter-finals. They were handicapped by injuries to key players, and were finally eliminated by a French team that had two of the tournament's major stars in Raymond Kopa and Just Fontaine. With Real Madrid maestro Kopa providing the passes, Fontaine helped himself to a World Cup record thirteen goals. He later lived in a house in France called *Treize*.

Wales, Ninian Park, 19.10.57. England won 4-0 (1 own goal)

Wales were in trouble from the moment early in the game when left-back Mel Hopkins passed the ball wide of goalkeeper Jack Kelsey and into his own net. Missing the powerful influence of the absent John Charles, Wales caved in to two goals from Johnny Haynes and a brilliant strike from Tom Finney. Goalkeeper Eddie Hopkinson, right-back Don Howe and outside-right Bryan Douglas (hailed as the 'new Matthews') all made impressive debuts. Douglas said later: 'Imagine how excited I was, making my debut in place of my boyhood hero Stanley Matthews and playing alongside the only other player in his class, the great Tom Finney. I was a bag of nerves before the game, but got them under control when Tom quietly told me that he needed to be nervous before a match to perform at his best. It was typical of him that he would say something like that to help put me at my ease.' There was another debutant. Middlesbrough's Harold Shepherdson was having his first match as trainer, a job he would hold for sixteen years. *Team: Hopkinson Howe Byrne Clayton Wright* Edwards Douglas Kevan Taylor Haynes (2) Finney (1)*

Northern Ireland, Wembley, 6.11.57. England lost 3-2

Skipper Danny Blanchflower and goalkeeper Harry Gregg were carried off shoulder high by celebrating Irish fans after this unexpected victory that ended England's sixteen-match unbeaten run. Burnley schemer Jimmy McIlroy gave Ireland a first-half lead with a penalty shot that hit a post and then went into the net off the back of goalkeeper Hopkinson. The penalty had been conceded by Billy Wright with one of the few fouls he ever committed in an England shirt. Liverpool winger Alan A'Court, making his debut in place of the injured Tom Finney, equalised soon after half-time before McCrory and Simpson (with a goal hotly disputed by England) put the Irish 3-1 clear. Duncan Edwards pulled back a goal, but Ireland went on to their first victory over England since 1927 and the first on English soil since 1914. Doncaster Rovers goalkeeper Harry Gregg, later to join Manchester United and survive the Munich air crash, had a game to remember, making at least half a dozen crucial saves. The third Irish goal looked at least two yards off-side and England's defenders could not believe it when the linesman's flag stayed down. *Team: Hopkinson Howe Byrne Clayton Wright* Edwards (1) Douglas Kevan Taylor Haynes A'Court (1).*

France, Wembley, 27.11.57. England won 4-0

Bryan Douglas had a storming game, and three of the four England goals came from his crosses. Bobby Robson, winning his first cap, scored two goals as did Tommy Taylor. Tragically, they were to be his last for England. The game was so one sided that it was almost reduced to French farce, with England hammering in twenty shots to none from France in the last twenty minutes. Only one of them produced a goal, Bobby Robson hitting the back of the net at the end of a seven-man movement to underline his arrival as a force in international football. Three months later England lost three of their major players, Roger Byrne, Duncan Edwards and Tommy Taylor, to the Munich air crash that decimated the Manchester United team. Manager Walter Winterbottom said: 'We owe it to the memory of the United players to do the very best we can.' **Team: Hopkinson Howe Byrne Clayton Wright* Edwards Douglas Robson (2) Taylor (2) Haynes Finney.**

Scotland, Hampden Park, 19.4.58. England won 4-0

Bobby Charlton, a Munich survivor, electrified the first of his 106 England appearances with a classical goal when he connected with a Tom Finney cross on the volley to send it flashing into the Scotland net from the edge of the penalty area. His wonder strike came in the sixty-second minute after Bryan Douglas had headed England into a first-half lead and then laid on the first of two goals for Derek Kevan. Fulham's Jim Langley made a commendable debut in place of the sadly missed Roger Byrne, with Wolverhampton's Bill Slater taking on the impossible job of following Duncan Edwards. The nearest Scotland came to scoring was when a Jackie Mudie header hit the bar midway through the second-half, by which time England were sitting on a cushion of three goals. Kevan wrapped it up for England fifteen minutes from the end after Johnny Haynes, Bobby Charlton and Bill Slater had cut open the Scottish defence with a procession of precise passes. Tommy Docherty, marking Charlton, said later: 'It was one of the great international goals. What a way to start. The ball was crossed by my all-time favourite player Tom Finney and was smashed on the volley by the player who was one of the few who could be mentioned in the same breath. It underlined what a fantastic prospect the young Bobby was and I just couldn't believe it when England ignored him for the World Cup matches. He was just as promising as any of the young Brazilians who were pitched into the tournament. You should not judge a footballer by his age but by his ability. Bobby was already a master of the game and I was proud to be there to see his first goal for England, even though I was on the receiving end. It was an absolute blinder.' *Team: Hopkinson Howe Langley Clayton Wright* Slater Douglas (1) Charlton (1) Kevan (2) Haynes Finney.*

Portugal, Wembley, 7.5.58. England won 2-1

Two goals from Bobby Charlton (the second, a scorching shot similar to that which rocked the Scots) rescued England from the brink of defeat. Portugal created enough chances to have won the game, but their finishing was feeble. Jim Langley failed to score from the penalty spot, one of only two misses throughout his career. It was the fourth penalty miss in a row in an international match at Wembley. Portugal played a tight defensive game as they set out to prove that they were unlucky not to have qualified for the World Cup finals. Portugal went into their defensive shell after taking a deserved lead early in the second-half. England might have had a more emphatic victory if Derek Kevan had not climsily made a mess of three excellent chances in the closing stages. For Bobby Charlton, the two goals were some consolation for Manchester United's FA Cup final defeat by Bolton at Wembley four days earlier. How United could have done with him. They had to go into their European Cup semi-final against AC Milan with their best man claimed by England. It threw up the ages-old club or country controversy. *Team: Hopkinson Howe Langley Clayton Wright* Slater Douglas Charlton (2) Kevan Haynes Finney.*

Yugoslavia, Belgrade, 11.5.58. England lost 5-0

All the confidence and cohesion built up in the England team pre-Munich had disappeared, and they found this World Cup warm-up match in Belgrade too hot to handle in more ways than one. The game was played in a heat wave with temperatures in the high nineties, and three of the Yugoslav goals came in the last ten minutes with several of the England players close to exhaustion. The match was a personal nightmare for Jim Langley, who was run ragged by three-goal right winger Petakovic. It was a particularly testing trip for Bobby Charlton, mentally more than physically. He was back in Belgrade where the Busby Babes had played their final match. The last leg of the flight had meant landing at and taking off from Munich. It was a defeat that underlined just how much England had gone back since the Munich air crash. They were disjointed and totally lacking any sort of team pattern. If anything, the final scoreline flattered England and it did severe damage to their confidence with the World Cup finals so close. *Team: Hopkinson Howe Langley Clayton Wright* Slater Douglas Charlton Kevan Haynes Finney.*

USSR, Moscow, 18.5.58. Drew 1-1

For this final match before the World Cup finals, Eddie Clamp came in at right-half to make an all-Wolves half-back line with clubmates Billy Wright and Bill Slater. Colin

McDonald took over in goal and Bolton's tough-tackling Tommy Banks was called in at left-back. After the defeat in Yugoslavia, England gave a much more disciplined performance in the new Lenin Stadium and a Derek Kevan goal just before half-time gave them a draw against a Russian side rated one of the best in Europe. England might have won but for the goalkeeping of the great 'Man in Black' Lev Yashin, and the intervention of the woodwork when first Tom Finney and then Derek Kevan struck shots against a post. The shock after the match was that Brian Clough, Middlesbrough's untried goal master, was told he was not needed for the World Cup squad. Cloughie had scored 42 goals that season and was in red-hot form. Cloughie made no secret of his displeasure. It made no sense to most people that the selectors decided to leave behind not only Brian Clough, but also the vastly experienced Nat Lofthouse and the living legend Stanley Matthews. Lofty had been in devastating form in the FA Cup final when his two goals virtually won the trophy for Bolton. The selectors could also have considered the young Chelsea whizkid Jimmy Greaves. For some reason they chose to take only twenty players, when twenty-two were allowed in each squad. England arrived in Sweden just two days before the kick-off to the tournament and were hardly the best prepared team going into the finals. *Team: McDonald Howe Banks Clamp Wright* Slater Douglas Robson Kevan (1) Haynes Finney.*

USSR, World Cup, Gothenburg, 8.6.58. Drew 2-2

Tom Finney coolly placed a penalty wide of Russian goalkeeper Lev Yashin six minutes from the end to give England a draw in their opening World Cup match against a Russian team much changed from the side they had played in Moscow the previous month. The Russians had led 2-0 with twenty minutes to go, and it looked all over for England until Bryan Douglas created a goal for Derek Kevan. After Finney had scored the equaliser from the spot, a furious Lev Yashin got hold of the referee and spun him around like a top. Incredibly, he was allowed to stay on the field. He was protesting over the award of the penalty because he considered the tackle had been made outside the box. In the closing moments a crushing tackle on Finney damaged his knee and put him out of the rest of the tournament. *Team: McDonald Howe Banks Clamp Wright* Slater Douglas Robson Kevan (1) Haynes Finney (1, pen).*

Brazil, World Cup, Gothenburg, 11.6.58. Drew 0-0

This was the only World Cup match in which eventual champions Brazil failed to score, and it was due mainly to the defensive tactics worked out by Walter Winterbottom's assistant Bill Nicholson, who had watched their opening match against Austria. The Brazilians were not allowed to get into their smooth rhythm. The nearest they got to

The great Tom Finney, a penalty-scoring hero against Russia.

breaking down the disciplined England defence was when Vava rocked the crossbar. Bill Slater played a key role, sticking close to their ball master Didi and not giving him room to produce his devastating passes. Liverpool left winger Alan A'Court gave a solid performance as deputy for the injured Finney. The result forced the Brazilians to re-think, and they were persuaded to call up two exceptional but untested individualists for their next match against Wales: Garrincha and Pele. Slater finished the match with bruises on the inside of both knees where he had kept banging them together to stop Didi pulling off his favourite trick of threading the ball through an opponent's legs, a trick now known as the nutmeg. *Team: McDonald Howe Banks Clamp Wright* Slater Douglas Robson Kevan Haynes A'Court.*

Austria, World Cup, Boras, 15.6.58. Drew 2-2

England, needing to beat Austria to qualify for the quarter-finals, were trailing 1-0 at half-time to a thunderbolt of a goal scored from thirty yards by left-half Koller. Johnny Haynes equalised ten minutes into the second half, and then the Austrians regained the lead following a corner. The ball was cleared to Koerner, who beat goalkeeper Colin McDonald with another long-range shot. Derek Kevan, whose bulldozing tactics had brought him severe criticism, pulled England level again ten minutes from the end after running on to a Johnny Haynes pass. Five minutes later they celebrated what they thought was a winning goal after Bobby Robson had breasted down the ball and shot all in one sweet movement. The referee ruled that Kevan had obstructed the goal-keeper. This draw meant England had to play off against Russia, their third meeting in a month. Most experts were expecting Bobby Charlton to be called in for his World Cup debut for the deciding match against the Russians, but the selectors decided the pressure would be too great for him. *Team: McDonald Howe Banks Clamp Wright* Slater Douglas Robson Kevan (1) Haynes (1) A'Court.*

USSR, World Cup, Gothenburg, 17.6.58. England lost 1-0

Chelsea winger Peter Brabrook came in for his debut along with Wolves inside-forward Peter Broadbent, but Bobby Charlton was again ignored. Brabrook almost became an instant hero with a shot that struck the Russian post and then bounced into Yashin's hands. In the second-half he had a goal disallowed before the Russians scored the winning goal when Ilyin's shot went in off a post to put England out of the World Cup. When England arrived back in London, Walter Winterbottom was met at the airport by his young son, Alan, who asked the question on the lips of thousands of football fans: 'Daddy, why didn't you play Bobby Charlton?' *Team: McDonald Howe Banks Clayton Wright* Slater Brabrook Broadbent Kevan Haynes A'Court.*

SUNDERLAND suffered a double blow. They were relegated for the first time after a record unbroken run in the First Division since their election to the Football League in 1890. And to add to the misery on Wearside, Clown Prince Len Shackleton was forced to retire because of a recurring ankle injury. A career that had started very briefly at Arsenal, took in skilled service with Braford Park Avenue, Newcastle and 320 appearances in ten years at Roker Park. He was the Great Entertainer, and the game would rarely see his like again.

Celtic were in seventh heaven. They crushed deadly rivals Rangers 7-1 in the Scottish League Cup final, the highest score in any British final. Hearts were the sensational side of the season, scoring a record 132 goals on the way to the Scottish First Division title. Jimmy Wardhaugh and Jimmy Murray each scored 28 goals.

After years of dithering, the Football League at last agreed to introduce Third and Fouth Divisions instead of the outdated Third Division South and Third Division North.

Stan (Thunderboots) Lynn became the first full-back to score a League hat-trick for Aston Villa against Sunderland in January 1958. He was huge favourite at Villa Park and later at deadly rivals Birmingham City.

In his first season in Italy, John Charles led Juventus to the league title and was the championship's top marksman with 28 goals in 34 games.

Hereford United equalled the record victory by a non-League team against League opponents when they hammered Queen's Park Rangers 6-1 in the second round of the FA Cup. First Division Newcastle United, the great FA Cup specialists of the 'fifties, were beaten 3-1 at home by Third Division Scunthorpe.

Second Division Cardiff City beat First Division Leeds for the third successive year in the FA Cup ... in the same round (the third) and by the same scoreline (2-1).

In the same season that the seniors were capturing the League title, Wolves won the FA Youth Cup in an amazing two-leg final against Chelsea. The Cullis Cubs were 1-5 down against Drake's Ducklings from the first leg, and went on to win 7-6 on aggregate!

First Division: Wolves, 64pts. Runners-up: Preston, 59 pts.
Wolves record: P42 W28 D8 L6 F103 A47 Pts64
Representative team: Finlayson; Stuart, Harris; Clamp, Wright (capt.), Flowers; Deeley, Broadbent, Murray, Mason, Mullen. Also: Slater (14), Wilshaw (12), Booth (13).
Top scorer: Murray (29). Manager: Stan Cullis.

Second Division: West Ham United, 57pts. Runners-up: Blackburn Rovers, 56pts.
Third Division (South): Brighton, 60pts. Runners-up: Brentford, 58pts.
Third Division (North): Scunthorpe, 66pts. Runners-up: Accrington Stanley, 59pts.

FA Cup final: Bolton Wanderers 2, Manchester United 0
Bolton: Hopkinson; Hartle, Banks; Hennin, Higgins, Edwards; Birch, Stevens, Lofthouse (capt.), Parry, Holden. Scorer: Lofthouse (2)
Manchester United: Gregg; Foulkes (capt.), Greaves; Goodwin, Cope, Crowther; Dawson, E. Taylor, Charlton, Viollet, Webster

Top First Division marksman: Bobby Smith (Tottenham), 36 goals
Footballer of the Year: Danny Blanchflower (Tottenham)
European Footballer of the Year: Raymond Kopa (Real Madrid)

Scottish First Division: Hearts, 62pts. Runners-up: Rangers, 49pts.
Scottish Cup final: Clyde 1, Hibernian 0

FA Amateur Cup final: Woking 3, Ilford 0

European Cup final: Real Madrid 3, AC Milan 2 (Brussels, after extra-time)
Real Madrid: Alonso (capt.); Atienza, Lesmes, Santisteban; Santamaria, Zarraga; Kopa, Joseito, Di Stefano, Rial, Gento. Scorers: Di Stefano, Rial, Gento
AC Milan: Soldan; Fontana, Beraldo, Bergamaschi; Maldini, Radice; Danova, Liedholm (capt.), Schiaffino, Grillo, Cucchiaroni. Scorers: Schiaffino, Grillo
Fairs Cup final: Barcelona beat London 8-2 on aggregate

World Cup final: Brazil 5, Sweden 2 (Stockholm, attendance: 49,737)
Brazil: Gilmar, Djalma Santos, Nilton Santos, Zito, Bellini (capt.), Orlando, Garrincha, Didi, Vava, Pele, Zagalo. Scorers: Vava (2), Pele (2), Zagalo
Sweden: Svensson, Bergmark, Axbom, Boerjesson, Gustavsson, Parling, Hamrin, Gren, Simonsson, Liedholm (capt.), Skoglund. Scorers: Liedholm, Simonsson
Referee: Maurice Guigue (France)
Third place: France 6, West Germany 3
Leading scorer: Just Fontaine (France) 13 goals in 6 games

THE LEAGUE TABLES
Where they finished in 1957-58

FIRST DIVISION

		P	W	D	L	F	A	Pts
1	Wolverhampton W.	42	28	8	6	103	47	64
2	Preston North End	42	26	7	9	100	51	59
3	Tottenham Hotspur	42	21	9	12	93	77	51
4	West Bromwich A.	42	18	14	10	92	70	50
5	Manchester City	42	22	5	15	104	100	49
6	Burnley	42	21	5	16	80	74	47
7	Blackpool	42	19	6	17	80	67	44
8	Luton Town	42	19	6	17	69	63	44
9	Manchester United	42	16	11	15	85	75	43
10	Nottingham Forest	42	16	10	16	69	63	42
11	Chelsea	42	15	12	15	83	79	42
12	Arsenal	42	16	7	19	73	85	39
13	Birmingham City	42	14	11	17	76	89	39
14	Aston Villa	42	16	7	19	73	86	39
15	Bolton Wanderers	42	14	10	18	65	87	38
16	Everton	42	13	11	18	65	75	37
17	Leeds United	42	14	9	19	51	63	37
18	Leicester City	42	14	5	23	91	112	33
19	Newcastle United	42	12	8	22	73	81	32
20	Portsmouth	42	12	8	22	73	88	32
21	Sunderland	42	10	12	20	54	97	32
22	Sheffield Weds.	42	12	7	23	69	92	31

SECOND DIVISION

		P	W	D	L	F	A	Pts
1	West Ham United	42	23	11	8	101	54	57
2	Blackburn Rovers	42	22	12	8	93	57	56
3	Charlton Athletic	42	24	7	11	107	69	55
4	Liverpool	42	22	10	10	79	54	54
5	Fulham	42	20	12	10	97	59	52
6	Sheffield United	42	21	10	11	75	50	52
7	Middlesbrough	42	19	7	16	83	74	45
8	Ipswich Town	42	16	12	14	68	69	44
9	Huddersfield Town	42	14	16	12	63	66	44
10	Bristol Rovers	42	17	8	17	85	80	42
11	Stoke City	42	18	6	18	75	73	42
12	Leyton Orient	42	18	5	19	77	79	41
13	Grimsby Town	42	17	6	19	86	83	40
14	Barnsley	42	14	12	16	70	74	40
15	Cardiff City	42	14	9	19	63	77	37
16	Derby County	42	14	8	20	60	81	36
17	Bristol City	42	13	9	20	63	88	35
18	Rotherham United	42	14	5	23	65	101	33
19	Swansea Town	42	11	9	22	72	99	31
20	Lincoln City	42	11	9	22	55	82	31
21	Notts County	42	12	6	24	44	80	30
22	Doncaster Rovers	42	8	11	23	56	88	27

THIRD DIVISION (NORTH)

		P	W	D	L	F	A	Pts
1	Scunthorpe United	46	29	8	9	88	50	66
2	Accrington Stanley	46	25	9	12	83	61	59
3	Bradford City	46	21	15	10	73	49	57
4	Bury	46	23	10	13	94	62	56
5	Hull City	46	19	15	12	78	67	53
6	Mansfield Town	46	22	8	16	100	92	52
7	Halifax Town	46	20	11	15	83	69	51
8	Chesterfield	46	18	15	13	71	69	51
9	Stockport County	46	18	11	17	74	67	47
10	Rochdale	46	19	8	19	79	67	46
11	Tranmere Rovers	46	18	10	18	82	76	46
12	Wrexham	46	17	12	17	61	63	46
13	York City	46	17	12	17	68	76	46
14	Gateshead	46	15	15	16	68	76	45
15	Oldham Athletic	46	14	17	15	72	84	45
16	Carlisle United	46	19	6	21	80	78	44
17	Hartlepools United	46	16	12	18	73	76	44
18	Barrow	46	13	15	18	66	74	41
19	Workington	46	14	13	19	72	81	41
20	Darlington	46	17	7	22	78	89	41
21	Chester	46	13	13	20	73	81	39
22	Bradford Park A.	46	13	11	22	68	95	37
23	Southport	46	11	6	29	52	88	28
24	Crewe Alexandra	46	8	7	31	47	93	23

THIRD DIVISION (SOUTH)

		P	W	D	L	F	A	Pts
1	Brighton & Hove A.	46	24	12	10	88	64	60
2	Brentford	46	24	10	12	82	56	58
3	Plymouth Argyle	46	25	8	13	67	48	58
4	Swindon Town	46	21	15	10	79	50	57
5	Reading	46	21	13	12	79	51	55
6	Southampton	46	22	10	14	112	72	54
7	Southend United	46	21	12	13	90	58	54
8	Norwich City	46	19	15	12	75	70	53
9	Bournemouth	46	21	9	16	81	74	51
10	Queens Park R.	46	18	14	14	64	65	50
11	Newport County	46	17	14	15	73	67	48
12	Colchester United	46	17	13	16	77	79	47
13	Northampton Town	46	19	6	21	87	79	44
14	Crystal Palace	46	15	13	18	70	72	43
15	Port Vale	46	16	10	20	67	58	42
16	Watford	46	13	16	17	59	77	42
17	Shrewsbury Town	46	15	10	21	49	71	40
18	Aldershot	46	12	16	18	59	89	40
19	Coventry City	46	13	13	20	61	81	39
20	Walsall	46	14	9	23	61	75	37
21	Torquay United	46	11	13	22	49	74	35
22	Gillingham	46	13	9	24	52	81	35
23	Millwall	46	11	9	26	63	91	31
24	Exeter City	46	11	9	26	57	99	31

DOWN in London town and up in the North East two young footballers were runnng parallel with each other in a prolific chase for goals that has rarely been surpassed in the history of the domestic game. Both were to become and remain household names: Jimmy Greaves and Brian Clough.

Greavsie – his nickname – was the more precocious. Cloughie – his nickname – was the more powerful, a biff-bang merchant out of the old school, who would push his granny out of the way to get a goal.

Jimmy was a goal-scoring machine from the moment he netted a wonder goal for Chelsea in his 1957 debut against Tottenham at the age of seventeen. Those of us of a certain age who watched him in those crew-cut teenage days at Chelsea will tell you he was the greatest goalscorer we had ever seen. He was nearly as productive but not quite as quick in his later days with Spurs after a brief flirtation with football in Italy. His career output speaks for itself: 491 goals, including a record 357 in the old First Division, a feat that will never ever be surpassed because that league no longer exists.

He also helped himself to 44 goals in 57 England matches, second in his day only to Bobby Charlton (49 goals in 106 matches). Nobody has equalled his post-war haul of six First Division hat-tricks in a single season, and three times at the top level he netted five goals in a single match.

Cloughie, five years older than Greavsie, was just as prolific with his hometown club Middlesbrough and, later, Sunderland, but the majority of his foraging for goals came in the Second Division. He netted 251 goals in just 275 League games before a knee injury brought a premature end to his career at the age of twenty-eight. In the 1958-59 season Cloughie was leading Second Division marksman for the second successive year with 42 goals. It was the third season that he averaged a goal a game, and he raced to 100 League goals in fewer games than any other player before him.

Both Cloughie and Greavsie had more fame ahead of them, Brian as one of the finest club managers ever and Jimmy as a television personality whose quick Cockney wit alongside his straight man Ian St John (Saint and Greavsie) pulled in record numbers of viewers for a football television programme. He was great in the box or on the box.

Jimmy and Brian laid the foundation to their careers in the *Footballing Fifties*, which they would look back on as the summertime of their lives. It screamed out for them to be paired on the football pitch but the England selectors were running scared of their individual styles and allowed them only two matches together. With a little patience, the Clough and Greavsie goal show could have run and run.

A treasured autographed photograph of Cloughie from the author's personal collection. It was signed by the great man himself on an old Charles Buchan Football Monthly *magazine from the fifties when we became good friends in the 1960s. The picture shows him banging in one of his many goals for Middlesbrough in what he described as the greatest years of his life. 'There was nowt to beat playing the game,' he said.*

THE LEAGUE CHAMPIONSHIP
1958-59: Centurion Billy Wright quits at the top

BILLY WRIGHT, England's man for all seasons, elected to get off at the top of the mountain in 1959 after completing a unique double. He had captained Wolves to their second successive League championship and had become the first player in the world to collect one hundred international caps.

His decision to retire had been hurried by an embarrassing experience at Stamford Bridge on 30 August 1958. Chelsea took the Wolves defence apart on the way to scoring six goals, and Billy spent much of the afternoon chasing the shadow of a whizkid who helped himelf to five of the goals and had another legal-looking one waved off-side. It was, of course, Jimmy Greaves, and Billy – feeling every one of his thirty five years – could get nowhere near him.

'That was when I decided to give it one more season,' Billy told me later when I used to ghost a *Daily Express* column for him after he had become manager of Arsenal. 'I realised I couldn't keep up with the pace of the First Division for much longer. Mind you, Jimmy gave every defender he came up against in that season the run around. I always considered that his very best years were at Chelsea because he had no fear and just did what came naturally.'

Many years later Billy gave Jimmy his first full-time job in television when an executive at ATV (Central Television). 'I made him sit down and sign the contract,' Billy joked. 'I didn't want to risk him selling me a dummy.'

Wolves retained the championship in 1959 with a six point cushion between them and their perennial rivals Manchester United. Jim Murray (21 goals), Peter Broadbent (20) and Norman Deeley (17) were the main marksmen as the team again topped the century mark with 110 First Division goals.

The title triumph made Billy wonder if perhaps he should continue and help Wolves go for the hat-trick, but his mind was finally made up for him by, of all people, the Home Secretary of the time, R.A. 'Rab' Butler. Journey with me back to the year of 1959. It was a beautiful summer's day and June was busting out all over in the garden of the imposing Stansted Hall, Essex, home of Mr. Butler, one of the most distinguished politicians of his generation and a powerhouse in the Harold Macmillan government.

The previous day Billy had heard he was to be made a Commander of the British Empire for his services to football (why oh why not a knighthood?), and the previous month he had played England international match 105 while creating a record of seventy successive appearances. Just a month earlier he had led Wolves to their second successive League championship. He was on top of the world.

Billy and his lovely wife of eleven months, Joy of the singing trio the Beverley

For all his record 105 caps Billy Wright's success never ever went to his head.

Sisters, were being shown around the Stansted Hall garden by Mr. Butler, who had invited them over for the opening ceremony of a new stand at his local Halstead football club. Billy recalled:

> *'Suddenly, Mr. Butler turned the conversation to the subject of retirement. There had been conjecture in the press about how long I would carry on playing. I was thirty-five and was considering at least another season or two before I hung up my boots. "The timing for retirement is so important," he said. "I speak as somebody who once got it wrong. I had four years as Chancellor of the Exchequer. For the first three years I was proud of my record but then for the next twelve months I had to take unpopular measures. If I had stepped down after three years I would have been hailed as a successful Chancellor, but one more year changed many opinions about the job I had done. Take advice from me, Billy, and don't leave retirement too late. You have set standards that should never ever be lowered."*
>
> *I took his advice on board, and then after struggling to conquer the hills in our pre-season training I went to see Stan Cullis to discuss my future. He made it clear that he would be looking to gradually move George Showell into the centre-half position. It was as clear a hint as I could expect that one of my most respected mentors felt I was past my best.'*

Billy decided there and then that the time was right to retire. He could have collected a fat fee from any national newspaper for the exclusive news. But, showing the loyalty that was his trademark, he contacted his friend on the Wolverhampton *Express & Star*, Phil Morgan, and gave him the story for nothing.

Phil exclusively revealed in the paper that Billy's final match would be the public pre-season practice match at Molineux between the first team and the reserves on 8 August 1959: The Colours v The Whites. An astonishing crowd of more than twenty thousand turned out for what was a fairly meaningless match. They were all there to say a fond farewell to their idol, Wolverhampton's man for all seasons. For the rest of the country, it was goodbye to an England hero for all seasons.

No player gave more to the *Footballing Fifties* than Billy Wright. He played 491 League matches for Wolves between 1946 and 1958, and captained England 90 times on his way to the then record 105 caps. Bobby Moore, who was just starting an apprenticeship with West Ham as Billy stepped off the stage, later exactly equalled Billy's achievement of captaining England in 90 games.

Last word on Billy to Jimmy Greaves, who helped chase him into retirement: 'Billy was one of my idols when I was a schoolboy with dreams of becoming a professional footballer, and it was a pleasure to play with and against him at the back end of his fabulous career. England had never had a greater or more loyal servant, and his exploits with Wolves and England lit a torch for many young players, myself included. On top of everything else, he was a bloody nice bloke.'

THE 1959 FA CUP FINAL
Ten-man Forest beat the Wembley hoodoo

THE Wembley injury jinx struck yet again in the 1959 FA Cup final, but Nottingham Forest overcame the handicap of losing winger Roy Dwight with a broken leg to beat Luton Town 2-1.

Dwight was stretchered off after thirty-two minutes, with Forest two goals up and in complete control. On the terraces schoolboy Reg Dwight cried as he watched his cousin being carried off. Twenty five years later he would shed tears at Wembley again, this time in the Royal Box as the Watford club he owned was beaten by Everton in the 1984 FA Cup final. By then, Reg Dwight had become better known as Elton John.

Before his injury, Roy Dwight had been running the Luton defence into disarray with rapid raids down the right wing. It was Dwight who powered Forest into the lead after ten minutes when he suddenly cut in and met Stewart Imlach's pass on the half volley.

Four minutes later Forest took a stranglehold on the game when Tom Wilson rose at the far post to head in a perfectly placed pass from Billy Gray.

Luton, stacked with experienced big-match players lik Billy Bingham, Allan Brown and Footballer of the Year Syd Owen, had started the match as betting favourites, but they were being rushed off their feet by a Forest side playing smooth, confident and flowing football that bore the imprint of manager Billy Walker.

Then came the harmless-looking tackle by Brendan McNally from which Dwight emerged with a broken leg that brought a hush to the huge stadium as everybody thought of the well-publicised Wembley jinx. As he left for hospital treatment, Dwight said to team captain Jack Burkitt: 'Keep them going, skip.'

It was Burkitt and his side-kick Bobby McKinlay who led what now became a Forest rearguard action. From being virutally outplayed, Luton gradually got on top but struggled to pierce a Forest defence in which goalkeeper Charlie Thomson was an assured last line.

Hard as Luton tried they could come up with only one goal against the ten heroes of Forest, David Pacey scoring from close range following a Billy Bingham corner in the sixty-fifth minute.

Syd Owen, Luton's veteran centre-half and captain, was playing his last game, but there was to be no fairytale end to his twenty-year career before becoming Luton manager and then an outstanding coach at Leeds. He was big enough to admit: 'Forest thoroughly deserved their victory. They paralysed us in the first thirty minutes, and then didn't give us an inch when down to ten men.'

A MAN TO REMEMBER
The Lawman starts his adventure

THOSE of us from a certain generation get a Manchester United red mist come down when we hear Eric Cantona described as The King of Old Trafford. That title belonged to only one man. Bend the knee to Denis Law, who laid the foundation to his astonishing career in the *Footballing Fifties*.

When, in the early 1960s, I first met Denis in person away from the football pitch I fully expected to get a shock as we shook hands. He was *that* electric as a striker. Law had the quickest reflexes of any British player I have ever seen. I make no apologies for giving him more space than most in this stroll back into the past because he gave me, and millions of other spectators, more entertainment than most.

'Denis the Menace' – an obvious yet fitting nickname – was best known as an icon of the swinging 'sixties, the showman and the swordsman in the celebrated Best-Charlton-Law trio that dismantled defences in such stunning style. George Best was the genius, Bobby Charlton the commander, and Law the executioner.

He would score with a rapier thrust, turning a half chance into a goal in the blinking of an eye. Then the showman would emerge, his right arm punched into the air and held there in a salute that spawned a procession of imitators (Allan Clarke and Rodney Marsh were just two who admitted copying their idol in the way they autographed goals).

A straw-haired assassin who was pencil slim and built for speed, he had an uncanny ability to hover in the air when heading the ball. He stood 5 feet 9 inches, but could make much taller defenders seem about as mobile as lampposts as he soared above them. As well as doing conventional things well at lightning speed, the Electric Heel was a master of the hook shot and the overhead bicycle kick. He was extrovert, flamboyant, provocative and spectacular, and never ever dull. How dare they try to take away his title of The King!

His temper was as quick as his reflexes, and he was often in trouble with referees for retaliating. I once saw him involved in a full-blooded fist fight with Arsenal centre-half Ian Ure at Old Trafford. Both got their marching orders, and long suspensions. What made it even more of a compelling spectacle is that they were good pals who roomed with each other when on Scottish international duty. Friend or foe, Denis refused to concede a penalty area inch to any opponent. A Red Devil, if ever there was one.

Born on 24 February 1940 (in the same week as Jimmy Greaves was having his first kick of life in East London), Denis was the son of an Aberdonian trawlerman, who would have followed his father to sea but for his prodigious talent as a schoolboy footballer. We go back to the 'fifties for his introduction to the professional game.

Scouts working for Huddersfield Town were first to spot him, and it has gone down in football folklore how he arrived in Yorkshire from Aberdeen at the age of fifteen in the early summer of 1955 looking like a comic figure out of *The Beano*. He had a squint, wore National Health glasses and weighed no more than eight stone wet through.

Denis was picked up at Huddersfield station by the club's assistant manager, who was another legend in waiting – the one and only Bill Shankly. 'I could nae believe my eyes when I first saw him,' Shanks told me years later. 'He looked like a case for Oxfam rather than a young footballer. The first thing we did was get his squint sorted out so that we knew who he was looking at when we talked to him. Then we got some steaks inside him and he started to fill out. Once we let him loose on the football pitch he suddenly became a tiger. It was awesome to be there at the start of one of the great football careers. We had bred a footballing monster!'

Denis made his League debut with Huddersfield at the age of sixteen in 1956, and two years later he became Scotland's youngest ever player at the age of eighteen years 236 days. He marked his debut with a goal in a 3-0 victory against Wales at Ninian Park on 18 October 1958 at the launch of an international career that brought him a record 30 goals in 55 appearances. The first manager to pick him for Scotland was Matt Busby, who never made any secret of his belief that Denis was one of the finest players ever to come south of the border.

His transfer to Manchester City for £55,000 in 1960 was a British record, and his 21 goals in 44 games alerted Italian clubs who were throwing money at British players following the success of the great Welshman John Charles at Juventus. Within a year of Denis arriving at Maine Road, City sold him to Torino for £110,000 in another record deal.

For 21-year-old Denis, the following twelve months were the most miserable of his life. 'I was never happy with Torino,' he told me. 'Perhaps if I had been older I could have handled it, but I suffered terrible home sickness. They treated their players as if they owned them body and soul, and I felt like a prisoner. There was little satisfaction on the pitch because the Italian game was totally negative, and I used to have two or three defenders marking me every time I went on the pitch. My big bust up with the club came when they refused to release me to play for Scotland. I knew then that I just had to get back to Britain or go mad.'

He tried to get rid of his homesick blues by enjoying himself off the pitch in the company of his Torino team-mate Joe Baker, the Englishman from Hibernian who had a thicker Scottish accent than Aberdonian Denis. Their exploration of the Turin nightlife very nearly cost them their lives. Joe was at the wheel of a flash new Alfa Romeo with Denis beside him when they were involved in a high-speed crash. Both were dragged unconscious from the wreckage, but thankfully their injuries were not long term.

It was Matt Busby who came back into Law's life to rescue him from his dismal

Denis Law used to insist on extra-long sleeves so that he could hold the cuffs in the palms of his hands. He was a character all the way down to his fingertips.

exile. For a third time, the transfer record was broken as he made the move to Old Trafford in the summer of 1962 for £116,000.

Over the next ten years, Denis ignited the United attack with his fire and flair. He was an FA Cup winner in 1963, European Footballer of the Year in 1964, and a League championship winner in 1965 and 1967. He remains the only Scot to have been elected European Footballer of the Year.

Sadly, he missed the ultimate prize of the European Cup winners' medal in 1968. A knee injury reduced him to the role of hospital bed observer as he watched the Wembley triumph on television. Brian Kidd took his place, and celebrated his nineteenth birthday with a goal as he fed off the probing passes of another Scot, Pat Crerand, whose skilled support had been an important part of the Lawman's success story at Old Trafford.

He scored 171 League goals for United in 309 matches, and took his FA Cup goals haul to what was then a record 40 goals. This total did not include the six he scored for Manchester City against Luton in a 1961 tie that was abandoned because of rain.

A fiercely proud Scot, Denis just could not stomach the prospect of England winning the World Cup in 1966. On the day of the final at Wembley he took himself off to the golf course rather than watch the game on television. When news filtered through to him that England had beaten West Germany he threw his golf bag to the floor in disgust.

A year later he had the satisfaction of being a goal scoring member of the Scottish team that beat world champions England 3-2 at Wembley. I always put him in his place by reminding him of a game in which he played at Wembley on 15 April 1961 … England 9, Scotland 3.

His Manchester United career ended in rancour in 1973 when Tommy Docherty let him go on a free transfer. 'The first I knew about it was when I saw the news being announced on television,' an aggrieved Law said. 'I thought I would end my career at Old Trafford.'

Shrugging off a recurring knee problem, Denis returned to Manchester City and in the last game of the following season almost reluctantly back heeled the goal that helped push Manchester United down into the Second Division.

He had the satisfaction of making his World Cup finals debut in the last season of a magnificent career in which he inspired hundreds of youngsters to try to play the Lawman way. They could copy his style but few could get close to imitating his awareness and anticipation that always put him a thought and a deed ahead of the opposition.

A good family man with five sons, Denis is now a sixty something, and after beating cancer is a regular meeter and greeter at Manchester United and an amusing after dinner speaker with scores of stories up those famous sleeves of his .

It has been quite a voyage of adventure for the trawlerman's son from Aberdeen.

A MATCH TO REMEMBER
Harmer the Charmer sparks 10-goal Spurs

ON the morning of Saturday 11 October 1958 Bill Nicholson was officially appointed manager of Tottenham Hotspur. In the afternoon he was given the most remarkable start there has ever been to a manager's career.

Providing the opposition were Everton, who were struggling three from the bottom of the First Division, a point behind sixteenth-placed Spurs.

Tottenham were in the transition period between their push-and-run triumphs of the early 1950s (in which right-half Nicholson played a key role) and the 'Super Spurs' of the 1960s.

The first decision Nicholson made as manager was to recall Tottenham's impish inside-forward Tommy Harmer, known to the White Hart Lane fans as 'Harmer the Charmer.' But that afternoon Everton found him more like 'The Harmer' as he pulled them apart with an astounding individual performance. He had a hand – or rather a well-directed foot – in nine goals and scored one himself as Everton were buried under an avalanche of goals. The final scoreline was 10-4. It might easily have been 15-8!

Harmer was the 'Tom Thumb' character of football. He stood just 5ft 2in tall and was a bantamweight who looked as if he could be blown away by a strong wind. But he had mesmeric control of the ball and when conditions suited him could dominate a match with his passing and dribbling. Born in Hackney on 2 February 1928, he joined Tottenham from amateur club Finchley in 1951 and over the next eight years played 205 League games and scored 47 goals.

For the record, the teams that day were:

Tottenham: Hollowbread, Baker, Hopkins, Blanchflower, Ryden, Iley, Medwin, Harmer, Smith, Stokes, Robb.

Everton: Dunlop, Sanders, Bramwell, King, Jones, Harris (B), Fielding, Harris (J), Hickson, Collins, O'Hara.

There was a hint of what was to come in the opening moments when Spurs took the lead through Alfie Stokes after an inch-perfect diagonal pass from Harmer had split the Everton defence. The Merseysiders steadied themselves and equalised eight minutes later when Jimmy Harris side footed in a Dave Hickson centre.

The unfortunate Albert Dunlop, deputising in goal for the injured Jimmy O'Neill, then suffered a nightmare thirty minutes as Spurs ruthlessly smashed five goals past him through skipper Bobby Smith (2), George Robb, Stokes again and Terry Medwin.

The foundation for all the goals was being laid in midfield where Harmer and Danny Blanchflower, both masters of ball control, were in complete command.

Jimmy Harris gave Everton fleeting hope of a revival with a headed goal to make it 6-2 just after half-time, but bulldozing Bobby Smith took his personal haul to four and the irrepressible Harmer helped himself to a goal that was as spectcular as any scored during this gourmet feast. Bobby Collins lost possession just outside the penalty area, and the ball bobbled in front of Harmer. He struck it on the half volley from twenty yards and watched almost in disbelief as the ball rocketed into the roof of the net. It was the first time Tommy had scored a League goal from outside the penalty area.

Everton refused to surrender and the industrious Harris completed his hat-trick from a centre by dashing centre-forward Dave Hickson. Then Bobby Collins, just an inch taller than Harmer, showed that this was a magical match for the wee people when he hammered in a 25-yard drive as both teams crazily pushed everybody forward.

All the goals were scored by forwards until Spurs centre-half John Ryden, limping on the wing, scrambled in Tottenham's tenth goal – the fourteenth of the match – in the closing minutes.

Bill Nicholson, who went on to become the greatest manager in Tottenham history, said: 'I have never believed in fairy tales in football, but this came close to making me change my mind. In many ways it was a bad advertisement for football because so many of the goals were the result of slip-shod defensive play. But I have to admit it was magnificent entertainment. Little Tommy Harmer played the game of his life. On his day he was as clever a player as I have ever seen, but he was too often handicapped by his small physique. On this day, he was a giant.'

Jimmy Harris commented: 'It was a good news, bad news day for me. I was able to tell people that I had scored a hat-trick against Spurs, and would then mumble the bad news that we had lost 10-4. It's no exaggeration to say we could have had at least four more goals. I don't know who were the more bewildered by it all – the players or the spectators, who got tremendous value for their money. Tommy Harmer was the man who won it for Tottenham. It was as if he had the ball on a piece of string.'

Hero Harmer said: 'I had been out of the League team for the previous four matches and was half expecting to be left out again when I reported to White Hart Lane for the match with Everton. But Bill Nick told me I was in, and it became one of those games when just everything went right for me. I particularly remember my goal because it was about the only time I ever scored from that sort of range.'

As Tommy came off the pitch to a standing ovation, he said to Bill Nicholson: 'I hope you're not going to expect ten goals from us every week, Boss.'

Only three players from the Spurs team that scored the knockout ten goals survived as regular members of the 'double' winning side of 1960-61– right-back Peter Baker, artistic right-half Danny Blanchflower and cenre-forward Bobby Smith. The fourteen goals equalled the aggregate First Division record set in 1892 when Aston Villa annihilated Accrington Stanley 12-2.

THE EUROPEAN CUP 1958-59
A South American carnival in Belgium

BACK in the 1950s the European Cup was a pure knockout competition involving just the champions of each country, and the Cup holders were allowed to defend their crown. In 1958-59 the Uefa organisers were prepared to bend their own rules to allow Manchester United to compete along with champions Wolves. It was a mark of respect for what happened on that dreadful day in Munich the previous season.

Matt Busby eagerly and gratefully accepted the invitation in the spirit it was intended, and saw it as a way of helping to heal the huge mental scars caused by Munich. But the spirit of goodwill was shattered by a joint Football League and FA commission that decreed that United could not compete, with the excuse that rules were there to be obeyed! They had never heard of the saying, 'charity begins at home.'

So it was left to Wolves to carry the English challenge alone. It was fitting that they were competing in Europe because it was their exploits in the floodlit friendlies of the early 1950s that had inspired the idea of the Eurpean Cup.

Sadly, Wolves made a complete mess of their baptism. They were held 2-2 by the German club Schalke 04 in the home leg of the first round match at Molineux, and went down 2-1 in the second away leg that was scarred by bad temper and brutal tackling by both teams.

Champions Real Madrid, chasing a fourth triumph, had been strengthened by the arrival of a portly player rejoicing in the name of Ferenc Puskas. The Galloping Major, who had joined the mass defections from revolution-torn Hungary, was putting a final flourish to his playing career in the Spanish sunshine and with football that was as good as anything he had played with Honved and Hungary.

The final was an echo of the first tournament in 1956, with Real facing Reims in Stuttgart. There was one major difference. French legend Raymond Kopa, who had first made his name with Reims, was now wearing the white colours of Real Madrid.

Puskas missed the final because of injury, but Real were always on a victory path from the moment in the second minute when Mateos sold a massive dummy to the Reims defence before shooting just inside the right-hand post.

Mateos, who had been the outstanding forward with his darting work on the right, missed from the penalty spot before the ambling Alfredo di Stefano clinched yet another European Cup for Real two minutes after the interval. He played a series of wall passes with team-mates as he strolled almost arrogantly upfield before steering the ball into the net with pinpoint accuracy.

Real remained undisputed kings of Europe. But their finest hour was yet to come.

French master Raymond Kopa, the Real deal. He was the engineer and Just Fontaine the executioner for the French team that finished third in the 1958 World Cup.

Northern Ireland, Windsor Park, 4.10.58. Drew 3-3

Northern Ireland and England concocted a thriller on a waterlogged, mudheap of a pitch. Bobby Charlton, playing at centre-forward, scored with two thunderbolt shots to add fuel to the arguments that he should have been let off the leash in the World Cup. The Irish bravely led three times through Cush, Peacock and Casey as they searched for their first victory over England in Belfast since 1927. Bobby Charlton's two equalising goals sandwiched England's second goal by Tom Finney. This was a memorable milestone for the Preston Plumber. It was his thirtieth goal for England, a new all-time scoring record. Two Manchester United youngsters took the eye. Twenty-year-old Wilf McGuinness, another of the Busy Babes, won the first of what would surely have been many England caps but for a broken leg virtually ending his career in 1961. Wilf, later to have an uncomfortable spell in charge at Old Trafford, would have been on the Munich flight but for staying behind in Manchester for a cartilage operation. The star of the match was Bobby Charlton, and it revived the question that had been asked so many times in Sweden, 'Why oh why was he not selected for at least one game in the World Cup finals?' *Team: McDonald Howe Banks Clayton Wright* McGuinness Brabrook Broadbent R Charlton (2) Haynes Finney (1).*

USSR, Wembley, 22.10.58. England won 5-0

This was hollow revenge against the Russians for the defeat in the match that really mattered in the World Cup. Johnny Haynes, the pass master, turned goal snatcher with his one and only international hat-trick. Four of England's goals came in the second-half as goalkeeper Belayev, deputising for the injured Lev Yashin, flapped under non-stop pressure from the lion-hearted Lofthouse, who had been recalled after two years in the international wilderness. He revealed a flash of his old power with a crashing left foot shot for the fifth goal despite a Russian defender having a handful of his shirt. Bobby Charlton's goal came from the penalty spot. Ronnie Clayton, who was eventually to succeed Billy Wright as skipper, had an outstanding game with his driving performance from midfield, and Graham Shaw made a sound debut at left-back. The BBC television Sportsview team, led by Kenneth Wolstenholme, had been campaigning to have Johnny Haynes replaced. When they reported the match and Johnny's hat-trick, they appeared in front of the cameras in sackcloth and ashes. This was notable as Tom Finney's seventy-sixth and final game for England. No better player ever wore the white shirt. He left the stage quietly when what he deserved was a farewell of fireworks and praise for all he had achieved for England. Tommy was as modest as they come, and he should have received better treatment from the selectors who just suddenly ignored him after an injury and a run of bad form. He deserved a knighthood (and many years later he would get one). *Team: McDonald Howe Shaw Clayton Wright* Slater Douglas Charlton (1 pen) Lofthouse (1) Haynes (3) Finney.*

Wales, Villa Park, 26.11.58. Drew 2-2

Like Johnny Haynes, Peter Broadbent was more a schemer than a scorer. But, standing in for the injured hat-trick hero, he twice netted equalising goals against a spirited Welsh team. Arsenal winger Danny Clapton was given the impossible job of following Tom Finney. He performed with spirit, but no player could stand comparison with the Preston footballing master. Wales had taken a fifteenth minute lead through Derek Tapscott, who gave Billy Wright a tough time at the heart of the defence. Broadbent neatly lobbed the ball over goalkeeper Jack Kelsey to make it 1-1 just before half-time. Despite the handicap of having injured skipper Dave Bowen as a passenger on the wing for much of the game, Wales continued to press forward in search of their first victory over England for twenty-three years. Ivor Allchurch restored their lead with a shot on the turn in the seventieth minute. England struck back for a second equaliser when Broadbent rose at the far post to head in a centre from Alan A'Court. This was the final England appearance for Nat Lofthouse. He finished with a record-equalling thirty international goals from just thirty-three matches. The Lion of Vienna used to terrorise goalkeepers in an era when the shoulder charge was still accepted as a legitimate weapon. Who can ever forget his treatment of Manchester United goalkeeper Harry Gregg in the 1958 FA Cup final? A few years later, the shoulder charge that put Harry and the ball into the net would have brought Lofty an instant dismissal. For Bolton, it brought them their second decisive goal. It's a different game now. *Team: McDonald Howe Shaw Clayton Wright* Flowers Clapton Broadbent (2) Lofthouse Charlton A'Court.*

Scotland, Wembley, 11.4.59. England won 1-0

An historic day for Billy Wright when he became the first footballer in the world to win one hundred international caps. A closely fought game was won for England by an acrobatic header from Bobby Charlton after Bryan Douglas had sent over a precise centre in the sixty-second minute. At the final whistle, the England skipper was carried shoulder high to the Wembley dressing-room by his team-mates Don Howe and Ronnie Clayton. Johnny Haynes collected a painful memento of Billy's historic match when a fierce tackle by Dave Mackay left him with a broken little finger on his left hand, and Bryan Douglas limped through much of the game with damaged knee ligaments. Bolton winger Doug Holden won the first of his five caps, and played with pace and fire against a Scottish defence in no mood to concede an inch. Dundee goalkeeper Bill Brown was the man of the match, denying Bobby Charlton a hat-trick of goals with magnificent saves. It was a performance that convinced Tottenham manager Bill Nicholson that he should sign Brown for Spurs, and he became a key man in their double year of 1960-61. As he was carried the length of the Wembley pitch, Billy Wright was given the sort of ovation reserved only for true sporting gods. His wife Joy, of Beverley Sisters fame, had given birth to their first daughter, Victoria, just six days earlier and had been allowed out of hospital to watch the game. The Scots did their best to spoil the party by playing their hearts out, but nothing could ruin Billy's big day. *Team: Hopkinson Howe Shaw Clayton Wright* Flowers Douglas Broadbent Charlton (1) Haynes Holden.*

Italy, Wembley, 6.5.59. Drew 2-2

England were reduced to ten men when Ron Flowers went off with a broken nose with England leading 2-0. The goals were scored in the first-half by Manchester United team-mates Bobby Charlton and Warren Bradley, a schoolmaster who was making his debut on the right wing. By the time Flowers returned to the defence seventeen minutes later the young, experimental Italian team had drawn level. The Italians were fielding the first all home-born team for twenty-five years following a ruling from FIFA that in future teams could not include players capped by another country. There was an embarrassing start to the game. When they stood to attention before the match the Italian players were astonished to hear the banned Mussolini-era national anthem being played. This had been replaced after the war. Every Italian restaurant in Britain must have been short of staff because Italy had thousands of supporters in the crowd, and they whistled and hooted as the anthem was played. But for some superb saves by goalkeeper Eddie Hopkinson the Italian fans would have had a victory to cheer. *Team: Hopkinson Howe Shaw Clayton Wright* Flowers Bradley (1) Broadbent Charlton (1) Haynes Holden.*

Brazil, Rio de Janeiro, 13.5.59. England lost 2-0

England's first match of a four-game summer tour was a major test against the new world champions in front of 185,000 screaming fans in the Maracana Stadium in Rio. Bobby Charlton and Johnny Haynes rapped shots against the post after England had gone 2-0 down to early goals against a Brazilian team that featured both Didi and Pele

England's favourite football son Bobby Charlton ... the power growing, the hair going.

in a rare appearance together. Blackpool's Jimmy Armfield was given a chasing he will not forget by Julinho in what was a baptism of fire for the Blackpool defender. He was called in to partner Don Howe in an out-of-club position at left-back. Norman Deeley, small, direct Wolves winger, was the fifth player to wear the number seven shirt since the departure of the one and only Tom Finney. Goalkeeper Eddie Hopkinson saved two certain goals from Pele, but could do nothing to stop a thunderbolt from Julinho, who had been picked in preference to the great Garrincha. As Eddie Hopkinson lay on the ground after being beaten all ends up by Julinho's shot, a posse of Brazilian radio commentators rushed on to the pitch to try to interview him. It is just as well that they could not translate his direct comments delivered in Lancastrian tones! England were soundly beaten by the world champions and did well to keep their score down to just two goals. Didi and Pele together was just about the most potent combination that any team in the world could put together. Ronnie Clayton clattered into Pele with a tackle that led to the king being carried off on a stretcher for treatment. He soon came back, but for the rest of the game Clayton's life was made hell by the Brazilian fans who would not forgive him for hurting their hero. Shortly before he was carried off Pele missed a sitter right in front of an open goal. He was human, after all. *Team: Hopkinson Howe Armfield Clayton Wright* Flowers Deeley Broadbent Charlton Haynes Holden.*

Peru, Lima, 17.5.59. England lost 4-1

Jimmy Greaves, nineteen-year-old idol of Chelsea, arrived on the international stage with a neatly taken second-half goal, drawing the goalkeeper off his line before slotting a left foot shot just inside a post. But it was the only bright moment in a miserable England performance. England looked unfamiliar in blue shirts and proceeded to play like passing strangers. The Peruvians, leading 2-0 at half-time, were helped to four goals by mistakes from a strangely lethargic England defence which had no answer to the thrusting left wing runs of Seminario, who helped himself to a hat-trick. In a purple patch just after half-time England had their best moments of the match, with Ron Flowers striking a shot against a post and Bobby Charlton having a shot cleared off the line. Then Greavsie combined neatly with Johnny Haynes and Charlton before shooting the first of his 44 England goals. It was a ten minute spell that petered out as man of the match Seminario completed his hat-trick. He might easily have doubled his contribution but for some excellent saves by goalkeeper Eddie Hopkinson. Greavsie said later: 'We were knackered after all the travelling in what was a crazy itinerary. I was happy to get my first goal for England, but in truth we got a good hiding. I had never heard of Seminario. But what a player.' *Team: Hopkinson Howe Armfield Clayton Wright* Flowers Deeley Greaves (1) Charlton Haynes Holden.*

Mexico, Mexico City, 24.5.59. England lost 2-1

England scored first through Derek Kevan, but were burned out within an hour of kicking off in high-altitude Mexico City. Despite officially using substitutes for the first time they were run off their feet in the last 30 minutes. Jimmy Greaves swept the ball into the net just after half-time, but the referee ruled it off-side. Moments later Mexico snatched a second goal and from then on England were on the retreat as they struggled to breathe in Mexico's thin air. Eddie Hopkinson performed wonders in the England goal, but he was often confused by the flight of the ball. Wilf McGuinness was the first player to be substituted after half an hour. He was affected by the heat and had to go to the dressing-room for an emergency intake of oxygen. Doug Holden was the next player hit by the heat, and he was replaced in the fifty-seventh minute by Warren Bradley. It was a match that Ronnie Clayton would never forget. He had been so badly burned while sunbathing that his back came up in a mass of blisters. They burst during the game, and in the dressing-room afterwards the Mexican doctor bathed the Blackburn skipper's back with menthylated spirits. It was this more than anything that finally convinced the FA that they should follow Walter Winterbottom's advice and always travel with a team doctor. It was hardly the best organised tour. Ron Flowers at one stage found himself sharing a hotel room with six complete strangers! *Team: Hopkinson Howe Armfield Clayton Wright* McGuinness (Flowers) Holden (Bradley) Greaves Kevan (1) Haynes Charlton .*

USA, Los Angeles, 28.5.59. England won 8-1

This runaway victory in Billy Wright's 105th and final match helped wipe out the memory of the 1-0 defeat by the United States in the 1950 World Cup finals. The Americans had an early goal disallowed and then took the lead, and at 1-1 at half-time the football writers were preparing head-chopping stories that were hurriedly rewritten as Bobby Charlton led a second-half goal rush with a hat-trick. The pitch, rarely used for soccer, was gravel at one end and grass at the other. England scored seven of their goals while attacking the grassy end. Charlton's first hat-trick for England included a penalty. The suspect American goalkeeper was beaten by four shots from outside the penalty area. The only forward who did not get his name on the scoresheet was one Jimmy Greaves! It was Billy Wright's farewell game. His England career had started in front of a 57,000 crowd in Belfast in 1946. The finish came in front of just 13,000 fans at Wrigley Field in Los Angeles. But what a journey he had between the two games, setting a then world record of 105 international appearances. *Team: Hopkinson Howe Armfield Clayton Wright* Flowers (2) Bradley (1) Greaves Kevan (1) Haynes (1) Charlton (3, 1 pen).*

ASTON VILLA needed to beat neighbours West Bromwich Albion on the last day of the season to be certain of staying in the First Division. They conceded a goal in the last seconds of the match when leading 1-0. Manchester City beat Leicester City 3-1, dumping Villa into the Second Division.

Albert Quixall was called 'the man worth his weight in gold' when Manchester United bought him from Sheffield Wednesday for a British record £45,000 on 18 September 1958. The blond inside-forward won the first of five England caps while completing his National Service, but had not been called into the international team since 1955.

Norwich City were again the shock side of the FA Cup. The Third Division Canaries humbled Manchester United 5-0 at Carrow Road in the third round, beat Second Division Cardiff City 3-2, and then eliminated Tottenham in a replayed fifth round tie. Goalkeeper Ken Nethercott played the last half hour of a sixth round tie against Sheffield United at Bramall Lane with a dislocated shoulder as City held on for a 1-1 draw. They won the replay 3-2 until finally falling at the semi-final hurdle to a single goal from Luton Town's Irish international winger Billy Bingham.

Joe Baker, Scottish-based English centre-forward, banged in 25 League goals for Hibernian, but it was Rangers who took over from Hearts as champions. Runners-up Hearts had the consolation of the League Cup after thumping Partick Thistle 5-1 in the final. St Mirren beat Aberdeen 3-1 to win the Scottish FA Cup final for the first time since 1926.

League champions Wolves continued to be pioneers of floodlit football. They played the first Saturday night League match under lights at Molineux on 4 October 1958, beating Manchester United 4-0.

Aldershot inside-forward Albert Mundy scored the fastest Football League goal of the fifties at Hartlepools on 25 October 1958. He had the ball in the back of the net in six seconds.

Crystal Palace goalkeeper Vic Rouse became the first Fourth Division player to win an international cap when capped by Wales against Northern Ireland at Belfast. The Irish won 4-1.

First Division: Wolves, 61pts. Runners-up: Manchester United, 55 pts.
Wolves record: P42 W28 D5 L9 F110 A49 Pts61
Representative team: Finlayson; Stuart, Harris; (from) Slater, Clamp, Wright (capt.),
Flowers; Lill, Mason (Booth), Murray, Broadbent, Deeley.
Top scorer: Murray (21).
Manager: Stan Cullis.

Second Division: Sheffield Wednesday, 62pts. Runners-up: Fulham, 60pts.
Third Division: Plymouth Argyle, 62pts. Runners-up: Hull City, 61pts.
Fourth Division: Port Vale, 64pts. Runners-up: Coventry City, 60pts.

FA Cup final: Nottingham Forest 2, Luton Town 1
Nottingham Forest: Thomson; Whare, McDonald; Whitefoot, McKinlay, Burkitt (capt.);
Dwight, Quigley, Wilson, Gray, Imlach. Scorers: Dwight, Wilson
Luton: Baynham; McNally, Hawkes; Groves, Owen (capt.), Pacey; Bingham, Brown,
Morton, Cummins, Gregory. Scorer: Pacey

Top First Division marksmen: Jimmy Greaves (Chelsea), Bobby Smith (Spurs), 32
Top Second Division marksman: Brian Clough (Middlesbrough), 42 goals
Top Third Division marksman: Jim Towers (Brentford), 32 goals
Top Fourth Division marksman: Arthur Rowley (Shrewsbury Town), 37 goals
Footballer of the Year: Syd Owen (Luton Town)
European Footballer of the Year: Alfredo di Stefano (Real Madrid)

Scottish First Division: Rangers, 50pts. Runners-up: Hearts, 48pts.
Scottish Cup final: St Mirren 3, Aberdeen 1
Scottish League Cup final: Hearts 5, Partick Thistle 1

FA Amateur Cup final: Crook Town 3, Barnet 2

European Cup final: Real Madrid 2, Stade de Reims 0 (Stuttgart)
Real Madrid: Dominguez; Marquitos, Zarraga (capt.); Santisteban, Santamaria, Ruiz;
Kopa, Mateos, Di Stefano, Rial, Gento. Scorers: Mateos, Di Stefano
Stade de Reims: Colonna; Rodzik, Giraudo; Penverne, Jonquet (capt.), Leblond; La-
martine, Bliard, Fontaine, Piantoni, Vincent

THE LEAGUE TABLES
Where they finished in 1958-59

FIRST DIVISION

		P	W	D	L	F	A	Pts
1	Wolverhampton W.	42	28	5	9	110	49	61
2	Manchester United	42	24	7	11	103	66	55
3	Arsenal	42	21	8	13	88	68	50
4	Bolton Wanderers	42	20	10	12	79	66	50
5	West Bromwich A.	42	18	13	11	88	68	49
6	West Ham United	42	21	6	15	85	70	48
7	Burnley	42	19	10	13	81	70	48
8	Blackpool	42	18	11	13	66	49	47
9	Birmingham City	42	20	6	16	84	68	46
10	Blackburn Rovers	42	17	10	15	76	70	44
11	Newcastle United	42	17	7	18	80	80	41
12	Preston North End	42	17	7	18	70	77	41
13	Nottingham Forest	42	17	6	19	71	74	40
14	Chelsea	42	18	4	20	77	98	40
15	Leeds United	42	15	9	18	57	74	39
16	Everton	42	17	4	21	71	87	38
17	Luton Town	42	12	13	17	68	71	37
18	Tottenham Hotspur	42	13	10	19	85	95	36
19	Leicester City	42	11	10	21	67	98	32
20	Manchester City	42	11	9	22	64	95	31
21	Aston Villa	42	11	8	23	58	87	30
22	Portsmouth	42	6	9	27	64	112	21

SECOND DIVISION

		P	W	D	L	F	A	Pts
1	Sheffield Weds.	42	28	6	8	106	48	62
2	Fulham	42	27	6	9	96	61	60
3	Sheffield United	42	23	7	12	82	48	53
4	Liverpool	42	24	5	13	87	62	53
5	Stoke City	42	21	7	14	72	58	49
6	Bristol Rovers	42	18	12	12	80	64	48
7	Derby County	42	20	8	14	74	71	48
8	Charlton Athletic	42	18	7	17	92	90	43
9	Cardiff City	42	18	7	17	65	65	43
10	Bristol City	42	17	7	18	74	70	41
11	Swansea Town	42	16	9	17	79	81	41
12	Brighton & Hove A.	42	15	11	16	74	90	41
13	Middlesbrough	42	15	10	17	87	71	40
14	Huddersfield Town	42	16	8	18	62	55	40
15	Sunderland	42	16	8	18	64	75	40
16	Ipswich Town	42	17	6	19	62	77	40
17	Leyton Orient	42	14	8	20	71	78	36
18	Scunthorpe United	42	12	9	21	55	84	33
19	Lincoln City	42	11	7	24	63	93	29
20	Rotherham United	42	10	9	23	42	82	29
21	Grimsby Town	42	9	10	23	62	90	28
22	Barnsley	42	10	7	25	55	91	27

THIRD DIVISION

		P	W	D	L	F	A	Pts
1	Plymouth Argyle	46	23	16	7	89	59	62
2	Hull City	46	26	9	11	90	55	61
3	Brentford	46	21	15	10	76	49	57
4	Norwich City	46	22	13	11	89	62	57
5	Colchester United	46	21	10	15	71	67	52
6	Reading	46	21	8	17	78	63	50
7	Tranmere Rovers	46	21	8	17	82	67	50
8	Southend United	46	21	8	17	85	80	50
9	Halifax Town	46	21	8	17	80	77	50
10	Bury	46	17	14	15	69	58	48
11	Bradford City	46	18	11	17	84	76	47
12	Bournemouth	46	17	12	17	69	69	46
13	Queens Park R.	46	19	8	19	74	77	46
14	Southampton	46	17	11	18	88	80	45
15	Swindon Town	46	16	13	17	59	57	45
16	Chesterfield	46	17	10	19	67	64	44
17	Newport County	46	17	9	20	69	68	43
18	Wrexham	46	14	14	18	63	77	42
19	Accrington Stanley	46	15	12	19	71	87	42
20	Mansfield Town	46	14	13	19	73	98	41
21	Stockport County	46	13	10	23	65	78	36
22	Doncaster Rovers	46	14	5	27	50	90	33
23	Notts County	46	8	13	25	55	96	29
24	Rochdale	46	8	12	26	37	79	28

FOURTH DIVISION

		P	W	D	L	F	A	Pts
1	Port Vale	46	26	12	8	110	58	64
2	Coventry City	46	24	12	10	84	47	60
3	York City	46	21	18	7	73	52	60
4	Shrewsbury Town	46	24	10	12	101	63	58
5	Exeter City	46	23	11	12	87	61	57
6	Walsall	46	21	10	15	95	64	52
7	Crystal Palace	46	20	12	14	90	71	52
8	Northampton Town	46	21	9	16	85	78	51
9	Millwall	46	20	10	16	76	69	50
10	Carlisle United	46	19	12	15	62	65	50
11	Gillingham	46	20	9	17	82	77	49
12	Torquay United	46	16	12	18	78	77	44
13	Chester	46	16	12	18	72	84	44
14	Bradford Park A.	46	18	7	21	75	77	43
15	Watford	46	16	10	20	81	79	42
16	Darlington	46	13	16	17	66	68	42
17	Workington	46	12	17	17	63	78	41
18	Crewe Alexandra	46	15	10	21	70	82	40
19	Hartlepools United	46	15	10	21	74	88	40
20	Gateshead	46	16	8	22	56	85	40
21	Oldham Athletic	46	16	4	26	59	84	36
22	Aldershot	46	14	7	25	63	97	35
23	Barrow	46	9	10	27	51	104	28
24	Southport	46	7	12	27	41	86	26

A S we come to the end of our magical carpet ride through the Footballing Fifties we bridge to the swinging 'sixties by recalling the 1959-60 European Cup final when Real and Eintracht Frankfurt conjured one of the greatest club games ever.

The footballing aristocrats of Real had dominated the European Cup since its inception in 1955. They were bidding to win the trophy for a fifth successive year when they journeyed to Glasgow for the 1960 final against Eintracht.

Hampden Park was heaving with 127,621 spectators, many of them Rangers fans still flabbergasted by the way Eintracht had blasted Rangers to defeat on an aggregate of 12-4 in the semi-finals.

They were convinced that any team capable of twice scoring six goals against their Ibrox idols could topple the old masters of Madrid.

Real were a team of soccer mercenaries, drawn from all points of the compass to give them punch and panache. It is commonplace now to have multi-national teams. Back then it was a rarity.

The forward line was under the intoxicating influence of Alfredo di Stefano, who had come from Colombia via his native Argentina and, at thirty-four, was still one of the world's premier exponents of the footballing arts.

He pulled the strings for an attack that included the whiplash left-footed shooting of the incomparable Hungarian Ferenc Puskas, the pace and dribbling skills of homegrown heroes Luis Del Sol and Paco Gento and the invention of Brazilian winger Canario.

Eurovision was a new enterprise that brought the game 'live' to an armchair audience of millions, and across Europe viewers watched in awe.

For nineteen minutes the two teams sparred, and then Richard Kress scored for Eintracht to open the floodgates – and it was goals from Real that came pouring through.

Di Stefano, gliding across the Hampden turf like a Nureyev on grass, equalised eight minutes later and by half-time di Stefano and Puskas had made it 3-1 to Real.

For thirty minutes in the second half Real produced football so majestic and so artistic that it could have been set to music. A symphony by Strauss perhaps, with a passage for Hungarian violins and another for some red-hot flamenco, plus of course traditional Argentinian tango rhythms.

By the seventieth minute it was Real 6, Eintracht 1 – and the peerless Puskas had lifted his personal tally to four goals, including a penalty.

Eintracht hit the woodwork twice before centre-forward Erwin Stein scored with a stinging shot in the seventy second minute.

Real Madrid's Famous Five, photographed in 1958: Raymond Kopa (France), Hector Rial (Argentina), Alfredo di Stefano (Argentina, via Colombia), Ferenc Puskas (Hungary), Francisco Gento (Spain).

Almost from the restart di Stefano scored Real's seventh goal, and then the alert Stein had the final word in the ten-goal extravaganza.

The breathless crowd gave both teams an ovation that lasted a full fifteen minutes after a marvellous match that has been preserved on film as evidence of how the game of football can be played at the highest level.

Puskas said later: 'Stef and I have our names on the scoresheet, but this match was a triumph for everybody on the pitch – including the Eintracht players who helped make this game a victory for football. I must also pay tribute to the spectators. Most of them were neutral but they encouraged us to keep raising the standard of our play.'

Di Stefano commented: 'I was lucky to play in many fine matches but none greater than the 1960 European Cup final. Everything we tried worked to perfection. It was an honour and a privilege to be part of it.'

For the record: Real Madrid scored 112 goals and conceded 42 in 37 European Cup matches from 1955 to 1960 during which they won all five finals. They were beaten finalists in 1962 and 1964 and won the Cup for a sixth time in 1966 when beating Partizan Belgrade 2-1 in Brussels. They had to wait until 1998 for their next triumph by which time the tournament had become the Champions' League, but no champions since have touched the Everest-high performances of the di Stefano-Puskas-Gento era back in the magical *Footballing Fifties*.

THE LEAGUE CHAMPIONSHIP
1959-60: Burnley time their run to perfection

TALK about going down to the wire! In what was a unique championship race, Burnley did not lead the table until the last Monday of the season and found themselves having to beat Manchester City at Maine Road to take the title from under the noses of hat-trick-hoping Wolves.

If they had drawn with City, Burnley would have handed the title to Wolves on goal average. But they played out of their skins to master City 2-1 and so overtake Wolves at the top of the table. Just five weeks earlier they had been slammed 6-1 by the defending champions. Now they were top for the first time and nobody could knock them off.

Burnley's first title triumph since 1921 was an advertisement for British football at its best. They were a well organised side that played the game in a purist way that contrasted greatly with the long-ball tactics of Wolves, who for a third successive season reached a century of League goals.

It was in the midfield engine room where Burnley found the key to the championship. In tandem partners Jimmy Adamson and Jimmy McIlroy they had the perfect balance between poetry and motion.

Northern Ireland international McIlroy was the poet, steering the Burnley attack with passes that could not have been placed more accurately had he carried them to his teammates on a silver salver. Alongside him in midfield Adamson was the main motivator, inspiring those around him with his energy, enthusiasm and driving power.

Together, Adamson and McIlroy set up the chances that were eagerly taken by England's thrusting right winger John Connelly (20 goals), crash-bang centre-forward Ray Pointer (19 goals) and plundering inside-forward Jimmy Robson (18 goals). Jet-paced left winger Brian Pilkington (9 goals) and schemer McIlroy (6 goals) were also prominent marksmen in what was a true team effort. Pilkington knew he had to play flat out because waiting in the wings to steal his number eleven shirt was the promising Gordon Harris.

Burnley were smooth as well as solid in defence, with goalkeeper Adam Blacklaw always safe and reliable. There were not better full-back partners in the League than the solid John Angus and the elegant Alex Elder, and Tommy Cummings and Brian Miller were uncompromising yet fair at the heart of the defence.

They all took their cue from manager Harry Potts, a long-time Turf Moor stalwart who had been brought up in the claret and blue traditions of playing the game on the ground and with brains as well as brawn. His final instructions to the team as they went out were always the same: 'Play football and enjoy your game.'

THE 1959-60 FA CUP FINAL
Wee Deeley the hero as the jinx sinks Rovers

WHAT a load of rubbish took on new meaning when Wolves won the FA Cup as consolation for just missing out on the League and Cup double and also a hat-trick of titles. As the players went up the thirty-nine Wembley steps to collect their medals they were pelted with rubbish by furious Blackburn supporters incensed by what they had witnessed.

They considered that two of the goals scored by Wolves in their 3-0 victory should have been disallowed, and they also thought that the tackling by the men in old gold shirts had bordered on the brutal. One innocent collision with two-goal Wolves hero Norman Deeley left Blackburn left-back Dave Whelan with a broken leg just before half-time, and Rovers had to battle on with ten men as the Wembley injury jinx struck again (Whelan's career was virtually finished by the injury, and he decided to stay on the periphery of the game by selling sports goods ... a business he developed into JJB Sports, and he later liked Wigan Athletic so much that he bought the club).

The match-marring injury happened just after Wolves had taken a fortunate lead when defender Mick McGrath turned the ball into his own net. Little Norman Deeley, short in inches but with a giant heart, kept running the overstretched Blackburn defence into panic stations and was rewarded for his Herculean effort with two second-half goals. He later revealed that he too had been injured in the collision with Whelan but was determined to carry on despite a huge bruise on his shin.

Both Deeley goals were disputed by Blackburn, who played the off-side game in such a negative way that it helped ruin the match as a spectacle. Kevin Howley, thirty-five and making history as the youngest referee to handle a Wembley Cup final, was hugely criticised. He disallowed Wolves goals by Ron Flowers and Jim Murray and had fans of both sides arguing about his decisions.

All in all, it was a shocker of a final and ended on the sour note of Blackburn supporters throwing orange peel, programmes and cartons at the Wolves players and the referee. It was the first time there had been such bad-tempered behaviour at a Wembley final.

On paper, Blackburn had the players to sparkle: an all-star forward line in Bimpson, Dobing, Dougan, Douglas and MacLeod, and the midfield probing of Clayton. But on the pitch they just did not function, and this was even before the Whelan crisis.

It later became obvious there was a poor team spirit in the Blackburn dressing-room. Controversial centre-forward Derek Dougan, who would light up the 'sixties with his goals and personality, revealed he had posted a transfer demand on his way to the ground. He was soon 'on his bike' to Aston Villa. Ironically, his best playing days lay ahead of him at Molineux with Wolves.

Two of the outstanding players of the Footballing Fifties come together in a painful meeting at Wembley as Wolves goalkeeper Malcolm Finlayson dives across Blackburn Rovers ball master Bryan Douglas. The 1960 FA Cup final was one of severe physical contact and precious few moments of skill. Such a game today would be greeted with a forest of red cards.

A MAN TO REMEMBER
Walter Winterbottom's world of football

IT is impossible to paint an accurate picture of the *Footballing Fifties* without positioning prominently in the foreground the donnish figure of Walter Winterbottom. He was appointed the first England team-manager in 1946 and held the post until handing over to Alf Ramsey in 1962. Yet he was almost a stranger to the general public, and could walk down the street with few people recognising him. Have a good look at the picture on the right. Would you have picked him out in an identity parade?

Throughout the 1950s he put his faith at the feet of Billy Wright, the man he picked as skipper in 90 games and made football's first 100-cap international. Billy was an extension to Walter out on the pitch, carrying his orders and encouraging his team-mates to put into practise all the things that the England manager preached.

Winterbottom and Wright were about as alike as grass and granite. Billy, though quietly intelligent, was hardly an academic after leaving school at fourteen, and he would have worked in an iron foundry if it had not been for football. Walter, educated at Oldham Grammar School and then Chester College, combined a teaching job with playing football as an amateur for Royston and Mossley. In 1934 he signed professional for Manchester United, a playing career cut short by a spinal injury.

He became a college lecturer, and then, on the outbreak of the war, Walter qualified as a wing commander in the RAF and was seconded to the Air Ministry where he was appointed Head of Physical Training. He resumed his playing career as a guest for Chelsea and was twice called up as an England reserve for wartime international matches, understudying master centre-half Stan Cullis.

Walter had arranged to return to teaching after the war when he got a call from FA secretary Sir Stanley Rous inviting him to take over as the supremo of English football, responsible for the development of the game at all levels. He was just 33.

In the first half of his sixteen year reign as England's first full-time manager Walter was given access to arguably the greatest English footballers of all time. As well as Billy Wright, the names of the prominent players of that era echo like a roll call of footballing gods: Stanley Matthews, Tom Finney, Tommy Lawton, Raich Carter, Len Shackleton, Wilf Mannion, Nat Lofthouse, Stan Mortensen, Jackie Milburn, Frank Swift, and a poised and purposeful right-back called Alf Ramsey.

With players of that quality to call on, England should have cemented their traditionally held reputation as the masters of world football. It is an indictment of the overall system rather than Winterbottom's management that even with all this talent on tap English international football went into a decline.

A scientist? A schoolteacher? Laurence Olivier in character? No, this is Walter Winterbottom, who was England international football manager throughout the fifties yet little known to the general public.

Despite the stature of his job, the bespectacled, scholarly-looking Winterbottom managed to keep a low public profile. The only time he used to make it into the headlines was when the football writers lined up like a firing squad after any defeat. It was a standing joke in Fleet Street that the sports desks of the newspapers had *'Winterbottom Must Go'* headlines set up for every match.

Some of the old pros took a cynical view of his coaching. Once he chalked on a blackboard how he wanted his five forwards to move in unison down the field and then to shoot from the edge of the penalty area. Len Shackleton casually raised a hand and asked: 'In which corner of the net would you like us to put the ball?'

Walter's influence on post-war English football, particularly throughout the 'fifties, was greater than almost anybody's. It was as a coach that he made his most telling contribution, combining the role of England manager with that of the FA's Director of Coaching. In fact it was made clear to him right from the off that he was the FA coach first and England manager second. The forward-looking Sir Stanley Rous said: 'Most of the FA councillors did not want a national team manager, but I persuaded them to, rather reluctantly, appoint one. They gave Walter the responsibility, but saw to it that they retained the power. Anybody assessing what Walter achieved for English football must think of him first and foremost as a coach and an organiser *extraordinaire.*'

Winterbottom was the 'Father' of English coaching. He set up a nationwide network of FA coaching schools, and among his many disciples were outstanding coaches such as Alf Ramsey, Ron Greenwood, Bill Nicholson, Bobby Robson, Dave Sexton, Malcolm Allison, Don Howe and a young bearded Fulham forward called Jimmy Hill.

Sir Stanley, who later became the all-powerful President of the world-governing body, FIFA, had been impressed by Winterbottom when they met on an experimental coaching course that the visionary Rous had set up in 1937. They formed a strong alliance that had wide-ranging impact on post-war English football.

Winterbottom, knighted for his services to sport in his 1970s role as chairman of the Central Council for Physical Recreation, was handcuffed throughout his sixteen-year reign as England manager by amateur selectors. 'When I first took the job,' he told me, 'each selector would arrive at our meetings with his personal list of who should play. We used to discuss and discuss until we were down to, say, two goalkeepers and then a straight vote would decide. Then on to the next position, and so on through the team. Before they made their final decision I would be asked to leave the room while they deliberated. I would be called back in and told the line-up. It was asking almost the impossible to get the right blend with this way of selecting. At least in the later years I was able to present my team and then let them try to argue me out of it.'

Winterbottom, a deeply sincere and honest man, had the full respect of most of his players, despite a habit of being long-winded with his instructions. English football has rarely had a more faithful and loyal servant.

ENGLAND FOOTBALL DIARY
Summary of their 1959-60 matches

Wales, Ninian Park, 17.10.59. Drew 1-1

For the first time in 71 matches, England kicked off without the indomitable Billy Wright leading them out. Brian Clough at long last got the England chance his stack of goals with Middlesbrough deserved. Into the team with him from the England Under-23 squad came Tony Allen, John Connelly, Cloughie's clubmate Eddie Holliday and, taking the place of Wright, Birmingham centre-half Trevor Smith. It was a mix that did not work, and it was a first-half Jimmy Greaves goal that saved England from defeat against a Welsh team operating without either of the Charles brothers. The unfortunate Smith spent much of his debut limping with a calf muscle injury in what were pre-substitute days, and he could not prevent twenty-year-old Graham Moore from scoring a late equaliser for Wales. Driving wind and incessant rain made conditions intolerable, and Cloughie later described it as 'one of the most frustrating games of my life.' Jack Kelsey, the exceptional Arsenal goalkeeper, made a series of magnificent saves in a weather-wrecked game that rarely rose above the mediocre. Bobby Charlton, for England, and Phil Woosnam, for Wales, occasionally brightened the gloom with flashes of brilliance, but it was a match that would be quickly erased from the memory. *Team: Hopkinson Howe Allen Clayton* Smith Flowers Connelly Greaves (1) Clough Charlton Holliday*

Sweden, Wembley, 28.10.59. England lost 3-2

An unchanged team was given a second chance, but a defeat by Sweden signalled the end of the international road for Hopkinson, Smith and Cloughie. They carried the can for a poor performance that brought rare jeers from England supporters. The Swedes, World Cup runners-up to Brazil when host nation in 1958, played a smooth, walkabout game punctuated with sudden changes of pace that had England's defenders exposed to the perils of panic. It all started promisingly for England when John Connelly put the finishing touch to a swift five-man movement, but this was one of the few memorable moments from England for the 72,000 Wembley spectators. The Swedes rattled the England woodwork twice in the first-half as warning signs of what was to follow. Within 15 minutes of the second-half Sweden were 2-1 in the lead as they tore the England defence apart, and man-of-the-match Agne Simonsson made it 3-1 in the seventy-fifth minute. The skilful Swedish centre-forward made such an impression that the next day he was signed by Real Madrid. Jimmy Greaves cleverly created an opening for Bobby Charlton to make it 3-2, but there were plenty of witnesses to the fact that England had been flattened by the Swedes and flattered by the scoreline. It might easily have been a repeat of the six-goal drubbing received from Hungary six years earlier. The 'dream team' pairing of Greaves and Clough rarely got out of nightmare territory. Both were instinctive predators, and continually found themselves being drawn to the same place. There was room for only one of them, and it was Greaves who survived. It was short-sighted by the selectors, who surely should have given these two natural goal scorers more time to grow accustomed to each other's pace. Cloughie was thrown on the scrapheap, and it left him embittered that he was never given another chance. At one stage he had the embarrassment of falling and sitting on the ball close to the Swedish goal-line. 'It was as if I was trying to hatch the bloody thing,' Cloughie said later. *Team: Hopkinson Howe Allen Clayton* Smith Flowers Connelly (1) Greaves Clough Charlton (1) Holliday*

Northern Ireland, Wembley, 18.11.59. England won 2-1

Joe Baker, the Englishman from Hibernian with the broad Scottish accent, and Bolton's Ray Parry were two of nine new caps tried in three matches. Baker gave England the lead with a brilliantly worked goal which was equalized with three minutes to go by Billy Bingham. The match was into its final seconds when Parry snatched the winner. West Ham centre-half Ken Brown gave a solid performance in the middle of the England defence, but was quickly dumped as the selectors continued their hunt for a successor to Billy Wright. Ron Springett marked his impressive first game in the England goal with a first-half save from a Jimmy McIlroy penalty. It was Baker's debut performance that took the eye. He exhibited speed and strength to go with good skills on the ground, and his non-stop probing gave the Northern Ireland defence a thorough testing. It was fitting that it was Baker who set up Parry's late winner which England just about deserved against a gallant Irish team in which Danny Blanchflower and Jimmy McIlroy were a class double act in midfield. *Team: Springett Howe Allen Clayton* Brown Flowers Connelly Haynes Baker (1) Parry (1) Holliday*

Scotland, Hampden Park, 19.4.60. Drew 1-1

Tottenham brought the club-or-country issue to boiling point by refusing to release their three Scots, Dave Mackay, Bill Brown and John White, for this match. The referee awarded fifty-five free-kicks and three penalties, two of which were missed. Bobby Charlton converted from the penalty spot, and failed to find the net with a second twice-taken penalty. Graham Leggat, partnered by Ian St John and Denis Law, scored

Scotland's goal following a suicidal back pass from Bill Slater. This gave Scotland a half-time lead over England for the first time since the war, but Charlton's successful second-half penalty meant they had now gone since 1937 without beating the auld enemy on home territory. Ray Wilson, starting his distinguished England career at left-back, played on despite collecting a broken nose in the second minute, and Joe Baker battled on with a dislocated shoulder. Surely somebody would one day see the sense for substitutes, even if only for injured players? Walter Winterbottom agreed. 'There is an easy case to be made out for using substitutes,' the England team manager said. 'Even if it is only to replace an injured player this surely has to make more sense than a team having its balance thrown completely. You only have to study the evidence of what has happened in recent FA Cup finals to realise that an injury can wreck a game as a spectacle for the paying public.' For all this sensible talk, it would still be another five years before substitutes would at last be introduced by the stubborn authorities. *Team: Springett Armfield Wilson Clayton* Slater Flowers Connelly Broadbent Baker Parry Charlton (1, pen)*

Yugoslavia, Wembley, 11.5.60. Drew 3-3

England were trailing 3-2 with 90 seconds to go when Joe Baker crashed the ball against the bar, and Johnny Haynes swept in the rebound. Straight from the kick-off an England attack ended with Baker again heading against the bar but this time there was nobody able to turn the ball back into the goal. An England victory would have been an injustice to a Yugoslavian side that played some excellent football, with two-goal Galic continually turning the defence inside out. England led 2-1 after forty-eight minutes following neatly taken goals either side of half-time by Bryan Douglas and Jimmy Greaves after the Yugoslavs had taken a thirtieth minute lead. It was a tough debut for the latest candidate for the No. 5 shirt, Peter Swan of Sheffield Wednesday. He replaced Bill Slater, who heard that he was dropped just a few minutes before being told that he had been elected 'Footballer of the Year'. Swan was stranded as Yugoslavia equalised on the hour, and a clever back heel by Galic gave Kostic the chance to make it 3-2 with 10 minutes to go. This set up the dramatic climax to one of the most exciting international matches witnessed at Wembley. The emergence of the tall, commanding Swan promised to give England stablity at the heart of the defence for the first time since the retirement of Billy Wright. How tragic that a career so promising would be wrecked by the gambling scandal that rocked English football in 1963. Swan, along with gifted England team-mate Tony Kay, were among the players kicked out of football for their involvement in a throwing-matches-for-money betting sensation. *Team: Springett Armfield Wilson Clayton* Swan Flowers Douglas (1) Haynes (1) Baker Greaves (1) Charlton*

England team-mates Bobby Robson and Johnny Haynes reveal England's secret weapon during a 1958 training session: the wheelbarrow technique. Perhaps it was team manager Walter Winterbottom's version of push-and-run.

Spain, Madrid, 15.5.60. England lost 3-0

Johnny Haynes took over from the dropped Ronnie Clayton as captain. The rain in Spain was mainly on the pitch and England got bogged down in a midfield that was a mass of mud. Alfredo di Stefano played a reluctant part in the Spanish victory. He wanted to save himself for Real Madrid's European Cup final date with Eintracht Frankfurt at Hampden Park four days later. Alfredo had a long-running argument on the touchline with the Spanish coaches as he begged to come off, but he was persuaded to play on and help Martinez clinch victory with two goals in the last ten minutes. Di Stefano and his colleagues Gento and del Sol then flew off to Glasgow to join the Real team that conjured one of the great performances of all time in their 7-3 victory over Eintracht. With Jimmy Armfield playing magnificently to control Gento, England gave as good as they got for the first hour, but one of the youngest teams ever picked by Walter Winterbottom and the selectors ran out of steam in the heavy conditions. Spain bossed the last third of the game, and tantalised and teased England with their keep-ball tactics before striking forward to snatch two goals in the last ten minutes. For Haynes it was the first of a run of twenty-two games as captain There was a big reward coming his way within a year when Fulham made him England's first £100-a-week footballer following the long overdue lifting of the maximum wage. Players who had been 'soccer slaves' throughout the 'fifties were suddenly set free. Sadly it was too late for many of the great players who had lit up the decade with their skill and endeavour. *Team: Springett Armfield Wilson Robson Swan Flowers Brabrook Haynes* Baker Greaves Charlton*

Hungary, Budapest, 22.5.60. England lost 2-0

England missed a sackful of goals because of feeble finishing, but the approach play was an encouraging sign of things to come. They might easily have had the ball in the Hungarian net at least three times in the first-half, but the chances were wasted. Florian Albert, Hungary's new eighteen-year-old centre-forward discovery, scored both goals in the second-half. Dennis Viollet, Manchester United's quick and clever inside-forward, won the first of two caps. With better luck, he might have marked his debut with two goals. It was England's third and final close-season tour match and though they came home without a victory there was a feeling of optimism that better things were round the corner. It's interesting to note that just two of this team were in the side at Wembley Stadium in 1966 on the historic July 30 day when England won the World Cup. Bobby Charlton and Ray Wilson collected winners' medals, while Ron Springett, Jimmy Armfield and Ron Flowers were non-players in Alf Ramsey's 22-man squad. *Team: Springett Armfield Wilson Robson Swan Flowers Douglas Haynes* Baker Viollet Charlton*

FACTS, STATS AND TRIVIA
The winners and losers of 1959-60

TOM FINNEY retired at the end of the 1959-60 season after twenty-four years with Preston, 472 matches and 76 England caps. He played his last match for Preston against Luton Town on 30 April 1960, but in 1963-64 made the briefest of comebacks with Irish club Distillery. He helped them to a 3-3 draw in their European Cup home tie against Benfica, but declined to travel for the return, which Distillery lost 5-0!

The Soviet Union won the first ever European Nations' Cup final when they beat Yugoslavia 2-1 after extra-time in Paris on 10 July 1960. The tournament had kicked off in 1958! The four home countries deigned not to take part.

Jock Stein started his career as a manager at Dunfermline in March, with the club stranded way at the bottom of the table. Amazingly, they won their first six matches under Jock's direction and stayed up. The Jock Stein legend was under way.

Cliff Holton, ex-Arsenal centre-forward, scored hat-tricks on consecutive days for Watford in their Fourth Division Easter matches against Chester and Gateshead. He netted a club record 48 goals for Watford in 1959-60.

Blackburn Rovers beat Blackpool 1-0 in the final Christmas Day League match on 25 December 1959. Blackpool won the Boxing Day return 1-0 at Bloomfield Road. The last full Christmas Day programme was in 1957.

European champions Real Madrid became the first winners of the World Club Championship, beating South American champions Penarol of Uruguay 5-1 on aggregate. All the goals were scored in the second leg in Spain.

Motherwell's Ian St John scored a hurricane hat-trick in two and a half minutes against Hibernian in a Scottish League Cup tie on 15 August 1959. He would join Liverpool in May 1961 for an Anfield record transfer fee of £37,500.

Gerry Baker, younger brother of Joe, scored ten goals in St Mirren's 15-0 slaughter of Glasgow University in the first round of the Scottish Cup on 30 January 1960.

Tottenham were held to a 2-2 draw in a fourth round Cup tie at Fourth Division Crewe on 30 January 1960, and won the replay four days later at White Hart Lane 13-2.

1959-60 WHO WON WHAT
All the champions and runners-up

First Division: Burnley, 55pts. Runners-up: Wolves, 54 pts.
Burnley record: P42 W24 D7 L11 F85 A61 Pts55
Representative team: Blacklaw; Angus, Elder; Adamson (capt.), Seith (Cummings), Miller; Connelly, McIlroy, Pointer, Robson, Pilkington.
Top scorer: Connelly (20). Manager: Harry Potts.

Second Division: Aston Villa, 59pts. Runners-up: Cardiff City, 58pts.
Third Division: Southampton, 61pts. Runners-up: Norwich City, 59pts.
Fourth Division: Walsall, 65pts. Runners-up: Notts County, 60pts.

FA Cup final: Wolverhampton Wanderers 3, Blackburn Rovers 0
Wolves: Finlayson; Showell, Harris; Clamp, Slater (capt.) Flowers; Deeley, Stobart, Murray, Broadbent, Horne. Scorers: McGrath (o.g.), Deeley (2)
Blackburn: Leyland; Bray, Whelan; Clayton (capt.), Woods, McGrath; Bimpson, Dobing, Dougan, Douglas, MacLeod.

Top First Division marksmen: Dennis Viollet (Manchester United), 32
Footballer of the Year: Bill Slater (Wolves)
European Footballer of the Year: Luis Suarez (Barcelona)

Scottish First Division: Hearts, 54pts. Runners-up: Kilmarnock, 50pts.
Scottish Cup final: Rangers 2, Kilmarnock 0

FA Amateur Cup final: Hendon 2, Kingstonian 1

European Cup final: Real Madrid 7, Eintracht Frankfurt 3 (Hampden Park)
Real Madrid: Dominguez; Marquitos, Pachin; Vidal, Santamaria, Zarraga (capt.); Canario, Del Sol, Di Stefano, Puskas, Gento. Scorers: Di Stefano (3), Puskas (4)
Eintracht Frankfurt: Loy, Lutz, Hoefer; Weilbacher (capt.), Eigenbrodt, Stinka; Kress, Lindner, Stein, Pfaff, Meier. Scorers: Kress, Stein (2)
Fairs Cup final: Barcelona beat Birmingham 4-1 on aggregate
World Club championship: Real Madrid beat Penarol 5-1 on aggregate

European Nations' Cup final: USSR 2, Yugoslavia 1 (aet, Paris, attendance: 17,966)
USSR: Yashin, Chokheli, Krutikov; Voinov, Maslyonkin, Netto (capt.); Metreveli, Ivanov, Ponedelnik, Bubukin, Meshki. Scorers: Metreveli, Ponedelnik
Yugoslavia: Vidinic; Durkovic, Jusufi; Zanetic, Miladinovic, Perusic; Sekularac, Jerkovic, Galic, Matus, Kostic. Scorer: Netto (o.g.)
Third place: Czechoslovakia 2, France 0

THE LEAGUE TABLES
Where they finished in 1959-60

FIRST DIVISION

		P	W	D	L	F	A	Pts
1	Burnley	42	24	7	11	85	61	55
2	Wolverhampton W.	42	24	6	12	106	67	54
3	Tottenham Hotspur	42	21	11	10	86	50	53
4	West Bromwich A.	42	19	11	12	83	57	49
5	Sheffield Weds.	42	19	11	12	80	59	49
6	Bolton Wanderers	42	20	8	14	59	51	48
7	Manchester United	42	19	7	16	102	80	45
8	Newcastle United	42	18	8	16	82	78	44
9	Preston North End	42	16	12	14	79	76	44
10	Fulham	42	17	10	15	73	80	44
11	Blackpool	42	15	10	17	59	71	40
12	Leicester City	42	13	13	16	66	75	39
13	Arsenal	42	15	9	18	68	80	39
14	West Ham United	42	16	6	20	75	91	38
15	Everton	42	13	11	18	73	78	37
16	Manchester City	42	17	3	22	78	84	37
17	Blackburn Rovers	42	16	5	21	60	70	37
18	Chelsea	42	14	9	19	76	91	37
19	Birmingham City	42	13	10	19	63	80	36
20	Nottingham Forest	42	13	9	20	50	74	35
21	Leeds United	42	12	10	20	65	92	34
22	Luton Town	42	9	12	21	50	73	30

SECOND DIVISION

		P	W	D	L	F	A	Pts
1	Aston Villa	42	25	9	8	89	43	59
2	Cardiff City	42	23	12	7	90	62	58
3	Liverpool	42	20	10	12	90	66	50
4	Sheffield United	42	19	12	11	68	51	50
5	Middlesbrough	42	19	10	13	90	64	48
6	Huddersfield Town	42	19	9	14	73	52	47
7	Charlton Athletic	42	17	13	12	90	87	47
8	Rotherham United	42	17	13	12	61	60	47
9	Bristol Rovers	42	18	11	13	72	78	47
10	Leyton Orient	42	15	14	13	76	61	44
11	Ipswich Town	42	19	6	17	78	68	44
12	Swansea Town	42	15	10	17	82	84	40
13	Lincoln City	42	16	7	19	75	78	39
14	Brighton & Hove A.	42	13	12	17	67	76	38
15	Scunthorpe United	42	13	10	19	57	71	36
16	Sunderland	42	12	12	18	52	65	36
17	Stoke City	42	14	7	21	66	83	35
18	Derby County	42	14	7	21	61	77	35
19	Plymouth Argyle	42	13	9	20	61	89	35
20	Portsmouth	42	10	12	20	59	77	32
21	Hull City	42	10	10	22	48	76	30
22	Bristol City	42	11	5	26	60	97	27

THIRD DIVISION

		P	W	D	L	F	A	Pts
1	Southampton	46	26	9	11	106	75	61
2	Norwich City	46	24	11	11	82	54	59
3	Shrewsbury Town	46	18	16	12	97	75	52
4	Grimsby Town	46	18	16	12	87	70	52
5	Coventry City	46	21	10	15	78	63	52
6	Brentford	46	21	9	16	78	61	51
7	Bury	46	21	9	16	64	51	51
8	Queens Park R.	46	18	13	15	73	54	49
9	Colchester United	46	18	11	17	83	74	47
10	Bournemouth	46	17	13	16	72	72	47
11	Reading	46	18	10	18	84	77	46
12	Southend United	46	19	8	19	76	74	46
13	Newport County	46	20	6	20	80	79	46
14	Port Vale	46	19	8	19	80	79	46
15	Halifax Town	46	18	10	18	70	72	46
16	Swindon Town	46	19	8	19	69	78	46
17	Barnsley	46	15	14	17	65	66	44
18	Chesterfield	46	18	7	21	71	84	43
19	Bradford City	46	15	12	19	66	74	42
20	Tranmere Rovers	46	14	13	19	72	75	41
21	York City	46	13	12	21	57	73	38
22	Mansfield Town	46	15	6	25	81	112	36
23	Wrexham	46	14	8	24	68	101	36
24	Accrington Stanley	46	11	5	30	57	123	27

FOURTH DIVISION

		P	W	D	L	F	A	Pts
1	Walsall	46	28	9	9	102	60	65
2	Notts County	46	26	8	12	107	69	60
3	Torquay United	46	26	8	12	84	58	60
4	Watford	46	24	9	13	92	67	57
5	Millwall	46	18	17	11	84	61	53
6	Northampton Town	46	22	9	15	85	63	53
7	Gillingham	46	21	10	15	74	69	52
8	Crystal Palace	46	19	12	15	84	64	50
9	Exeter City	46	19	11	16	80	70	49
10	Stockport County	46	19	11	16	58	54	49
11	Bradford Park A.	46	17	15	14	70	68	49
12	Rochdale	46	18	10	18	65	60	46
13	Aldershot	46	18	9	19	77	74	45
14	Crewe Alexandra	46	18	9	19	79	88	45
15	Darlington	46	17	9	20	63	73	43
16	Workington	46	14	14	18	68	60	42
17	Doncaster Rovers	46	16	10	20	69	76	42
18	Barrow	46	15	11	20	77	87	41
19	Carlisle United	46	15	11	20	51	66	41
20	Chester	46	14	12	20	59	77	40
21	Southport	46	10	14	22	48	92	34
22	Gateshead	46	12	9	25	58	86	33
23	Oldham Athletic	46	8	12	26	41	83	28
24	Hartlepools United	46	10	7	29	59	109	27

COME back with me to New Year's eve, 31 December 1959, to be reunited with the main characters in the cast of thousands who made the 'fifties one of the most exciting and memorable in the history of British football. This is what they were doing as the curtain fell on the decade ... and with a potted history of what each of them went on to achieve.

JIMMY ADAMSON was midway through the season in which he led Burnley to the Football League championship. Within three years he would turn down the England manager's job. Footballer of the Year in 1962, he coached and managed Burnley, and later Dutch side Sparta, Sunderland and Leeds, but without ever making the same successful impact he had as a player. It remains a mystery how this cultured, upright skilful midfield player never managed to catch the eye of the England selectors.

IVOR ALLCHURCH took his League goals haul to 46 in 143 games for Newcastle before returning to Wales in 1962 with Cardiff. He then moved back to his first club Swansea where he lifted his goals record to 164 in 445 games. Awarded the MBE in 1966, he later played for Worcester City, had a spell as player-manager of Haverford West and was still playing at 50 with Pontardawe Athletic. Ivor died on 10 July 1997 aged sixty-seven. There's a statue in his honour outside Swansea's Liberty Stadium.

RONNIE ALLEN lifted his goals collection with West Bromwich Albion to 234 in 458 games before winding down his playing career with Crystal Palace (1961-64). Steered Wolves back to the First Division as manager in 1967 and then became a globe-trotter with Athletic Bilbao, Sporting Club of Portugal, then to Walsall, West Brom again, Saudi Arabia, Panathinaikos and finally back to West Brom in 1981-82. Ronnie died on 9 June 2001 aged seventy-two.

MALCOLM ALLISON was coming to terms with his playing days being ended by tuberculosis. He started a coaching/managerial career with Bath City and then followed a path littered with success, failure, fame and controversy that took in Plymouth Argyle (1964-65), Man City (1965-73), Crystal Palace (1973-76), Galatasaray (1976-77), Plymouth Argyle (1978-79), Man City (1979-80), Crystal Palace (1980-81), Sporting Club of Portugal (1981-82), Middlesbrough (1982-84) and Bristol Rovers (1992-93). He was never ever less than entertaining in all his posts, with his days at Maine Road with Joe Mercer his most successful. In the new Millennium, 'Big Mal' hit difficult times with drink-related problems. He will always be fondly remembered as one of football's most flamboyant characters, a candid TV pundit and a coach with few peers.

JIMMY ARMFIELD was on the verge of being voted Young Footballer of the Year at Blackpool, the club for which he played until his retirement in 1971. Voted the 'best right-back' in the world after the 1962 World Cup finals in Chile. Won 43 caps, 15 as captain. He managed Bolton and then Leeds, guiding them to the 1975 European Cup final. Later became a consultant to the FA and persuaded them to make Terry Venables England manager. Awarded the OBE, he wrote extensively for the *Daily Express* and became a regular pundit and co-commentator on BBC Five Live.

JOHN ATYEO took his goals record with Bristol City to 351 in 647 appearances before retiring in 1966 to concentrate full-time on his teaching career. He eventually became a headmaster. John died on 8 June 1993, aged 61. There is a John Atyeo stand at Ashton Gate in his memory.

EDDIE BAILY wound down his playing career with Orient, and then became Bill Nicholson's right-hand man at Tottenham where he had been the pass master of the push-and-run team. Continued to hold trenchant views on the way the game should be played ('Keep it simple and play the ball to feet') in his retirement years.

GORDON BANKS was the last line of defence for Leicester after joining them from Chesterfield in 1959. He became the goalkeeping hero of England's 1966 World Cup winning team and will be forever remembered for 'the save of the century' against Pele in the 1970 finals. Moved to Stoke when Leicester found a successor in Peter Shilton. Kept 35 clean sheets in 73 England games before losing the sight of an eye in a 1972 car smash. Played in the USA for two seasons and was voted Most Valuable Goalkeeper. Managed Telford United before switching to the corporate-marketing world.

BILLY BINGHAM had spells with Everton and Port Vale after his FA Cup adventure with Luton. He then had a long and eventful career in management with Southport, Linfield, Plymouth, Everton and Mansfield between international posts with Greece and, most memorably, Northern Ireland (1967-71 and 1980-94). Guided Northern Ireland to the quarter-finals of the 1982 World Cup.

DANNY BLANCHFLOWER was about to take over as Tottenham skipper and led them to the historic League and Cup double in 1960-61. Twice Footballer of the Year, he became an outspoken columnist with the *Sunday Express* after a knee injury forced his retirement in 1964. Had brief unsuccessful management experience with Northern Ireland (1978) and Chelsea (1978-79). Danny suffered Alzheimer's Disease and died on 9 December 1993 aged 67.

JOHN BOND helped West Ham win the FA Cup in 1965 before playing for Torquay. Then had a colourful management career with Bournemouth, Norwich City , Manchester City, Burnley, Swansea, Birmingham City and Swansea in between high-profile work as a television pundit. Even into his seventies he was helping out as a scout and consultant to Wigan Athletic.

Gordon Banks from the author's scrapbook, fresh faced right at the start of his career with Chesterfield. He was to develop into one of the world's greatest goalkeepers.

RON BURGESS was poised to switch to Watford manager after three years in charge at Swansea. The captain of the famous Spurs push-and-run team died on 14 February 2007 aged 87. Many of a certain age consider him the greatest player ever to pull on a Spurs shirt, and when managing he discovered the likes of Cliff Jones, Terry Medwin and all-time great goalkeeper Pat Jennings.

MATT BUSBY was busy laying the foundations to the Man United side that would win the European Cup in 1968. He lived long enough to see his fellow-Scot Alex Ferguson steer Man United to their first Premiership title in 1993. Knighted in 1968, Sir Matt died on 20 January 1994 aged 84.

ROGER BYRNE was one of the victims of the Munich air disaster on 6 February 1958 and tragically never got to see the new decade.

NOEL CANTWELL was drawing the interest of Man United after steering West Ham to the First Division as captain. He skippered the FA Cup-winning Man United team in 1963, switching four years later to management with Coventry and then Peterborough. He later coached with success in the United States before returning to Peterborough as manager and then a publican. Noel was capped 36 times by Eire, and scored 14 goals as a makeshift centre-forward. He died on 8 September 2005 aged 72.

RAICH CARTER managed Mansfield and then Middlesbrough (1963-66) after his surprise departure from Leeds United in 1958. Rated by his contemporaries the finest inside-forward of the thirties and forties, 'Silver Fox' Raich died on 9 October 1994 aged 81. There is a road in Hull and a sports centre in Sunderland named after him, and his name will live on in football folklore..

JOHN CHARLES was the toast of Italian football where he was wowing them with his goals and entertaining them with his bass voice, making several hit records. He briefly rejoined Leeds from Juventus before playing for Roma, Cardiff, Hereford and Merthyr Tydfil. In 1997 he was voted Italy's greatest foreign footballer ever, ahead of the likes of Maradona, Zidane and Platini. Big John died on 21 February 2004 aged 72. There is a John Charles stand at Elland Road.

BOBBY CHARLTON was the player around whom Matt Busby was building his great side of the 'sixties. He remains top England marksman with 49 goals in what was then a record 106 England games, and he still holds the Man United League goals (199) and appearances record (606). Knighted for his services to football, Sir Bobby flirted with player-management at Preston before concentrating on a successful business career in holiday travel and youth coaching. He remains a red-blooded Man United director.

RONNIE CLAYTON was poised to lead Blackburn Rovers to the FA Cup final. He captained England five times in his 35 appearances and played for Blackburn from 1951 to 1969. He became an all-knowing tour conductor at the Ewood Park ground where he is still a great local hero.

BRIAN CLOUGH was banging in goals right left and centre with Middlesbrough before joining Sunderland, where his career was tragically ended by a knee injury at the age of 28. He then became a household name as a manager with Hartlepools, Derby County, briefly Brighton, even more briefly Leeds and, gloriously, Nottingham Forest. There was no more popular or outspoken pundit on television. He suffered drink-related problems later in life and died on 20 September 2004 aged 69. After his OBE, he nicknamed himself Old Big 'Ead. We will not see his like again.

EDDIE COLMAN was one of the Busby Babes tragically killed in the Munich air disaster on 6 February 1958 and did not live to see the 'sixites.

STAN CULLIS was hoping for Wolves to clinch a hat-trick of First Division titles and the League and Cup double. He was disgracefully booted out by Wolves in 1964. A year later he became Birmingham manager, but his heart never left Molineux where there is a stand named after him. Stan died on 28 February 2001 aged 84.

TED DRAKE was coming to the close of his eventful reign as Chelsea manager. He later became reserve team manager and chief scout at Fulham and then a director of the Craven Cottage club. Spent a lot of time on the golf course and watching the Hampshire cricket team for which he played before the war. Ted died on 30 May 1995 aged 82.

JOHN DICK was enjoying a goal-gorged partnership with West Ham left winger Malcolm Musgrove (they were nicknamed 'Dick and the Duchess' after a popular TV comedy show). He took his lethal left foot to Brentford in 1963 before returning to Upton Park to coach the juniors. John died in 2000 aged 69.

JIMMY DICKINSON was on his way to taking his appearances record at Portsmouth to 845 games. 'Gentleman Jim' hung up his boots in 1965 after 48 England caps and continued to serve his beloved Portsmouth in various roles, finally as manager in 1977. Pompey's favourite son died on 8 November 1982 in Alton, Hampshire, aged 57.

TOMMY DOCHERTY was soon to leave Arsenal to start a headline-hitting managerial career with Chelsea after four games as player-coach. He then famously had 'more clubs than Jack Nicklaus': Rotherham, QPR (twice), Aston Villa, FC Porto, Hull City, Scotland team manager, Man United, Derby, Sydney Olympic (twice), Preston, South Melbourne, Wolves and Altrincham. Made the front pages when sacked by Man United for running off with the club physiotherapist's wife Mary Brown. They became happily married and eventually The Doc settled down to a life of celebrity as a radio pundit and an after-dinner speaker with a routine better than most stand-up comedians.

BRYAN DOUGLAS was in the middle of the season in which he helped to steer Blackburn to the FA Cup final after switching from traditional winger to scheming inside-forward. Scored 100 goals in 438 League games for Rovers before in 1969 gently winding down with non-League Great Harwood. Later became a sales representative before retiring in Blackburn where, like Ronnie Clayton, he remains an idol.

George Eastham, a rebel without a pause, leads Arsenal out at Highbury.

GEORGE EASTHAM had just refused to sign a new contract with Newcastle as he launched a one man war against the 'soccer slave' retain-and-transfer system. He won a High Court battle against Newcastle, claiming unfair restraint of trade. While all this was going on he joined Arsenal and became club captain under Billy Wright. Played 19 times for England and helped Stoke City win their first ever trophy, scoring the winning goal in the 1972 League Cup final at Wembley. Briefly managed Stoke in 1977-78 before emigrating to South Africa. He more than any other player triggered the revolution that forced the League bosses to kick out the maximum wage restrictions.

DUNCAN EDWARDS died at the age of 21 three weeks after being hauled from the wreckage of the Man United charter plane that crashed at Munich on 6 February 1958. English football had lost a player who many good judges considered potentially one of the all-time greats.

GEORGE FARM was winding down his goalkeeping career as player-manager of Queen of the South before becoming full-time manager He was later in charge at Raith Rovers, Dunfermline Athletic and Raith Rovers (twice). When he left football in 1974 he worked in local radio and also had a spell as a lighthouse keeper. George died on 18 July 2004, aged 80.

MALCOLM FINLAYSON was working as a representative for a steel company while playing in goal for a Wolves side just pipped for a hat-trick of League titles. On his retirement in 1963 he concentrated full time on the steel business and became one of the wealthiest of all ex-fifties footballers. Now retired, he gives much of his time to looking after his collection of classic E-Type and Aston Martin sports cars. He is a season ticket holder at Molineux.

TOM FINNEY was continuing to work in his electrical and plumbing business as he prepared to retire from football. Most 1950s pros would select him even ahead of Stanley Matthews as England's finest footballer of the decade. Belatedly knighted in 1998. He had a statue raised to him outside the National Football Museum, and he is the revered club president of Preston.

EDDIE FIRMANI was at the peak of his playing career at Sampdoria before returning to Charlton in 1963. He later played for Southend and then went back to Charlton as manager. In 1974 he moved to North America to boss Tampa Bay, New York Cosmos, Montreal Manic and the New York Metrostars. He then moved to Kuwait as a coach, managed to get himself imprisoned by the Iraqis for three months and on his release returned to Canada as general manager of Supra de Montreal. His son, John, became a lawyer and then a distinguished judge in the United States.

CHARLIE FLEMING became a globe-trotting manager and coach after finishing his playing days with non-League Bath . He worked in the USA, Canada and Australia before returning to Scotland and coaching schoolboys. Charlie died in 1997 aged 70.

RON FLOWERS was a key man in the Wolves team following the retirement of Billy Wright, and he was an FA Cup winner in 1960. Winning 40 of his 48 England caps in successive matches, he played for England in the 1962 World Cup finals in Chile and was a non-playing member of Alf Ramsey's 1966 squad. Six of his ten goals for England came from the penalty spot, including two in the 1962 World Cup finals. After a brief spell as player-manager of Northampton Town, he finished his career with non-League Wellington while building up a highly successful sports shop business.

TREVOR FORD wound down his playing career with Newport and then Romford after serving a suspension from the Football League following an investigation into illegal payments while at Sunderland. Rated the second greatest Welsh centre-forward after John Charles (who idolised him), he played in Holland with PSV Eindhoven until allowed back into the League. He later went into the car trade, fronting garages in Cardiff, Swansea and Sunderland. Trevor died on 28 May 2003 aged 79.

BILL FOULKES was helping to shore up the Man United defence after surviving the Munich air disaster, and was, fittingly, a member of the United team that won the European Cup at Wembley in 1968. He coached the United youth team for five years before travelling the world as a coach in the United States, Norway and Japan and then returning to Manchester, specialising in showing Japanese tourists around Old Trafford.

NEIL FRANKLIN came into the 'sixites regretting having joined the outlawed Colombian League. Arguably England's greatest ever centre-half, he had to serve a ban on his return to England and then played for Hull, Crewe and Stockport. He had some success as manager of Apoel in Cyprus and then came back into the English game as boss at Colchester. Disillusioned, he moved out of football and ran a pub called the Dog and Doublet in Sandon, Staffordshire. Neil died on 9 February 1996 aged 74.

RON GREENWOOD was coaching at Arsenal before taking over from Ted Fenton as West Ham manager in 1961. He was a tactical genius who helped turn Moore, Hurst and Peters into world beaters. Following Don Revie as England manager, he steered the team to the 1982 World Cup finals where they were eliminated without losing a game. Ron died on 8 February 2006 aged 84.

HARRY GREGG was a hero figure in Manchester after surviving the Munich air crash and continually going back into the wreckage to pull other passengers clear. A succession of football injuries prevented the Northern Ireland international winning any major medals with United, yet he was considered one of their all-time great goalkeepers and kept 48 clean sheets. He later played for Stoke before travelling the managerial roundabout with Shrewsbury, Swansea, Crewe and Carlisle. During the Dave Sexton reign at Old Trafford he was invited back as goalkeeper coach before teaming up with Lou Macari as assistant manager at Swindon.

JIMMY GREAVES was kicking himself for having agreed to join AC Milan in the defence-dominated Italian League. He would return to England with Tottenham and resume his barrage attack on goalkeepers. Later, he played for West Ham and then Brentwood, Chelmsford and Barnet while tackling and beating a drink problem. In tandem with Ian St John, he would become one of the nation's television favourites. He is now a much in-demand speaker on the after-dinner circuit.

JOHNNY HANCOCKS went into non-League football with Wellington Town as player-manager and then in 1960 joined Cambridge United. He was fleetingly with Oswestry Town before having the final shots of his career at the football outpost of GKN Sankeys. After hanging up his schoolboy-size boots, he worked at an ironworks in his hometown of Oakengates. He was one of the unlucky ones who never got to play with the maximum wage lifted. Johnny died on 19 February 1994 aged 74.

JOE HARVEY had started a managerial career with Barrow and then Workington, but when the job at Newcastle became vacant he lost out to Charlie Mitten. He finally got his wish to manage the Magpies in 1962, and led them back to the First Division and lifted the Fairs Cup (now the Uefa Cup) in 1969. He was forced out of the club after a run of bad results in 1974-75, but later got involved again in a scouting capacity while running a newsagent's business. Joe died in February 1989 aged 70.

JOHNNY HAYNES was on the verge of famously becoming British football's first £100-a-week player and continued to play for Fulham through the 'sixties. He reluctantly had two weeks in the manager's chair in 1968, but then went back to what he liked doing best, playing the game. Fulham turned down a 'name your price' offer from Milan and Spurs and Arsenal were always lusting after a player who could pass the ball like Beckham, but with *both* feet. He played with Johnny Byrne for Durban City in 1970 and lived in South Africa for fifteen years while building up a chain of betting shops that he sold to the Tote in 1976. He came home to live in Scotland among the 'auld enemy' against whom he led England to a 9-3 defeat at Wembley in 1961. John died the day after suffering a brain haemorrhage while at the wheel of his car driving through his adopted home town of Edinburgh on 17 October 2005, his 70th birthday.

JIMMY HILL was leading the PFA fight to get the maximum wage lifted. He then became an exceptional manager at Coventry before starting a 30-year career as an outspoken TV personality. He has owned clubs, been chairman at Fulham and has done just about everything in football including once running the line in a League game! There will never be another quite like the multi-tasking Mr Hill!

CLIFF HOLTON was surprisingly sold by Watford to Northampton where he continued to bang in the sort of goals that had made him a huge hero at Vicarage Road. He later played for Crystal Palace, Watford again, Orient and Charlton before leaving football to concentrate on an engineering job. Cliff died on 4 June 1996 aged 67.

DON HOWE was taking his service with West Brom to twelve years before moving to Highbury to play for his old England skipper Billy Wright. A broken leg against Blackpool virtually ended his career, and he developed as the coaching brains behind a succession of bright teams including Arsenal's double-winning side of 1970-71.

HARRY JOHNSTON was in the middle of a seven-season spell as manager at Reading before returning to his first-love club Blackpool as chief scout. The whole of Blackpool went into mourning when Harry died on 12 October 1973 aged just 54.

JACK KELSEY was still No 1 goalie for Arsenal and Wales, but a back injury hurried his retirement in 1962 after becoming a Highbury legend with 327 League appearances. He became Arsenal commercial manager. Jack died on 18 March 1992 aged 62.

DEREK KEVAN was on his way to 157 goals in 262 League games with West Brom before going on a have-boots-will travel journey with Chelsea, Man City, Crystal Palace, Peterborough, Luton, Stockport and then on the non-League circuit with Macclesfield, Boston, Stourbridge and Ancell's FC. Famous for always taking out his false teeth before going out on to the pitch, Derek had the poetic middle name Tennyson. Many defenders remember him as the most awkward forward they ever faced.

DENIS LAW, like Jimmy Greaves, was regretting taking the Italian job with Torino. He would soon be back in English football and building his legend with Manchester United before finishing with his old club Manchester City. Following his retirement in in 1973 he concentrated on outside business interests, keeping in touch with football as a pundit on radio and television. He won a well-publicised battle with cancer.

TOMMY LAWTON was something of a lost soul going into the 'sixties when his playing and then managing career ended. He hit hard times, and Everton staged a testimonial for him in 1972 and the *Nottingham Evening Post* gave him a weekly column. All his heading of the old leather ball had taken its toll and he had a long period of ill health. Tommy, arguably the greatest player ever to pull on the No 9 England shirt, died on 6 November 1996 aged 77.

BILLY LIDDELL was preparing himself for his final shots with Liverpool, for whom he scored 216 goals in 494 League games despite losing his peak years to the war. He became a Justice of the Peace and served as bursar at Liverpool University. Like so many of his generation who had headed the ball too many times, he became affected by Alzheimer's. Billy died on 3 July 2001 aged 79. *A note on the footballs of the 'fifties: They weighed exactly the same as today's balls at kick-off, but they were not water resistant and often weighed twice as much on muddy days.*

NAT LOFTHOUSE was about to retire after thumping footballs and goalkeepers into the net on behalf of his beloved Bolton, and after hanging up his boots he continued to serve the club in a variety of roles, including as manager before becoming life president of Wanderers.

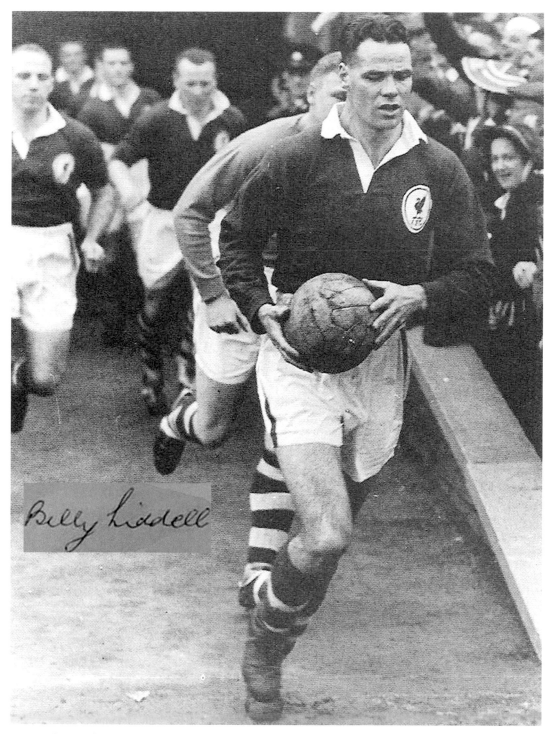

From the author's scrapbook, an autographed photograph of Billy Liddell, the flying Scot who turned Liverpool into Liddellpool.

JIMMY LOGIE wound down his playing career with Gravesend and Northfleet in 1960 after 68 goals in 296 League games for Arsenal. He missed out on the big-earning days with the lifting of the maximum wage and to make ends meet sold newspapers in Piccadilly Circus. Jimmy, who admitted to gambling problems, was rated second only to Alex James in the procession of great Scots who moved south to play for the Arsenal. The most he earned at Highbury was £17 a week, and he moved into non-League football in the season that the maximum wage was raised to £20 and a year before the lid on earnings was lifted completely. Jimmy died in April 1984 aged 64.

JIMMY McILROY was midway through the season in which his precise passes helped make Burnley League champions. Later played for and coached Stoke and then flirted with management at Oldham and Bolton before retiring to write about the game he had played so beautifully. There is a stand at Turf Moor named after him, and many good judges rate him the finest footballer ever to pull on the claret and blue shirt.

DAVE MACKAY was winding himself up for a major role in Tottenham's historic League and Cup double in 1960-61. He later drove Derby back up to the First Division, and managed at Swindon, Nottingham Forest, Derby County (lifting the League championship), Walsall and then at Doncaster and Birmingham City after a lucrative nine years in Kuwait. As good a player as ever came south o' the border.

ALF McMICHAEL was coming to the end of his 13-years service to Newcastle and left in 1962 to become manager of South Shields and later his hometown club Bangor. He ended his working days at Belfast's Harland and Wolffe shipyard. In 2004 he reluctantly put up for sale all the mementoes of his successful days at Newcastle when he was rated one of the great full-backs. Alf died on 7 January 2006 aged 78.

PETER McPARLAND was taking his final shots with Aston Villa (98 goals in 293 League games) before single season duty at Wolves and Plymouth and then a period with Atlanta Chiefs in the North American League. After managing the Cyprus national team, he returned home to Ireland as player boss of Glentoran. Later he established a property business in Bournemouth, travelling the world to visit one son in Australia and another in Japan. Peter has a park in Great Newry named after him to mark the impact he made on the 1957 FA Cup and the 1958 World Cup finals.

WILF MANNION is a sad example of what happened to the fabulous stars of the 'forties and 'fifties who played through the 'soccer slave' days. After struggling with management at Cambridge United and failing as a publican, one of the finest footballers of his generation was reduced to a series of mundane jobs. 'Golden Boy' Wilf had few skills apart from being able to make a football sit up and talk, and he finished up bankrupt and working on a car assembly line. Forced to sell his England caps to feed his family, he was given a long overdue testimonial by Middlesbrough in the 1980s. Wilf died close to penniless on 14 April 2000 aged 81 What a way to treat a hero.

STANLEY MATTHEWS was poised for a return to Stoke City where he added a new chapter to his legend by playing in the First Division at the age of 50. The first footballer knighted in 1965, he had an unhappy time as general manager of Port Vale when an illegal payments scandal threw a shadow over the club. He travelled the world as a football ambassador and coach and spent a long period in Malta before returning home to find himself still hero worshipped. February 1 (the Maestro's birthday) is Stanley Matthews Day in Stoke when people are encouraged to go to work and school wearing football shirts to raise money for the charitable Stanley Matthews Foundation. There is a statue in his memory outside Stoke City's Britannia Stadium and also in his birthplace of Hanley. The original King of football died on 23 February 2000 aged 85.

JOE MERCER was not enjoying the best of times as manager of Aston Villa, and the stress of the job led to him having a stroke. On his recovery the Villa directors sacked him and in 1964 he left football in disillusioned mood. But the game was in his blood and he was tempted back as manager of Manchester City in 1965. He appointed Malcolm Allison as his coach and together they steered City through golden years of success. In 1972, after falling out with Big Mal, he moved on to Coventry City and also took over as England manager in a caretaker capacity between the sacking of Alf Ramsey and the appointment of Don Revie. Football's favourite uncle served as a Coventry director up to his retirement in 1981 when he started being affected by Alzheimer's. Joe died on 9 August 1990 aged 76.

GIL MERRICK was on the brink of accepting the job of manager of Birmingham City for whom he had handled with care in more than 700 games. He had four years in the Blues hot seat but had only the newly introduced League Cup to show for all his effort, but boosted by the fact that Birmingham beat neighbours Aston Villa in the 1963 two-leg final. After leaving St Andrews he became a non-League manager with Bromsgrove Rovers and Atherstone United before working in Solihull with finance company S&U.

JACKIE MILBURN was managing Yiewsley before a nightmare season in charge of Ipswich Town as successor to Portman Road legend Alf Ramsey. He was far too nice to cut it as a manager, and became a North East football writer with the *News of the World*. His image as a hero on Tyneside never diminished and there is a stand and two statues in memory of 'Wor Jackie.' He died from cancer on 9 October 1988 aged 64.

BOBBY MITCHELL was coming to the end of his wing wandering days with Newcastle and was about to take over as player-manager at Gateshead. One of the great left wingers, 'Bobby Dazzler' later ran two pubs in Newcastle and used to regale customers with tales of the days when he, Bobby Cowell and Jackie Milburn were the only players to collect three FA Cup winners medals with Newcastle during the 'fifties. Bobby died in 1993 aged 68.

STAN MORTENSEN was about to make a brief comeback with Lancaster City after retiring in May 1959 while with Bath. He became involved in politics as a Tory councillor and had business interests that he shelved while enjoying a spell as Blackpool manager (1967-69). He continued to be idolised at Bloomfield Road after leaving football to go back to the business world. A stand at the ground bears his name and there is a statue in his memory. Morty died on 22 May 1991 aged 69. It was said by one cynic on the day that he was buried: 'I suppose they'll call this the Matthews funeral.'

JACKIE MUDIE was soon to move on to Stoke along with Stanley Matthews after scoring 144 League goals for Blackpool. He and Stanley helped steer Stoke to the First Division, and paired up again at Port Vale where Jackie was player-manager and Stanley general manager. He later travelled the lower leagues as a coach at Oswestry, Crewe, Northwich and Eastwood Town. Jackie died of cancer on 2 March 1992 aged 61.

JIMMY MULLEN took his goals haul for Wolves to 112 before hanging up his boots in 1959 as a loyal one-club man with 20 years service at Molineux. Geordie Jimmy, a groundstaff boy at Wolves the same time as Billy Wright, ran a sports shop in Wolverhampton until his sudden death in October 1987 aged 64.

BILL NICHOLSON was building his great Tottenham double side, and he continued to serve Spurs with such distinction that the club named a road after him (Bill Nicholson Way is part of the official Tottenham address). He spent a year in the mid-70s with West Ham in a consultancy role, but was recalled to Spurs to give the benefit of his experience to a succession of managers. He was made club president in 1991, and goes down in football history as one of the all-time great managers and tacticians. Bill died on 23 October 2004 aged 85.

SYD OWEN became Luton Town manager after winning the Footballer of the Year award in his final season as a player. In 1961 he joined Don Revie at Leeds where he became a respected coach. He later had spells with Birmingham City and Hull before coaching the youth squad at Old Trafford. Syd died in January 1999 aged 76.

BOB PAISLEY was a member of the Bill Shankly 'Boot Room' team at Anfield, little suspecting that in 1974 he would succeed the legendary Shanks. He became even more successful than his mentor, winning 13 major competitions in nine seasons, including six League championships and the European Cup three times. He is remembered at Anfield with the Paisley Gates complimenting the Shankly Gates. Yet another footballing old-timer who was affected by Alzheimer's. Bob died on 14 February 1996 aged 77.

BILL PERRY was struggling with a knee injury that eventually cost him his place in the Blackpool team. He played with Southport and Hereford and spent a short time in Australia before finally hanging up his boots. Bill set up a business in Blackpool selling washing machines and vacuum cleaners, and then started a successful printing business before settling to a comfortable retirement in his adopted hometown of Blackpool.

ALBERT QUIXALL was establishing himself at Manchester United with whom he would collect an FA Cup winners' medal in 1963. He later played for Oldham, Stockport County and Altrincham. After retiring Albert went into the scrap metal business.

ALF RAMSEY was building his reputation as an outstanding manager with Ipswich, and after lifting the Second and First Division championships in back-to-back seasons he took over as England manager. Knighted after guiding England to the World Cup in 1966, Sir Alf was uncerimoniously sacked after failing to qualify for the 1974 World Cup finals. He retired after running Birmingham City in a caretaker capacity and giving technical advice to Greek club Panathinaikos. There have been few in the history of British football to match his tactical genius. He has a statue and a road named after him in Ipswich. Another of the old-timers affected by Alzheimer's, Sir Alf died on 28 April 1999 aged 79.

DON REVIE was about to be appointed player-manager at Leeds at the start of an adventurous career in management. He made Leeds one of the most feared and famous teams in the land during the 1960s and early 1970s before taking over from Alf Ramsey as England manager. He became the centre of controversy when he walked out on England in 1977 to take a hugely lucrative job in the United Arab Emirates. Don later managed Al Nasr and Al Ahly in Egypt before returning home to fight the FA in court after they had suspended him on a charge of bringing the game into disrepute. He won his case but not before being accused in court of being consumed by greed. In 1987 he revealed he was suffering from motor neurone disease. It was only in these tragic circumstances that he was given the credit he deserved as being one of the greatest of all club managers. The old kop at Elland Road was named after him. Don died on 26 May 1989 aged 61.

GEORGE ROBLEDO was winding down his playing career with Club Deportivo in his native Chile, and in later years kept involved with football as youth coach in Vina Del Mar. George, who will always be remembered for his goal-scoring feats with Newcastle United, died following a heart attack on 1 April 1989 aged 62.

BOBBY ROBSON was into his third season with West Brom between two periods with Fulham. After playing for Vancouver Royals he started his managerial career with Fulham in 1968. It was the beginning of an adventure that took him to Ipswich, PSV Eindhoven (twice), Sporting Club in Portugal, Porto, Barcelona and then, his dream job, manager of Newcastle United. In between he squeezed in an eventful eight years as manager of England, guiding them to the World Cup quarter-finals in 1986 and to the semi-finals in 1990. After he made a tearful departure from Newcastle in 2004 the 'Grandfather' of managers was appointed consultant to the Irish international team. Knighted in 2002, he has continually battled and beaten cancer. He remains an idol at Ipswich where he has a statue and also the position of honorary club president.

ARTHUR ROWE was preparing to return to football as manager of Crystal Palace after recovering from the illness that forced his retirement at Tottenham. He had two years in charge at Selhurt Park before ill health again made him retire from the game. He had a brief stand-in period at Crystal Palace in 1966 and then kept on the periphery as consultant for the short-lived London Football Hall of Fame. Gentleman Arthur, the master of push-and-run, died in November 1993 aged 86.

ARTHUR ROWLEY was continuing to score goals galore with Shrewsbury for a final career total of 434 goals in 619 League matches, a record unlikely ever to be approached let alone beaten. He later managed Shrewsbury, Sheffield United and Southend, and then went into non-League football with Telford United and Oswestry Town. Arthur died on 19 December 2002 aged 76. His older brother Jack, a scoring sensation with Man United, died on 28 June 1998 aged 77.

JIMMY SCOULAR was about to become player-manager of Bradford Park Avenue after his exploits with Portsmouth and Newcastle United. He later managed Cardiff City and Newport County. One of the hardest tacklers ever to step foot on a pitch, he scouted for Aston Villa and Wolves while involved in first the jewellery business and then the chemical industry. Jimmy died in 1998 aged 72.

MAURICE SETTERS was on the point of joining Manchester United as they rebuilt after Munich. He became a dynamo in their midfield and played a key role in the 1963 FA Cup final success. He played for Stoke, Coventry and Charlton and managed Doncaster before teaming up with Jack Charlton, first at Sheffield Wednesday and then as his right hand man during the glory days with the Eire international team.

JACKIE SEWELL had recently moved from Aston Villa to Hull, for whom he played 44 League games. In 1960 he went to Rhodesia for a three months coaching job and stayed there for 13 years! He coached in Zambia and what was then the Belgian Congo before returning to England and taking a job as a car salesman in Nottingham.

LEN SHACKLETON had been retired from football for three years and getting accustomed to a new life as a journalist, first with the *Daily Express* and then with the *Sunday People*. The most he had ever earned from the game was £17 a week, this for the most entertaining player of his generation. There is a Len Shackleton memorial at the Horsfall Stadium in his hometown of Bradford. Len, who retired to Grange-over-Sands, Cumbria, died on 27 November 2000 aged 78. They threw away the mould after the creation of the one and only Clown Prince of Football.

BILL SHANKLY was into his first season as Liverpool manager and about to start a Red revolution. It was a massive shock when he announced his retirement in the summer of 1974. It was Shanks who laid the foundation to everything that Bob Paisley achieved in succession to him, and he will always remain a giant in Anfield football folklore. Bill died on 28 September 1981 aged 68.

Arthur Rowley, who scored more League goals (434) than any other footballer in history.

ALF SHERWOOD was in the middle of his last season in League football with Newport County. He then went to the United States to first of all play for and then coach a team called New York Americans. The legendary full-back, capped 42 times by Wales, later settled back home in Cardiff where he first made his name as a club footballer. Alf died in March 1989 aged 68.

RONNIE SIMPSON was poised to leave Newcastle to join Hibs before becoming a goalkeeping legend at Celtic. He was one of the Lisbon Lions who became the first British team to lift the European Cup in 1967. He briefly managed Hamilton Academical after retiring from playing, and later served on the pools panel. Joker Ronnie once shared a cab with Gordon Banks in Liverpool, and the taxi-driver, recognising Gordon, said, 'You are the greatest goalkeeper I've ever seen.' 'Thanks very much,' said Ronnie, and then indicating Gordon: 'This feller wasn't bad either.' Ronnie died on 19 April 2004 aged 73.

BILL SLATER was midway through the season in which he captained Wolves to victory in the 1960 FA Cup final, celebrating also being named Footballer of the Year. He carried on for three more years before quitting as a part-time player to give all his attention to lecturing at first Liverpool and then Birmingham universities. He became President of the British Gymnastics Association, and his daughter, Barbara, was a top gymnast before becoming a respected BBCtv producer.

BOBBY SMITH was about to help Spurs win the League and FA Cup double as their main marksman. He then formed a winning partnership with Jimmy Greaves for club and country before finishing his career with Brighton. Bobby later became a painter and decorator and occasional after-dinner speaker. A double hip operation slowed him down as he entered his 70s.

BOB STOKOE started his managerial adventure with Bury at the beginning of the sixties and travelled the roundabout with Charlton, Rochdale, Carlisle (three times), Blackpool (twice), Bury (again), Rochdale and most memorably with Sunderland. It was at Sunderland where he entered the land of legend, leading them to a 1973 FA Cup final victory from the Second Division over the then mighty Leeds. A statue capturing his famous victory run towards goalkeeper Jim Montgomery at the final whistle stands at the Stadium of Light in memory of his finest hour. Sunderland and Newcastle fans (remembering his playing days at St James') were united in their grief when he died on 1 February 2004 aged 73.

ERNIE TAYLOR was playing for Sunderland as he wound down an eventful career, holding his passing out parade with non-league clubs Altrincham and Derry before a spell Down Under in New Zealand. He made a huge contribution to the footballing 'fifties, playing in FA Cup finals with Blackpool, Newcastle and Manchester United. Ernie died in April 1985 aged 59.

TOMMY TAYLOR was a victim of the Munich air disaster on 6 February 1958 and did not live to see the 'sixties. He scored 16 goals in 19 England appearances.

BERT TRAUTMANN was on his way to taking his appearances for Man City to 564 League games. When he left City in 1964 he played a few games for Wellington Town and then became general manager of Stockport County for the 1965-66 season. He then managed in Germany for two years before being sent on a tour of Africa as a football ambassador for the German FA. He retired with his second wife to Valencia where a foundation was set up in his name to foster British-German relationships through football. His work was rewarded with the OBE in 2004.

DENNIS VIOLLET was midway through the season in which he scored a club record 32 League goals for Man United in 36 games. He moved to Stoke in 1962 and won a Second Division championship medal before playing for a season with Balitmore Bays in the USA. On his return to the UK he played for Witton Albion and then as player-manager at Linfield, leading them to the Irish Cup in 1970. After coaching at Preston and Crewe he went back to the United States where he had considerable success coaching three clubs before settling down in his adopted hometown of Jacksonville, Florida. Dennis died of cancer on 6 March 1999 aged 65. The Viollet Cup is played for annually between the Universities of North Florida and Jacksonville in his memory.

CHARLIE WAYMAN was coming to terms with his career just having been prematurely finished by a recurring knee injury while with Darlington. He turned to coaching with Evenwood Town before landing what many would consider the dream job of sales manager for the Scottish and Newcastle Brewery. Even though standing only 5ft 6in, he was probably the greatest centre-forward never capped by England and unlucky to be at his peak at the same time as giants of the game in Tommy Lawton, Nat Lofthouse, Stan Mortensen, Jackie Milburn and Tommy Taylor. As well as his power on the ball, Charlie also had superb close control and had a favourite trick of flicking the ball over the centre-half and running round him to shoot on the volley, the sort of skill Pele revealed in the 1958 World Cup final. Spectators warmed to him because he always played with a smile on his face, but he could never get the selectors to share their enthusiasm. Charlie died on 26 February 2006 aged 85.

LEN WHITE was coming up for his final season with Newcastle before moving on to Huddersfield and then Stockport. Len was unfortunate to have to live in the shadow of a Tyneside legend in Jackie Milburn. He had to move across the forward line to win his place, with 'Wor Jackie' guaranteed the No 9 shirt. For several seasons his goals output kept pace with that of Milburn's and he contributed 142 goals in 244 League appearances for the Magpies. There are players around today with dozens of caps to their name who were nowhere near the class of Wayman and White, two forgotten men of England. Len died of cancer in June 1994 aged 70.

RAY WILSON was poised to win the first of his 63 England caps. He got 30 while defending for Huddersfield, and the rest after moving to Everton in 1964. The peak of his career came in 1966 when he was left-back in the England team that became World Cup winners. A knee injury hurried his retirement after he had briefly played for Oldham and Bradford City. He eventually moved full-time into his father-in-law's funeral director's business. He retired in 1997 to live quietly in Halifax after belatedy receiving an MBE for the part he played in making England world champions.

BERT WILLIAMS came into the 'sixties with a new life ahead of him after retiring in 1959 with 420 matches with Wolves and twenty-four England caps behind him. 'The Cat' became a highly respected goalkeeping coach while running a sports shop in his hometown Bilston. He realised there was a call for sporting facilities away from the professional clubs and opened a sports centre in the town, with his goalkeeping school as the main attraction. His pupils could not have been in better hands.

WALTER WINTERBOTTOM was making plans for England's 1962 World Cup challenge, his fourth tilt at the title. When England were knocked out by eventual champions Brazil in the quarter-finals he resigned to make way for his successor Alf Ramsey. There was a move to make him FA Secretary in place of Sir Stanley Rous, who had become Fifa President. But he was blocked following a lot of politcal in-fighting and lost out to Denis Follows. Walter left the FA after sixteen years for an executive role with the Central Council of Physical Education, and it was his work with that organisation that earned him a knighthood. Walter died on 16 February 2002 aged 89.

RAY WOOD played one more game for United after surviving the Munich air distaster. He was in goal for 207 League games for Huddersfield before playing in Toronto and then with Bradford City and Barnsley. Ray became a globe-trotting manager and coach, working in the USA, Ireland, Zambia, Canada, Greece, Kenya, Kuwait, UAE and Cyprus. Ray died on 7 July 2002 aged 71 in Bexhill-on-Sea, East Sussex.

BILLY WRIGHT was working with the Football Association and heir apparent to Walter Winterbottom when he got an offer he could not refuse to manage Arsenal. He was never comfortable in the Highbury hot seat and was sacked in 1966, just before the World Cup finals. Many expected him to return to Wolves in some capacity, but instead he accepted a job as a sports television executive with ATV (now Central Television). He became a high-powered force in the television industry where the pressures of his job drove him to drink. He beat a battle with the bottle and became a popular figure back at Molineux as a club director and enjoying a wonderful marriage to Joy of the Beverley Sisters. There is a Billy Wright statue and a stand in his memory. Billy died of cancer on 3 September 1994.

The curtain comes down. Now for the verdict as to who were the greatest of the players in the Footballing Fifties.

BOOKS

THE GREAT FOOTBALLING FIFTIES POLL

We asked visitors to the www.footballingfifties.co.uk website and readers of The Judge column in The Sun *to vote for their favourite footballers and teams from that dramatic decade. We close this journey back into the days when the beautiful game was in black and white with the poll results. We do not pretend that this is a definitive view of football in the fifties but it's interesting to see which players, teams and managers have remained monumental in the memory or have made the biggest impact on the consciousness of those too young to have been there.*

THE GREAT FOOTBALLING FIFTIES POLL
The Top 10 goalkeepers

These, in order of votes received, were the ten top-rated goalkeepers of the *Footballing Fifties* .... with the summary of each player as it appears on the website to guide voters.

1. BERT TRAUTMANN Manchester City. The ex-German Prisoner-of-War became the master of the Maine Road goalmouth, and many old-time City supporters will tell you that he was an even better goalkeeper than the legend he replaced, Frank Swift**.**

2. JACK KELSEY Arsenal. Played in goal for Wales in 41 internationals, and considered by many good judges to have been Arsenal's greatest ever goalkeeper — even ahead of David Seaman. Key man in the Welsh team that reached the 1958 World Cup quarter-finals.

3. BERT WILLIAMS Wolves. 'The Cat' wins his place in this top ten a fingertip ahead of the man who took over from him on the Wolves goal-line, **Malcolm Finlayson**. A greatly respected coach, Bert won 24 England caps and played more than 400 League and Cup games for the Molineux club.

4. GORDON BANKS Leicester City. Established himself in the Leicester City defence in the late 'fifties after starting his career with Chesterfield. England's last line of defence in the 1966 World Cup, but remember you are judging him as a young 1950s 'keeper.

5. HARRY GREGG Manchester United. Played 210 League games for United after taking over from England international Ray Wood in 1957. Won hero status in Manchester after surviving the Munich air disaster and then going back into the wreckage to rescue other passengers.

6. TED DITCHBURN Tottenham Hotspur. The last line of defence in the famous push-and-run Spurs that won back to back Second and First Division titles at the start of the 'fifties. His England caps were restricted to six because of the powerful presence of Frank Swift.

7. GIL MERRICK Birmingham City. Unlucky to be hit by the Hungarian hurricane, conceding 13 goals in two matches against the Magical Magyars. He let in 45 goals in 23 England internationals, and played in more than 500 League and Cup games for Birmingham City before becoming their manager.

8. GEORGE FARM Blackpool. Commanding goalkeeper throughout Blackpool's FA Cup exploits of the 1950s. Capped ten times by Scotland, he played more than 500 League and Cup matches for Blackpool after joining them from Hibernian reserves.

9. EDDIE HOPKINSON Bolton. Won 14 England caps, and played more than 500 League games for Bolton as a solid goalkeeper with great reflexes. Collected an FA Cup winners' medal against Man United at Wembley in 1958.

10. **SAM BARTRAM** Charlton Athletic. Played in the shadow of Frank Swift, who does not make this shortlist because he retired in 1949. Sam was agile and a great character who bossed his area with authority and, often, humour.

THE GREAT FOOTBALLING FIFTIES POLL
The Top 10 full backs

These, in order of votes received, were the ten top-rated full-backs of the *Footballing Fifties* .... with the summary of each player as it appears on the website to guide voters.

1. ROGER BYRNE Manchester United. Was established as England's regular No 3 at the time of the Munich air crash in which he lost his life. Captained the Busby Babes, and showed skill to go with the speed that he developed when starting his career as a left winger.

2. ALF RAMSEY Tottenham. He was 'The General' of the famous push-and-run Spurs team and was always looking to organise the defence. He made up for a slowness on the turn with a solid tackle, and he always used the ball with intelligence. Capped 32 times by England, and skipper three times.

3. JIMMY ARMFIELD Blackpool. A fast, thinking man's right-back who was one of the pioneers of overlapping runs. Motivated by starting his career playing behind Stanley Matthews, he won 43 England caps and was the regular skipper before the emergence of Bobby Moore.

4. RAY WILSON Huddersfield. He was hugely influenced by manager Bill Shankly before having his peak years with Everton. England's untouchable left-back in the 1966 World Cup winning team on his way to collecting 63 caps.

5. BILL ECKERSLEY Blackburn Rovers. Played 17 times for England, with Alf Ramsey as his regular full-back partner. He had a thundering tackle and collected spectacular goals with powerful left foot shots. Played 406 League games for Rovers and scored 20 goals.

6. NOEL CANTWELL West Ham. One of the outstanding left-backs of his generation. Led West Ham to the First Division as captain in 1957-58 before switching to Old Trafford and skippering the 1963 FA Cup-winning Man United side.

7. ALF McMICHAEL Newcastle. He was a key member of the outstanding Northern Ireland team of the fifties and many considered him the finest left-back in the Football League. He played more than 500 League and Cup matches for the Magpies.

8. ALF SHERWOOD Cardiff City and Newport County. He was known as the 'king of the sliding tackle' and surprised many wingers with his powers of recovery. Played 41 times at left-back for Wales. Stanley Matthews described him as his most difficult opponent.

9. DON HOWE West Bromwich Albion. A composed and constructive right-back, he was capped 23 times by England. He was well-established in the West Brom defence with 342 League appearances when Billy Wright took him to Arsenal where a broken leg brought a premature end to his playing days.

10 WALLEY BARNES Arsenal. A cultured, thoughtful left-back who was handicapped through much of his career by a recurring knee injury. Capped 22 times by Wales, he was a key man in the Arsenal defence on the way to the 1952 FA Cup final.

The most popular combinations in the dream team selections were 1. Ramsey and Byrne; 2. Armfield and Byrne; 3. Ramsey and Wilson.

THE GREAT FOOTBALLING FIFTIES POLL
The Top 10 wing-halves

These, in order of votes received, were the ten top-rated wing-halves of the *Footballing Fifties* .... with the summary of each player as it appears on the website to guide voters.

1. DUNCAN EDWARDS Man United. The colossus who had not reached his peak when cut down by the Munich air disaster. He was the oustanding player for the Busby Babes, and an all-rounder who could play in any position. For this Poll, we shortlist him as a left-half.

2. DANNY BLANCIIFLOWER Tottenham. A creative right-half with Barnsley and Villa before his golden years with Spurs, leading them to the 1960-61 League and FA Cup double. Had impressive partnerships with Dave Mackay and Jimmy McIlroy.

3. DAVE MACKAY Tottenham. Made his name at Hearts before joining Tottenham and later Derby County. He had a shuddering tackle, could distribute the ball with precision and motivated the players around him with his all-action attitude. Capped 22 times by Scotland.

4. JIMMY DICKINSON Portsmouth. Helped Portsmouth win back to back League championships and won 48 England caps as a totally dependable left-half. His 764 appearances for Pompey was a League record for many years.

5. EDDIE COLMAN Man United. A victim of the Munich air crash, he was a beautifully skilled right half whose positional play and imaginative passes made him stand out with the Busby Babes. Nicknamed 'snake hips', he had excellent ball control and was very competitive.

6. JIMMY SCOULAR Portsmouth and Newcastle. He was an aggressive right-half who inspired team-mates with his hard-tackling style. Capped nine times by Scotland, he helped Pompey to the League title double before skippering 1955 FA Cup winning Newcastle.

7. RON BURGESS Tottenham . Skipper and powerhouse left-half in the push-and-run Spurs. He won 32 Welsh caps despite losing much of his career to the Second World War and finished his playing days in his home country with Swansea.

8. TOMMY DOCHERTY Preston. The Doc was an energetic, tough tackling right-half who inherited Bill Shankly's shirt at Preston and with Scotland. Capped 25 times, he finished the 'fifties as a midfield dynamo in the Arsenal team.

9. RONNIE CLAYTON Blackburn Rovers. Driving right-half who made his debut for Rovers at sixteen on his way to becoming captain of his club and country. He was capped 32 times and played more than 600 League and Cup matches for Rovers.

10. JIMMY ADAMSON Burnley. He had a strong tackle, and always used the ball with care. He left the pretty football to his midfield partner Jimmy McIlroy, and concentrated on giving solid support to the forwards and was quick to switch to defence when necessary. Amazingly, never capped.

The most popular combinations in the Dream Team selections were: 1. Blanchflower and Edwards; 2. Colman and Edwards; 3. Scoular and Edwards.

These, in order of votes received, were the ten top-rated centre-halves of the *Footballing Fifties* .... with the summary of each player as it appears on the website to guide voters.

1. JOHN CHARLES Leeds United. Spent his greatest years with Juventus in Italy but achieved enough with Leeds United and Wales to establish himself as one of the all-time British greats. Equally at home in the middle of the defence or at centre-forward. The Gentle Giant played 38 times for Wales.

2. NEIL FRANKLIN Stoke City. Was widely considered the finest centre-half to play for England, but literally walked out on club and country to join the outlawed Colombian league. Returned to play for Hull but was banned from playing for Engand after 27 successive caps.

3. BILLY WRIGHT Wolves. Switched from right-half to centre-half for club and country after Neil Franklin had walked out. At 5ft 10in, he was short for the centre-half role, but more than made up for his lack of inches with his positional play and sheer determination.

4. JACK CHARLTON Leeds United. He was called into the centre of the Leeds defence to allow John Charles to move to centre-forward. It was the start of a long career which had its peak at Wembley in 1966 when he wore the No 5 shirt in England's World Cup winning team.

5. HARRY JOHNSTON Blackpool. Captain of the team that entered the land of legend by winning the 1953 'Matthews final'. He won ten England caps, an international career ended when Hidegkuti scored a hat-trick against him the same year as the FA Cup final triumph.

6. BILL SLATER Wolves. A utility player who was at home in almost any position, he took over as England and Wolves centre-half following the retirement of Billy Wright. He won twelve England caps, yet never became a full-time pro because he wanted to concentrate on his university lecturing.

7. BOB STOKOE Newcastle United. He was a strong and solid centre-half with the Magpies before adding to his legend as manager of Sunderland. The highspot of his playing career was collecting an FA Cup winners medal in the middle of the Newcastle defence in 1955.

8. JACK FROGGATT Portsmouth. One of the most versatile of all players, he won caps for England at outside-left and as a commanding centre-half. He played more than 300 League and Cup matches for Portsmouth in a variety of positions before transferring to Leicester City.

9. LESLIE COMPTON Arsenal. The oldest player to make his England debut at the age of 38, he was a solid and commanding influence in the middle of the Gunners defence. His cricketing and footballing brother Denis got most of the headlines, but the tall, imposing Leslie was industrious and reliable.

10. SYD OWEN Luton Town. A resolute centre-half for Luton, he found fame late in his career when he was elected Footballer of the Year in his final season after guiding Luton to the FA Cup final at Wembley. Capped three times by England following Neil Franklin's defection.

THE GREAT FOOTBALLING FIFTIES POLL
The Top 10 wingers

These, in order of votes received, were the ten top-rated wingers of the Footballing Fifties .... with the summary of each player as it appears on the website to guide voters.

1. STANLEY MATTHEWS Blackpool. The most famous footballer of his generation, he set an all-time record by playing for Stoke in the First Division at the age of 50. The 'Wizard of Dribble' won 54 caps over a space of 22 years, and was the first footballer to be knighted.

2. TOM FINNEY Preston. He was equally effective on either wing, but won most of his England caps at outside left with Stanley Matthews on the right. He was two footed and played in four different forward roles for England. Netted 30 goals in his 76 England games.

3. BILLY LIDDELL Liverpool. In his peak years at Anfield he was such a formidable force that Liverpool were known as Liddellpool. He was effective in all the forward roles, but at his most devastating when cutting in from the left wing. Scored 216 goals in 495 League games.

4. BRYAN DOUGLAS Blackburn Rovers. He was considered the 'new' Stanley Matthews when he made his breakthrough into the Rovers team, and he scored eleven goals in 36 England internationals as a right winger with superb dribbling skills.

5. BOBBY MITCHELL Newcastle. Nicknamed 'Bobby Dazzler,' he along with Bobby Cowell and Jackie Milburn were the only players to collect three FA Cup winners' medals with Newcastle in five years. He scored 95 goals for the Magpies.

6. JOHNNY HANCOCKS Wolves. He wore schoolboy-size boots but packed a thundering shot in his right foot. Capped just three times because of the presence of Matthews and Finney, he scored 158 goals in 343 League games for Wolves.

7. BILLY BINGHAM Sunderland. Fast and direct, Billy was a huge favourite with Sunderland and then Luton Town and Everton fans. He played 56 times for Northern Ireland and was feared by defences for the way he would suddenly cut inside and plunder goals.

8. PETER McPARLAND Aston Villa. A darting, dangerous left winger, he scored many decisive winning goals for Villa and Northern Ireland. He was capped 34 times, and scored more than 100 League and Cup goals for Villa before moving on to Wolves.

9. JIMMY MULLEN Wolves. He zipped down the left wing for Wolves while Hancocks was dancing down the right touchline, and the width they gave the Molineux club was one of the reasons for all their success. Caped 12 times by England, he scored more than 100 goals.

10. BILL PERRY Blackpool. A South African capped by England, he was a fast and direct left winger who was a good finisher as he proved by scoring the winning goal in the famous 'Matthews FA Cup final' at Wembley in 1953. He scored two goals in his three England appearances.

The most popular combinations in the Dream Team selections were: 1. Matthews and Finney; 2. Matthews and Liddell; 3. Matthews and Mitchell.

THE GREAT FOOTBALLING FIFTIES POLL
The Top 10 inside-forwards

These, in order of votes received, were the ten top-rated inside-forwards of the *Footballing Fifties* .... with the summary of each player as it appears on the website to guide voters.

1. BOBBY CHARLTON Man United. It was difficult to know where to place England's favourite footballing son. He was equally devastating in four forward roles, but was at his most effective when scheming from deep and coming through and bombarding goalkeepers.

2. JIMMY GREAVES Chelsea. A goal scoring genius, he netted a record 357 First Division goals and also 44 in 57 games for England. Many consider his greatest days were as a teenage Chelsea player, dancing through defences and pick-pocketing goals.

3. DENIS LAW Huddersfield/Manchester City. He had his peak years with Man United in the 1960s, but was already established as a star of the 'fifties with Huddersfield. He had lightning-fast reflexes in the penalty area and could turn a half chance into a goal in the blinking of an eye.

4. LEN SHACKLETON Newcastle/Sunderland. 'The Clown Prince' was one of the most entertaining footballers ever to step on a football field, but his clowning was frowned on by the selectors and he was picked for a meagre five England internationals.

5. JOHNNY HAYNES Fulham. The pass master who could hit a ball like Beckham but with both feet. Captained England in 22 of his 56 appearances, and was the key midfield player in the World Cup campaigns of 1958 and 1962.

6. WILF MANNION Middlesbrough. He had his greatest days in the 1940s, but was still an effective player for Middlesbrough with his stunning ball control and ability to ghost through defences. The Ayresome Park 'Golden Boy' scored 11 goals in 26 England games.

7. JIMMY McILROY Burnley. A wonderfully composed schemer for club and country. He was always beautifully balanced, and could find a team-mate with passes that were delivered with uncanny accuracy. Capped 55 times by Northern Ireland, he had a potent midfield partnership with Danny Blanchflower.

8. IVOR ALLCHURCH Newcastle. Idolised at Swansea, Newcastle and Cardiff, he was the perfect all-round forward who could scheme and score. He passed with pride and precision for Wales in 68 international matches.

9. GEORGE EASTHAM Newcastle/Arsenal. Football's 'Matchstick Man,' he was only a bantamweight but difficult to knock off the ball. His close control was superb and he could unlock the tightest defences with well-placed passes.

10. EDDIE BAILY Tottenham Pulled the strings in midfield for the famous push-and-run Spurs team that won the Second and First Division titles in successive years. A wonderful passer of the ball with either foot, he scored five goals in nine England games.

The most popular combinations in the Dream Team selections were: 1. Greaves and Charlton; 2. Greaves and Law; 3 Mannion and Shackleton.

THE GREAT FOOTBALLING FIFTIES POLL
The Top 10 centre-forwards

These, in order of votes received, were the ten top-rated centre-forwards of the *Footballing Fifties* .... with the summary of each player as it appears on the website to guide voters.

1. NAT LOFTHOUSE Bolton. The Lion of Vienna who bashed his way into football legend with a one-man show in Austria, but he was much more than a one-game hero. A master of the old school of mixing raw power with subtle skills. Scored 30 goals in 33 England games.

2. TOMMY TAYLOR Manchester United. He was at the peak of his career when killed in the Munich air disaster. Excellent in the air and a fine positional player, he plundered 112 goals in 166 League games for the Busby Babes and netted 16 times in 19 England games.

3. JACKIE MILBURN Newcastle. An idol on Tyneside, he had the appropriate initials JET because he was jet paced and a deadly finisher. Three FA Cup finals in five years was just part of his legend. Ten goals for England in 13 games, and equally effective on the right wing.

4. BRIAN CLOUGH Middlesbrough/Sunderland. One of the most prolific goal scorers in League history (251 in 274 games), his scoring stage was usually the Second Division. He was awarded just two England caps and had his career cut short by injury at the age of 28.

5. TOMMY LAWTON Notts County. Was past his peak in the 1950s but still a formidable force, as he proved with Brentford and Arsenal at the back end of his career. If judged on his 1930s and 1940s form he would be a shoe-in for the dream team, but this is a 'fifties side.

6. STAN MORTENSEN Blackpool. Forever remembered for his hat-trick in the 1953 FA Cup final, he was fast, direct , brave in the air and had power in both feet. He could play in any of the three inside forward positions and netted 197 League goals for Blackpool and 23 in 25 England games.

7. TREVOR FORD Aston Villa/Sunderland. He combined power with skill, and was a handful for the best centre-halves. Averaged a goal every two games before returning home to Wales for his final shots. Netted 23 goals in 38 internationals.

8. DON REVIE Manchester City. He perfected the deep-lying centre-forward role as devastatingly demonstrated by Hidegkuti for Hungary in the 6-3 slaughter of England at Wembley in 1953. A have-boots-will-travel player, he was a dependable goal scorer at each of his clubs.

9. JOHN ATYEO Bristol City. His phenomenal goal scoring feats with Bristol City (314 League goals in 596 League games) forced England to select him six times even though he did most of his hunting in the Third Division. Literally a head master, he combined teaching with football.

10. RONNIE ALLEN West Brom. He was the two-goal hero of the 1954 FA Cup final and was a centre-forward who played with brains more than brawn. Won five England caps and scored 208 goals in 405 League games for West Brom.

These, in order of votes received, were the ten top-rated managers of the *Footballing Fifties* .... with the summary of each player as it appears on the website to guide voters.

1. MATT BUSBY Man United. He inherited one team, built another (the Busby Babes) and bought a third championship-winning team. He survived the 1958 Munich air disaster and captured the European Cup ten years later, but you must judge him on his feats in the 'fifties.

2. STAN CULLIS Wolves. Managed Wolves in the same way that he used to play for them, with total commitment and the emphasis on power. His leaning towards long-ball tactics meant they were not always pretty to watch, but in the 'fifties they were the great untouchables.

3. TED DRAKE Chelsea. Brought a revolution to Stamford Bridge in an era when Chelsea were the butt of music-hall jokes. He swept aside the Pensioner image and guided them to their first League championship in 1954-55 before developing the headline-hitting Drake Ducklings.

4. ARTHUR ROWE Tottenham. The architect of push-and-run, he was a tactical genius who produced a Tottenham team that played pure football on the way to back-to-back Second and First Division championships. Greatly influenced future master managers Alf Ramsey and Bill Nicholson.

5. WALTER WINTERBOTTOM England. Though not a club manager, you may wish to consider him as manager of your dream team. He spent 16 years as England team manager without touching the heights of his successor Alf Ramsey. Walter was responsible for setting up a nationwide coaching network.

6. TOM WHITTAKER Arsenal. Promoted from club physiotherapist, the 'man with the magic hands' helped restore Arsenal's pride in the immediate post-war years and steered them to two FA Cup finals and a League championship.

7. BILL RIDDING Bolton. Took a Bolton team all the way to FA Cup final glory in 1958 that cost just £110 in signing-on fees. He liked his teams to mix beef with their skill and the take-no-prisoners Bolton defence of the 1950s was one of the most feared in football.

8. HARRY POTTS Burnley. Always insisted on his team playing perfect football, and finally got the deserved reward for his skill-at-all-times approach by lifting the League championship in 1959-60. This quiet man of football later become general manager at Turf Moor.

9. JOE SMITH Blackpool. A manager out of the old school, he produced a procession of exceptional Cup-specialist teams and in more than 20 years at the helm motivated the likes of Matthews and Mortensen to make the Seasiders a greatly respected club.

10. LES McDOWALL Man City. He was in charge at Maine Road for thirteen years from 1950, and had his peak season in the mid-1950s when steering City to successive FA Cup finals, losing the first in 1955 and then returning in 1956 to capture the coveted Cup.

These, in order of votes received, were the ten top-rated club teams of the *Footballing Fifties* .... with the summary of each player as it appears on the website to guide voters.

1. MANCHESTER UNITED They had three exceptional teams in the fifties, but are represented here by the unforgettable Busby Babes who won back to back First Division titles before tragically being wiped out by the Munich air disaster of 1958.

2. WOLVES Wolves created a record of topping 100 goals in four successive First Division seasons, and set Europe alight with their thrilling pioneering floodlit victories over the likes of Honved and Real Madrid. They more than any other club inspired the idea of the European Cup competition.

3. TOTTENHAM Their push-and-run team won back to back Second and First Division titles at the start of the 1950s, and played stylish fooball that was thoroughly enjoyable to watch for neutral spectators.

4. ARSENAL The Joe Mercer-motivated Arsenal of the early 1950s, featuring the scheming skills of Jimmy Logie, captured the League championship in 1953 after winning the FA Cup and finishing runners-up.

5. NEWCASTLE UNITED They collected the FA Cup three times in five years in the 1950s, with Bobby Cowell, Jackie Milburn and Bobby Mitchell the only ever-presents. Their highest end-of-season place in the First Division during the decade was fourth in 1950-51.

6. BLACKPOOL of Matthews, Mortensen and Mudie fame were FA Cup specialists, finally winning the trophy in the memorable 1953 final after finishing runners-up to Manchester United and Newcastle. Their best bid for the League championship during the 'fifties came in 1955-56 when they finished second to the Busby Babes.

7. CHELSEA They were the shock winners of the League championship in 1954-55 under the guiding influence of manager Ted Drake, who later introduced his Drake Ducklings featuring the likes of Jimmy Greaves, Bobby Tambling and Frank Blunstone.

8. BURNLEY Managed by Harry Potts, they pipped Wolves for the League championship in 1959-60 and won the admiration of neutral fans with the way they always chose to play pure football. Their tandem team partners in midfield, Jimmy Adamson and Jimmy McIlroy, was close to poetry in motion.

9. MANCHESTER CITY With Don Revie as their 'secret' weapon as a deep-lying centre-forward, they were runners-up for the FA Cup in 1955 and came back the following year to win it by beating Birmingham City 3-1. Their best League season was fourth in 1955-56.

10. LIVERPOOL The pre-Shankly side had the power of the legendary Billy Liddell to push them to a runners-up place in the 1950 FA Cup final three years after capturing the League championship.

These, in order of votes received, were the players selected for the *Footballing Fifties* Dream Team. The only instruction was that the side had to be picked in the old-style 2-3-5 formation. Duncan Edwards and Stanley Matthews were the heroes who collected most votes, both of them included in more than 90 per cent of the submitted teams. Next highest votes went to Jimmy Greaves, Tom Finney and Roger Byrne, who were in more than 80 per cent of the teams. Denis Law and Billy Liddell were the best supported Scots, making it into more than 60 per cent of the teams, and it is another great Scot, Sir Matt Busby, who would be the manager in charge. You can have YOUR say on the official website at www.footballingfifties.co.uk

Bert Trautmann

Alf Ramsey   *Roger Byrne*

Danny Blanchflower John Charles Duncan Edwards

Stanley Matthews Jimmy Greaves Nat Lofthouse Bobby Charlton Tom Finney

Just for fun, the author selected the following World XI from the *Footballing Fifties* to take on the cream of the Football League ...

Lev Yashin
(Russia)

Djalma Santos   *Nilton Santos*
(Brazil)   *(Brazil)*

Bozsik   *Santamaria*   *Ocwirk*
(Hungary)   *(Uruguay)*   *(Austria)*

Garrincha   *Pele*   *Di Stefano*   *Puskas*   *Gento*
(Brazil)   *(Brazil)*   *(Argentina)*   *(Hungary)*   *(Spain)*

The *Footballing Fifties*. Truly a dream decade. Thank you for making the journey with me.

PREVIOUS BOOKS BY NORMAN GILLER

Banks of England (with Gordon Banks)
The Glory and the Grief (with George Graham)
Football And All That (an irreverent history of the game)
The Seventies Revisited (with Kevin Keegan)
The Final Score (with Brian Moore) **ABC of Soccer Sense** (Tommy Docherty)
Billy Wright, A Hero for All Seasons (official biography)
The Rat Race (with Tommy Docherty) **Denis Compton** (The Untold Stories)
McFootball, the Scottish Heroes of the English Game
The Book of Rugby Lists (with Gareth Edwards)
The Book of Tennis Lists (with John Newcombe)
The Book of Golf Lists TV Quiz Trivia Sports Quiz Trivia
Know What I Mean (with Frank Bruno) **Eye of the Tiger** (with Frank Bruno)
From Zero to Hero (with Frank Bruno) **The Judge Book of Sports Answers**
Watt's My Name (with Jim Watt) **My Most Memorable Fights** (with Henry Cooper)
How to Box (with Henry Cooper) **Henry Cooper's 100 Greatest Boxers**
Mike Tyson Biography Mike Tyson, the Release of Power (Reg Gutteridge)
Crown of Thorns, the World Heavyweight Championship (with Neil Duncanson)
Fighting for Peace (Barry McGuigan biography, with Peter Batt)
World's Greatest Cricket Matches World's Greatest Football Matches
Golden Heroes (with Dennis Signy) **The Judge** (1,001 arguments settled)
The Great Football IQ Quiz Book (The Judge of *The Sun*)
The Marathon Kings The Golden Milers (with Sir Roger Bannister)
Olympic Heroes (with Brendan Foster)
Olympics Handbook 1980 Olympics Handbook 1984
Book of Cricket Lists (Tom Graveney) **Top Ten Cricket Book** (Tom Graveney)
Cricket Heroes (Eric Morecambe) **Big Fight Quiz Book TVIQ Puzzle Book**
Lucky the Fox (with Barbara Wright) **Gloria Hunniford's TV Challenge**
Comedy novels: **Carry On Doctor Carry On England Carry On Loving**
Carry On Up the Khyber Carry On Abroad Carry On Henry
A Stolen Life (novel) **Mike Baldwin: Mr Heartbreak** (novel) **Hitler's Final Victim** (novel)
Affairs (novel) **The Bung** (novel)

Books in collaboration with **RICKY TOMLINSON**
Football My Arse Celebrities My Arse Cheers My Arse
Reading My Arse (The Search for the Rock Island Line)

PLUS books in collaboration with **JIMMY GREAVES**:
This One's On Me The Final (novel) **The Ball Game** (novel)
The Boss (novel) **The Second Half** (novel)
Let's Be Honest (with Reg Gutteridge) **Greavsie's Heroes and Entertainers**
World Cup History GOALS! Stop the Game, I Want to Get On
The Book of Football Lists Taking Sides
Sports Quiz Challenge Sports Quiz Challenge 2
It's A Funny Old Life Saint & Greavsie's World Cup Special
The Sixties Revisited Don't Shoot the Manager